No Place Like Home, *Thank God*

A 22,000 MILE BICYCLE RIDE AROUND EUROPE

Steven Primrose-Smith

First published in 2014 by Rosebery Publications
1 Perwick Rise, Port St Mary, Isle of Man

Copyright © 2014 Steven Primrose-Smith
All rights reserved.
steven@primrose-smith.com

ISBN-13: 978-1501067983
ISBN-10: 1501067982

Except in the United States of America,
this book is sold subject to the condition
that it shall not, by way of trade or otherwise,
be lent, re-sold, hired out, or otherwise circulated
without the publisher's prior consent in any form
of binding or cover other than that in which it is
published and without a similar condition including
this condition being imposed on the subsequent purchaser.

Names have been changed where appropriate.

A route map along with photographs of all the
places visited, people met and food eaten can be found at
www.UniCycle50.com.

To my mum,
who told me all the ways this ride would kill me.

*I want a life that's bigger than me,
But I'm crushing myself to death.*
"Ordinary Angel" - Hue & Cry

*"The most important: Keep tranquillity.
Do not give in to the panic."*
Belarusian hotel fire notice

Table of Contents

Acknowledgements..7

Chapter 1: Dying to leave..9

YEAR ONE

Chapter 2: A mouthful of knobs.....................................19

Chapter 3: Eating poo sausage..33

Chapter 4: Doing drugs..48

Chapter 5: Take my breath away....................................60

Chapter 6: Dancing and dumplings..............................71

Chapter 7: It means nothing to me................................83

Chapter 8: A marmot for dinner.....................................91

Chapter 9: God loves me...102

YEAR TWO

Chapter 10: The brains in Spain...................................121

Chapter 11: The maggots go down...............................133

Chapter 12: Drinking holy water..................................146

Chapter 13: The world's worst philosophy tour....................164

Chapter 14: Let me polish your trainers 175

Chapter 15: The man who lived under a table 191

Chapter 16: Fires, tunnels and bulls 204

Chapter 17: Tobogganing in war zones 218

YEAR THREE

Chapter 18: Who let the dogs out?..............................235

Chapter 19: Stealing wine from church 256

Chapter 20: Warnings about Russians 283

Chapter 21: From Russia with fear 303

Chapter 22: The cost of being bored 312

Chapter 23: A fight in a holy land............................325

Chapter 24: A place like home.................................338

Epilogue..350

Acknowledgements

If you ever feel the world is a terrible place you should go on a long bike ride. You'll end your journey with a much improved view of humanity. Over the course of my 22,000 miles literally thousands of people helped me, providing support, directions, local knowledge, a friendly cheer, food, beer, entertainment or a roof over my head. Massive thanks to every one of them.

Many of these wonderful people appear in this book but there are some very generous ones who, for lack of space, don't and so I'd like to thank them here. They are Dewi Jones in Paris, the OU's European representatives – Jana and Lucie in Prague, Katarina in Bratislava, and Alexandra and Sarah in Vienna – social media guru Christian Payne aka Documentally in Graz, Jolanta and Dovas in Vilnius, Glen Grant in Riga, Anne and James Watt in Paulerspury, Lovely Linz in Cheltenham, and Neil Harrison, Susan Goodyear and the staff of BBC Wales in Cardiff.

I'd also like to thank Robyn Bateman and Jenny Bond at the Open University who helped to promote my ride. Katharine Jenner, Claire Austin and Mark Hooley at Blood Pressure UK (formerly The Blood Pressure Association) also did wonders to raise awareness of the trip.

Thank you to everyone who gave money to charity on behalf of the ride. Your valuable contributions have helped to make this world a better place.

Finally, I'd like to thank each and every person who followed me or my UniCycle50 page on Facebook. At the end of a long day in the saddle, stationed in a poky hotel room with no entertainment, your comments – encouraging, wise but more often daft – brought a smile to my face. Thank you.

Chapter 1: Dying to leave

Even if you're 39 years old, long past the age of cakes and balloons, there are better places to spend your birthday than in intensive care on the Isle of Man. It's intensive care that's the issue, by the way, not the Isle of Man.

I was lying very still. I'd been told to. As soon as someone tells you this it's hard not to start fidgeting. So I did.

"Stop moving around," the nurse said. "Any movement of your head might cause another bleed. The next one could be fatal."

Brilliant. It was May 2009. I'd been about to cycle from the Isle of Man to Spain's southern coast, a ride of over 1,500 miles, my first long distance bike ride. But something was seriously up with me. I was well sick, man.

I'd been feeling increasingly queasy for the last few months. I'd also re-developed travel sickness, something I thought I'd ditched at the same time as Top Trumps. Two days before I was due to leave, my vision went blurry. Internet research and lots of squinting at my monitor pointed worryingly to diabetes. The thought of cycling through a strange land with blurred vision and increasing nausea, asking lampposts for directions before throwing up on them, didn't appeal and I decided not to ride, wisely as it turned out.

The nausea increased and then serious vomiting kicked in, at first after each meal but later whenever I moved. The travel sickness appeared even if I only travelled from the living room to the kitchen. Normally I'd avoid seeing a doctor but it was now too bad to ignore and clearly wasn't going to get any better without attention. The doctor's surgery was closed for the weekend and so I went to A & E. A nurse took my blood pressure and looked at the monitor's digital display first quizzically and then worriedly.

"You're staying in!" she said. "Your blood pressure is 210 over 120." That goes off the scale of those charts at the bottom of hospital beds.

I learned a lot in hospital. First, I learned I didn't have diabetes. I'd had a brain haemorrhage – three in total – brought on by very high blood pressure. I'd been an idiot. I'd known for years my blood pressure was high but I hadn't taken it seriously. Pills for the rest of my life? That's for old people. I'd nearly paid the ultimate price for that complacency. Second, I learned that, as a result of long-term hypertension, my kidneys were now functioning at only 60% and probably wouldn't improve much if at all. The final thing I learned in hospital was that despite an entire town claiming otherwise the Frenchman I met in the patients' TV room absolutely definitely wasn't a paedophile. He may or may not have been telling the truth but, either way, to introduce yourself and then, apropos of nothing, immediately and categorically deny any pederast tendencies is a bold approach to making new friends.

As a result of the endless vomiting I was lighter than I'd ever been in my adult life. Lying in the hospital bed and looking down at my new, flat stomach, it was great to feel so slim. But once discharged and seeing myself properly in the bathroom mirror I saw a withered, spindly insect alien. Any muscles I'd had – and there hadn't been many of those to begin with – had vanished along with the fat. I looked like a pipe cleaner on hunger strike.

Being so skinny I did what I'd always imagined would be wonderful. I'd eat myself back to my ideal weight. I spent a summer recuperating in a hammock eating tub after luscious tub of toffee ice cream. Despite my low starting weight my ice cream diet was badly executed and I overshot the mark. By the end of summer I was two stone overweight. I had to get my body moving again. Besides, approaching the event horizon of Death's black hole has a way of focusing the mind. All the things I'd ever put off had come so close to never having been completed, or even started.

In September, three months after intensive care and against my family's wishes, I set off on the bike ride I'd postponed. I wanted to prove that having high blood pressure wasn't the end of living. So off I popped, with panniers containing five different types of blood pressure tablet. I took a rural route through the UK, France and Spain and had the best five weeks of my life.

If you're one of the Open University's 240,000 current students, or one of the millions that have passed through its virtual lecture halls, you'll probably know just how addictive their courses can be. I'm not sure what it is that motivates other people to keep plodding along with an OU degree but for me it's the sense of continual, if slow, progress. It fills every minute of your day. And then, after several, long years, you pass your final module and you now possess a shiny new degree. You dance happily around the living room for ten minutes and wonder what you'll do with all the free time that you once spent studying. The next two weeks will see you trying to fill this space – which now feels more like a void – with something vacuous on telly or you toss around on Facebook. Eventually you surf on over to the OU's website – just for old time's sake, mind – and before the evening is done you've signed up for another degree. The OU is crack for the brain.

After leaving school with disappointing A-levels and always feeling I should have done better I finally got an OU degree in English Language and Philosophy in the final days of 2008. I did the dancing around the living room and the telly watching and then, perhaps a little ambitiously, I immediately enrolled for three more degrees: one in Mathematics and another in Physical Science with the Open University, and an MA in Philosophy at Lampeter University. It's a plan that, now I've written it down for the first time, just looks stupid. Doing so many courses at once meant progress in each was slow but time itself wasn't a factor. I had until my hypertension killed me.

Money was a problem though. I'd done the odd hour of programming and tutoring while studying but I was basically living from savings and by the middle of 2010 funds were getting low. Progress with all three degrees would slow to a dripping tap if I had to go back to full-time work and, besides, I enjoyed student life. Mostly, it was the not-going-to-work part I enjoyed.

I looked at my finances and I looked at my life and I made what some might think was a brave move. Others will think it utterly stupid. Including my mum. You see, we're sold a lie. Work hard, save for your pension and reap your reward when you retire. You've earned it! But even if you reach retirement age – hardly a given – your body is unlikely to manage the things it could in its twenties, thirties and forties. We see advertisements for retirement plans with silver foxes and foxettes engaged in something mildly adventurous, perhaps trekking up a little hill in the Lake District and beaming radiantly at each other in pastel knitwear. Look, folks, we got there. We're having the time of our lives. Buy our plan. But the things you'd ideally do today if only you'd more time might not be possible decades down the line. One dodgy knee and any physical plans are buggered.

The father of a friend of mine is a good example. He was looking forward to his retirement. He didn't have the biggest of dreams but he and the missus planned to have days out at the coast – they loved Southport for some reason – and to go for drives in the country, stopping for a pie and a pint. A few weeks before he was due to retire, his wife died suddenly of an asthma attack. He was robbed of the woman who'd share his golden days. There was no joy in doing any of those things by himself and so he didn't. He lived to be seventy-five. Instead of eating ice cream and walking happily hand in hand along a chilly north-west beach he spent those last ten, lonely years watching orange-dyed daytime TV presenters sell pepper pots for a tenner. He'd paid into the system for fifty years and this was his reward.

I couldn't control what would happen in the future but I could control what happened now. I didn't want to wait until I was old and knackered. I'd paid a fair amount into a pension fund during my working life. If I liberated that money I could have three more years of full time study and another bike ride, a really big one. But it would mean no pension at all. I'd moved around a lot during my twenties and early thirties and hadn't paid enough into any country's scheme to qualify for their state pension. But having come so close to death I was pumped on life and it seemed like the best idea I'd ever had.

But what sort of bike ride and where? Open University courses are based in Europe and so my ride would have to be based there too. I'd have to post off assignments. The further away I was from the UK, the longer they'd take to reach my tutor and the further ahead in each course I'd have to be to compensate. But I wanted to do something massive, something that I hadn't heard anyone else do before. I wanted a bike ride as stupendously big and as juicily ambitious as my studies. If I was going to cash in my chips I couldn't waste them on anything less than monumental.

I decided I'd cycle from the Isle of Man to the Isle of Man. Admittedly, this doesn't sound like much. You could do it in an afternoon. But I was going the long way around. Before returning to the island I'd visit every capital in Europe in a continuous loop, only removing the bicycle from land when a ferry ride necessitated it. My wheels would see neither train, plane nor automobile. The capital count came to a nice, round fifty.

I estimated it'd take around eighteen months of cycling to do justice to this trip. It could obviously be done more quickly but I didn't want to rush. I wanted to see the sights, talk to the locals, drink their beer and eat their food, especially their weird food. However, I'd need to replenish my stock of blood pressure pills and there were exams each October. September was the perfect time to break off the ride each year. Besides, I didn't want to cycle in winter. Riding in snow is no fun. Six months per year for three years seemed ideal.

Importantly, my trip would build in excitement. To test if this concept was possible my first year would visit Europe's tamer places, the lands people go for fun rather than adventure. The second year would turn up the heat, crossing Turkey, Albania and the former Yugoslavian states including Bosnia and Kosovo. My final year would see me in Europe's Wild West, despite its being east, in Romania, Moldova, Ukraine, Belarus, and Russia itself.

I wouldn't plan a route or accommodation. I wouldn't plan much at all. I'd make it up as I was going along. All I knew was the order in which I'd see the capitals and where I'd finish each year. The bike had to end each leg at a friend's house for winter storage before being dusted off the following spring.

The most direct route between each capital in the order I'd chosen was about 19,000 miles but I wouldn't cycle the most direct route. There were other places to see and people to meet, family, friends and those who'd got in touch with me after hearing about the ride. This meant 19,000 miles would be the absolute minimum, although that distance was daunting enough.

I thought of the realities of my trip. Travelling in the warmer months meant camp sites would be open, reducing costs. Hotels would be allowed if cheap. Wild camping was also an option but that involves hiding yourself away and I only wanted to do this if there were no other possibilities. Therefore I'd need to carry a tent, a sleeping bag and a stove as well as all the usual things cycle tourists have to lug around but I'd also be carrying things not so common on long distance tours: a Kindle to read my course work, a laptop to write assignments and well over a thousand blood pressure pills.

But would it even be possible to cycle and study at the same time? I looked online for advice from people who'd done it and realised no one else had or, if they had, they'd kept it quiet. But even if I was the first, that didn't make it impossible. Others didn't seem as convinced. When I first mentioned the idea out loud my sanity was questioned. These accusations were made in jest – at least I think they were – but there's something worrying about proposing an idea and then being told you must be mad. I wasn't. What I planned to do was the sanest thing ever. The nutty ones are those who say they'd love to do an adventure but never get around to it.

But there was something else. My goal was to reach the capitals but the ride would take me through hundreds of other cities, towns and villages. I'd get to see what the whole of Europe looked like, how it sounded, how it smelled, how it tasted. I'd see Europe's wonders and blunders, its palaces and doss houses and I'd be able to discover something I'd pondered for a very long time: is Lancashire's Blackburn, my birthplace and home until the age of 25, really the worst place in Europe? I strongly suspected it might be.

YEAR ONE

Chapter 2: A mouthful of knobs

Capitals visited: 0
Total distance: 0 miles

The Isle of Man is an exceedingly beautiful place if it's a bright, sunny day. Apparently there's a woman in a care home in Peel who remembers such an occasion. She's 247 years old. Today wasn't bright and sunny.

It was 31st of March in Port Saint Mary, the Isle of Man. Day One had arrived. Outside it was very cold, extremely wet and horrendously windy. It was also five in the morning, a time of day when the cold seems colder, the wet wetter and the wind windier. On a more positive note, although the morning was as black as Piers Morgan's heart, luckily it was just possible to tell it was also foggy. It was reassuring to know that for the beginning of my ride I had nearly the full set of bad weather conditions. I was only missing a tornado and a shower of frogs. Both were forecast for later.

Despite the deathly conditions out of doors there was plenty of life inside my parent's house, the start point of my mammoth ride. Something was about to happen that'd never happened before. We were about to be interviewed for television. Or rather I was and so was my brother Dave, and probably my dad, but definitely not my mum. She didn't want any limelight, which made it difficult to explain why she was in full make-up so early in the morning. The man from ITV was due any minute and everyone was a little jumpy.

After giving up my rented flat to do the ride I'd been staying at my mum and dad's. Dave had come around for my last supper the previous evening. He was going to cycle with me as far as the ferry to the mainland or 'across' as it's called here in Manxland.

As well as the challenge of the ride itself a friend had dared me to eat something I'd never tried before in each country, preferably something local. The Isle of Man was one of my countries and so I had to find something new to eat here but having spent so much time on the island there really wasn't anything local left for me to try. Or was there?

My eye had been caught by Manx Knobs, a product available in a local tourist shop. I'd never eaten a knob before and so I bought myself a jar. I cracked it open and popped one into my mouth. I sucked gently and it tasted surprisingly pleasant. But ultimately Manx Knobs turned out to be a huge disappointment. They were, after all, nothing more than boring, old boiled sweets marketed with a slightly rude name in order to boost sales. It wasn't even a droll play on words, like a bar of Cockolate or a Toblerbone.

I'd have to look farther afield for something original. I'd been tipped off about a local source of gastronomic exotica and so I popped to the meat shop in Castletown and had a butcher's at its grand choice of jungle food and its various cuts of endangered species. Should I partake of a tasty hippo burger or maybe an elephant's rib, or something lighter like hyena on toast? I was slightly disappointed they'd sold out of panda and all their dodo meat was out of date but in the end I selected a lump of bison and a slab of wild boar.

The evening before setting off I cooked up the meat combo. The wild boar was delicious, like a liver-flavoured pork steak, but the bison had many of the properties of a power ball. If I'd been thinking clearly I'd have put it to better use and cut it into strips in case I needed to patch my tyres.

But that was last night. Now, my mum fussed around, fixing breakfasts, while I loaded my heavy panniers on to the bike. And then a car turned into the driveway and out climbed Paul with a video camera. He stuck it in my face and filmed as I chewed my words and gabbled like an arse. It was Dave's turn next to say what he thought about my trip. He was much more composed. Paul then interviewed my dad, whose strategy to get through this was to grunt monosyllabically like he'd had his brain removed.

"What do you think of what Steven is doing?" asked Paul.

My dad smiled shyly and took an age to answer.

"He's mad," he finally said. You could see Paul's face urging him on for more but that was all he was getting. Paul asked him a couple more questions but received similarly terse responses. It was like milking a hamster. While Paul packed his camera away, my mum piped up.

"If I'd known your dad was going to be that rubbish I'd have done it myself."

It was time to leave. The fog had mostly cleared and although it was still raining the strong winds were directly behind us propelling us along. This might have seemed like an auspicious start but in reality it wasn't. The ride to the ferry in Douglas was northwards. A wind blowing from the south wasn't going to help me once I'd arrived at Heysham and started pedalling in the opposite direction.

Paul stopped at various places along our route to capture what might have been called 'action shots'. With the complete blackness – the Isle of Man turns off its street lights at one each morning – it was going to look more like a crap version of *Close Encounters of the Third Kind*. Two plazzy-looking bicycle lights would emerge from the gloom and silently pass by the camera. It was hardly *Too Fast Too Furious*.

My girlfriend Nina had given me a good luck token, a two-inch high, ceramic figure. Despite looking like a panda – that's the figure, not Nina – the little statue had the ungrammatical "I love meerkat" painted on its chest, a cheap ploy to shift a warehouseful of unpopular toys by fabricating a link to the recently successful *Compare The Market* commercials. Knowing my rejection of all things religious, superstitious and supernatural, Nina likes to bring me into what she might call 'the spiritual realm'. My job this dark morning was to bury the panda under the famous Fairy Bridge en route to Douglas. It's when crossing this bridge by car that otherwise sane adults greet the fairies out loud in order not to skid off the road and burst into flames. Over the coming three years, would the fairies protect my panda and, by extension, me during my long journey? No, of course they wouldn't. Apart from obviously not ever existing, local folklore describes Manx fairies as evil, little sods who went around stealing babies and killing cattle. I'd be less surprised if instead of digging up a perfectly preserved figurine in three years' time it were hanging by a noose from one of the nearby trees.

A few miles down the road I ticked off the first of my fifty European capitals, Douglas. I'd made it! Just as I had done a hundred times before.

The ferry washed up in Heysham. For the last four hours the vessel and wind had joined forces in a titanic struggle to wrestle my breakfast from me. Despite coming out victorious my guts felt queasy for the first couple of hours of the forty remaining miles to Blackburn. The ride took me through Lancaster and along the mercifully flat A6. The wind still made it feel like a uphill climb, especially with my untested legs. Finally though, more tired than I had any right to be, I hauled my aching body up the hill to my auntie Rita's house in Blackburn. She plied me with potato pie and beer and gradually restored me to health.

Together we watched Granada Reports but I wasn't mentioned. ITV Paul had explained that he produces these films but it's up to HQ in Manchester to decide whether or not they're used. He hadn't seemed overly confident. Maybe with the darkness, my gabbling and my dad's verbal efficiency we'd been cut. Apparently it appeared a couple of days later. The female presenter who chipped in after the report said, "And he's going to lose so much weight, the fat git!" Although "the fat git" part may have only been in my head.

She was right though. In the previous six months I'd done no cycling at all. I was over sixteen stone and much heavier than I was the last time I'd toured. I was feeling it already. I was absolutely knackered. I really didn't want to continue tomorrow but that's one thing about announcing something massive to everyone you know. You can't give up, not after one day.

The next morning, after a huge bowl of Weetabix, I cycled away from Rita's into a day that promised more rain and wasn't lying. Riding out of town I got a proper chance to have a look at the Blackburn I'd left behind in the spring of 1996.

Some lives seem to be defined by a single moment: Caesar's crossing of the Rubicon, Einstein's imagining of special relativity, Josef Fritzl's first visit to The Ideal Home Exhibition. My defining moment occurred in 1995 on a Tuesday in November, close to midnight. I was sitting beneath Blackburn's rusting, hulking Darwen Street bridge at the wheel of my grubby Vauxhall Nova. I watched the traffic lights refuse to change from red. It was dark. It was raining. It was depressing. It was Blackburn.

I'd set off to the first of my three jobs at eight that morning. At a quarter past five in the afternoon I drove 45 minutes to my second job. Now, six hours later, I was close to home where I'd start my third job, one that'd keep me busy until three in the morning. It took three jobs and four hours' sleep a night to scrounge just enough to live a meagre existence. It was hardly *Angela's Ashes* but nor was I eating any swan butties for tea.

As the wipers scraped across the windscreen beating out the seconds that edged me ever closer to inevitable death, a simple, obvious thought popped into my head. Everything I have done since that thought traces back to it. It's hardly profound and it's one that everyone has probably had at some point in their lives but the memory of that thought and every detail surrounding it has never left me. The thought was simply *There has to be more to life than this*. See, told you it wasn't profound.

Yes, there had to be more to life. More to life than working eighteen hour days for a pittance, more to life than wintery, mid-afternoon pitch black skies, more to life than near constant drizzle, more to life than grey, ugly Blackburn. There was a whole world out there. There were continents to discover, mountains to climb, deserts to cross. I was suddenly filled with a sense of my own destiny. I could change this. I could shake it all up. There was nothing I couldn't achieve. So I dreamed big, as big as it's possible to dream: I applied for a new job in, erm, Manchester. I didn't get it.

If Blackburn had seemed down back in 1996, now it looked well and truly out. It used to have a thriving pub scene but this seemed over, with public house after public house closed or converted into yet another mobile phone shop. Was the future really Orange? It looked grey to me.

Everyone looked ill. Wobbly teenage girls in tracksuits and scraped back hair pushed double prams. Blokes with shaved heads and vests exposing a tattoo-splattered torso prowled the grim streets with a taut lead attached at the other end to a fighting dog. It reminded me of how it'd been living here, avoiding eye contact so as not to get mashed. Those girls could be vicious.

I pedalled faster, glad to escape the town again, passing

places I'd known. There was Harwood Street, where the house into which I was born had long since been bulldozed to make way for a Tesco. I passed the end of Devon Road, the entrance to the council estate where my grandparents had lived and been terrorized by glue sniffers on the wasteland behind their house. And then I was out of Blackburn and moving into Accrington, which seemed to have fared better but not much.

I kept going, trundling on, with ever-wearying legs, bypassing Burnley, as every Blackburnian is supposed to do. Halifax and Huddersfield came and went, both much more rural than I'd expected. The roads got lumpier. I had to push the bike up a big hill. I was looking forward to the day when I was fit enough to ride these ascents. The sun came out briefly and I stopped for a rest. I lay on someone's garden wall and feel asleep for fifteen minutes. I didn't want to get up. It was only the threat of rain that roused me.

Back on the bike the scenery continued to improve. Utterly pooped I eventually reached a campsite near Holmfirth, better known as the location of *Last of the Summer Wine*. I couldn't have chosen a lovelier spot for my first tented night. I pitched my little house, a well-featured if hellishly expensive investment despite being second-hand, in the greenest of grass beside a bubbling river.

I popped to the site store and bought a tin of unpleasant lentil soup and a treat called Butter Farmhouse Fruit Cake. The lady who ran the shop told me I was the first camper of the year. I wonder how many days she'd been standing at that counter waiting for someone to arrive. Both the rubbish soup and the wonderful cake were devoured and then I made my first attempt at study on the road. I was asleep five minutes later.

It was the quacking that woke me. To reduce condensation

I'd left open the door flap of my tent. A party of ducks had seen this as an invitation to venture inside. I shooed them away and collapsed back into my sleeping bag. Despite a good night's sleep, or at least as good a night's sleep as a tent allows, I didn't feel refreshed. I didn't want to get up and get back on my stupid bike. What had I let myself in for? I'd be doing this every day for eighteen months of the next three years. I wanted to stay here forever, just me and the ducks and the little shop that sold Butter Farmhouse Fruit Cake.

I dozed, putting off the inevitable. By ten o'clock, after giving myself a good talking to, I was on the road but ten minutes into the ride my legs felt as leaden as they'd done at the end of yesterday. My 'best idea ever' was being continually evaluated and it came up short. It's at times like these the experience of previous rides is useful. There's no need to train for a long tour. It is its own training. Regardless of what a knacker you are on Day One, it doesn't take long before you've found your rhythm. I just hadn't found it yet.

Today though, this was little comfort. The contours started to bunch together. I cycled through the centre of Sheffield, past Hillsborough and then Bramall Lane. Over its hills I steeled myself, as you should in Sheffield. Two cyclists passed me, commenting on how heavy my bike looked. I hadn't weighed it but I knew it was at the limit of what was possible for me to carry.

About seven miles from that evening's campsite I passed through the lovely grounds of Chatsworth House before tumbling into Matlock, a town that feels and smells like a piece of Blackpool has detached itself and been washed inland. I arrived at an overpriced, under-facilitied site, basically a field and a pub toilet. Once again the field was mine alone. Early April obviously isn't a favourite time of the year with Britain's camping set.

*

Twenty four hours later I was in the Victoria Bikers' Pub in Coalville and I was soaked. The bikers you find here aren't lycra-clad softies like me. It's quite galling to be in surroundings frequented by burly, leathery motorcyclists when I'm sitting there with my nuts dangerously on display looking like an entrant in a wet T-shirt competition for fatties.

Today I'd got myself seriously lost in Derby. Luckily, the strong breeze was still blowing directly into my face, as it had done for the last four days. In the end all I needed to do to find my way again was head straight back into the wind. The terrain was flatter but the raindrops fatter. I walked into the pub squelching with every step. I looked as far from cool as it was possible to be, which was ironic really because I was freezing.

Ravenous after the day's exertion I asked the owner what was the biggest meal he served and within minutes he'd delivered it, a humongous pile of burgers, eggs, beans and chips. I sat there, watching something mindless on telly in the warmth, happily sipping my Old Speckled Hen while the rain slowly evaporated from my body. The pub was empty but my stomach was full and content. For the first time since setting off I was enjoying myself.

I disappeared into my portable home in the pub's back garden. I was glad I had an expensive tent. If one of this quality let in this much water just think how much more a cheap one would let in. My tent was a bit of an extravagance. It's a Hilleberg Nallo 2GT, a two man tent, but it also has a large porch area big enough to accommodate my bike. I figured if my bike wasn't visible to potential thieves it was less likely to be stolen. I'm not sure how important this precaution is when you're the only camper on the site.

Two days later – you don't need to hear about the intervening 48 hours of rain, wind and misery – I had an appointment in M.K., baby. That's Milton Keynes to you. I was meeting Robyn from the Open University. When you study remotely and your university is a pile of books and DVDs it's hard to believe the OU actually exists as a real campus. And when you speak to the people in M.K. it's even harder to believe it exists. No one knows where it is. The roadside builders didn't know but then again they didn't speak much English. And the woman on whose car window I tapped at a junction didn't know either. She didn't say much at all. I think I might have scared her. It doesn't help that the town is simply a grid of dual carriageways, each terminating in a roundabout. Each roundabout presents a choice of three further dual carriageways. Needless to say I got lost.

I stopped at a garage and asked for directions. A bloke there told me to turn right out of the garage and go for a mile. For some reason I wanted a second opinion and the next fella said that, yes, it was a mile away but I had first to turn left. With conflicting advice, I needed a third person to decide it.

"Turn left out of the garage," he started. So far so good. "And then it's about ten miles."

This wasn't getting me anywhere. On the garage forecourt a bloke sat in his car with his door open. I could see a satnav. He quickly found the location of the OU and explained where I needed to go. I'm sure I followed his instructions to the letter but ten minutes later I arrived back at the garage. I'd gone round in a big circle. The Open University is the Area 51 of education.

Robyn was my contact for *Platform*, the OU's community website, one of the places I was blogging this trip under the moniker *The UniCyclist*. We had a coffee while she interviewed me and I sweated all over her desk. This was the sixth time I'd been interviewed about the ride – I'd done some radio on the way down – but already I'd started to bore myself with the same old answers. I needed to start making up some shit.

The next morning I was back at the university to meet with Fenella and Annie, a couple of OU students I'd known via the internet for years but had never met in real life. You might know Fenella, or her voice at least. She used to read the news on Radio 2. Together we were going to cycle to London, capital number two. Also joining us was Mark from *Blood Pressure UK*, one of the charities for which I was raising money.

Britain has a strange attitude to challenges. Originally I'd no intention of doing the ride for charity. I just wanted to do it for myself. But whenever I told anyone about it – or more precisely whenever I told anyone British about it – their first question was always "Are you doing it for charity?" No other nationality I've come across does this and I don't know why. Are Brits more giving? Perhaps. The *Guardian* puts the UK close to the top of the World's Giving Index. Or do Brits feel you can only justify a trip like this if it benefits others, as though it would be too self-indulgent otherwise? I hope it's the former but perhaps the protestant work ethic frowns upon anyone who takes this much time off from the miserable drudgery that's supposed to constitute daily life. Once I'd learnt that people might donate something as a result of my ride I decided to choose a charity. Even if it only raised a tenner some worthy cause would get a few extra quid. Given what had happened in 2009, *Blood Pressure UK* was the obvious choice.

So there we were, four of us. Mark is a keen cyclist who'd already done Land's End to John o'Groats, Fenella often rode a bicycle and Annie believed she'd finally reached the fifteen mile mark on her gym's exercise bike a few days earlier but then realised she was on the wrong setting and it was only actually fifteen kilometres. And today, to the centre of

London, we'd be cycling sixty-odd miles. That's one hundred kilometres, Annie.

We decided to take the most traffic-free route, which, given we were in the south-east, was relative. After the highlight of traversing the world's most stupid roundabout in Hemel Hempstead, by late afternoon we hit the edge of London and, thanks to the lights on the Edgware Road, came to a halt every twenty metres. The traffic moved so slowly it wasn't the daunting experience I'd been expecting. In the early evening sunshine we arrived at Hyde Park. Given today's bizarrely tropical April weather it was crawling with people enjoying the last of the English summer.

After an ice cream and a cake it was only a death-defying ten minute scoot around central London to reach Trafalgar Square, where I was reunited with cool, refreshing beer and Nina, who'd flown out from her home in Spain to spend the weekend with me. Capital number two was in the bag.

Each member of the team had done magnificently, especially Annie. We said our goodbyes but before I could leave old London town there was something I had to do. I had to find some food I'd never eaten before.

By rights the UK should have been the hardest country on my trip to find something new to munch on. But since Nina is, in her own words, an Essex bird and had spent her youth in London she suggested something I'd never before contemplated and she knew just the place to find them.

"Here they are, jellied eels!" she said, presenting me with a Styrofoam cup of hideous grey lumps in aspic. She turned over the cup to tip its contents on to a plate. They remained stuck inside and had to be scraped out with a fork like a tin of dog food. She didn't tell me you're supposed to add vinegar. Without, it's like a horribly bland and lumpy Rowntree's fish jelly.

*

The most memorable thing about the ride from London to Portsmouth was the unfriendliness. Despite plenty of available space, a mean, old sod wouldn't let me camp on the site he'd block-booked because he said, "We have some seventy-year-olds in our group." What did he think I was going to do? Sit naked in the centre of the campsite playing *Anarchy in the UK* on an electric guitar while manically masturbating. That's daft. I don't even know the chords for *Anarchy in the UK*. And then a troubled youth threw a bottle at me from the passenger window of a car. I'd been going slowly up a hill on a narrow lane but had pulled over to let the traffic pass. A bottle at my face was his thanks. Luckily his aim was as impressive as his personality.

But I can't let these two ambassadors poison my opinion of humankind or even Britainkind, not when there are people like George. She – for George is a woman – is an OU student who'd read about my damp tent and offered a bed in Southsea, just around the corner from Portsmouth and my ferry.

Southsea is special to me. If it didn't exist then neither would I. Back in the late sixties my mum made the long trip from Blackburn to holiday there and she met a sailor on shore leave. Three years later I appeared.

Southsea is a great place for my existence but rubbish as a place to study, especially if you try to do it on a bench near the beach on a windy afternoon. I'd arrived a bit early and thought I should take advantage of this window in my schedule to do a little maths. Unfortunately, before I could finish them, the exercises I was doing were blown out to sea.

George was taking a gamble. She knew nothing about me except the persona I'd presented via Facebook, hardly a reliable indication of someone's true personality. For all she knew I could have been a cunning thirteen-year-old boy pretending to be forty simply to groom middle aged women.

The door was answered by George, a petite, smiley woman who looked in her mid-thirties although I later learned she was a good fifteen years older than that. Behind her was John, her boyfriend. They invited me in and found a safe place for the bike. After a cup of tea George and John went out for a run and left me in the house to finish off my maths. Luckily all the windows were closed and so nothing ended up on its way to France this time.

George and John had had it rough. Both had been married before, had kids and then lost their respective partners to illness very early. Recently, via the internet, they'd found each other and seemed to be bringing joy back into each other's lives. George and John's relationship was still very new. I've no idea if they're still together, but I hope that, wherever they are, whatever they're doing, they're happy. They deserve it.

After the best night's sleep since the ride began it was time for me to leave the shores of Blighty. I'd passed through the capital and plenty of towns and villages but I'd seen nothing to emulate the grimness I'd encountered in Blackburn. I'd have to look farther afield to find somewhere worse. Somehow I didn't expect the Channel Islands to provide it.

Chapter 3: Eating poo sausage

Capitals visited: 2
Total distance: 450 miles

Unlike the earlier ferry crossing the passage to Jersey was conducted in glorious sunshine on an English Channel that looked like an ice rink. On board I wandered on to the deck and got talking to a London banker on his way back home to Guernsey. When I told him why I was doing this trip he confessed to also having high blood pressure. Just as I'd foolishly done he too had been ignoring it. Hopefully now he'd do something about it. It felt nice to think I might have saved someone's life. It's just a pity it was a banker's.

After ten hours on the ferry I finally reached Saint Helier, capital number three. I was counting Saint Helier as the capital of the Channel Islands but please don't tell that to anyone from Guernsey. It was evening when I rolled down the ferry's ramp for my first visit to the land of Bergerac. This gave me just enough time not to find my campsite before it turned pitch black.

During the war there was a campaign in Britain to remove all road signs to confuse foreign spies. It appeared Jersey still operated this policy. One hundred metres from the ferry terminal all signage dried up. I might as well have navigated by magic crystal. I headed out boldly in what seemed like the right direction. I spent the next hour and a half biking around country lanes six feet wide with ten foot tall hedgerows on both sides. It was like cycling in Hampton Court Maze. I was lost. I asked several locals but no one could tell me the name of the road I was on, nor had they even heard of a campsite on this side of the island.

Eventually, with the sun long set, I got lucky and met a

fellow cyclist whose map was considerably better than mine, in that his was printed rather than copied from Google and drawn in pencil. My campsite was just around the corner. By now my head torch was on full blast and all my bike lights were blinking. Anyone looking out of their window would've thought they were being invaded by Christmas trees. Except they wouldn't have seen me because of all the sodding hedgerows.

I'd only given myself one full day to explore Jersey and so the next morning I went back "into town" as a visit to Saint Helier is called. It's a quaint, little place although I wasn't seeing it at its best with grey clouds scudding overhead. It felt a lot like the Isle of Man's Douglas in that you've the sneaking suspicion it's still 1955.

After a tour of the harbour I hunted for, and found, something I'd never eaten before. Black Butter isn't the French *beurre noir* but a Jersey speciality, a sticky syrup made from apples, cider, liquorice and spices. It's often eaten on bread but because I didn't think a large glass jar of treacle-like goo would be such an asset in my panniers I instead opted for fudge made from the stuff. The sweets were very much like Jersey: nice but expensive.

In the afternoon I had a bike around the coast, popping down to lovely Rozel Bay, where a semicircle of little, white houses kisses the sea. It's a pity I hadn't planned longer in Jersey as it seemed like a place worth exploring. Given more time I'd have hired a set of step ladders to peer over the hedgerows and have a proper look at the view.

Although I was nearly 500 miles into my ride I felt it hadn't actually started yet. That wouldn't happen until tomorrow when I arrived in France. You see, it's not travel unless everyone else is speaking in foreign. I was looking forward to arriving in Saint Malo the next morning and, armed with my 24-year-old French 'O' level, making a right tit of myself.

The ferry plopped me on to the mainland of Europe at nine in the morning. Having seen Saint Malo on my previous bike tour there was no reason to hang around. With the trip now finally started I set off like a priest after a school bus, haring away from Saint Malo's glorious walls. Then I realised that since today's ride was only around fifty miles I'd better slow down or else I'd be done before lunchtime.

The French get a bad rap in Britain but I've never understood their reputation for rudeness. They've always seemed friendly to me. None of them has ever thrown a bottle at my head. If you start a conversation in French, even ropey French, they'll help. Sometimes they'll help without even being asked. Around lunchtime, realising I was short of water, I pulled up outside a shop in La Boussac. Unfortunately it was closed but a man in the house opposite called out, asking me if I needed some food. I asked if I could have some water instead. Of course I could. And did I want it flavoured with peach syrup? How's that for *entente* cordial? I'd had my first French language transaction and I'd come out of it with enough juice to get me to the medieval town of Fougères, today's objective, on the border of Brittany and Normandy, a place full of cobbled streets, pâtisseries and boulangeries.

After looking down on the impressive 12th century castle from the colourful gardens of Saint Léonard's church, I popped into the supermarket and there I saw it for the first time, sitting innocently in the refrigerated section. For some of my countries on this trip I'd researched my foodie options for the Never Eaten Before challenge and tried to go as extreme as possible. I'd discovered a culinary horror story for France, a special sausage called *andouillette*, supposedly the worst of the wurst. It's made of intestines and tripe and has a reputation for giving off the subtle aroma of urine and faeces.

And there it was before me. I didn't need to buy one though. In a few days' time I'd be calling upon my cousin, and her husband Cyril had offered to cook one for me. And Cyril even claimed to like them, the weirdo.

Whoa! What the hell was happening? I was suddenly swimming, but not in water, in a thick, soupy blandness. I couldn't see but then vague shapes began to emerge. I was dreaming. No, I wasn't. Well, if I was, this was more real that any dream I'd ever had. And I was leaning at a bizarre angle, all my weight on my arms, my hands cold, my body feeling heavier than a car. I definitely wasn't dreaming. This was real. But where was I? It was a familiar place but I didn't know its name. I'd been here before. My body became lighter, but still heavier than normal. Eventually I could press my arms against the cool metal that my hands clasped and stand up straight. I was still wobbly and confused. Then I remembered why I didn't know the name of this place. Because only a few moments before I was cycling through it. Shit, I was in France, alone. I suddenly felt scared and very lonely.

At the village of Ambrières-les-Vallées a bridge crosses the river Varenne. It was lunchtime and I'd fancied a rest. I'd already bought a sandwich and it was time to eat. With the bike propped up against the metal railing that ran over the bridge I'd sat on the pavement beside it eating my baguette. A few mouthfuls later it was gone. Then I'd stood up.

Blood pressure is a strange bird. You almost never need to think about it. Your body sorts it out for you. But if you start messing with it by, say, taking loads of blood pressure-lowering pills, things can get freaky, especially if you take too many. While I was in hospital various medicinal cocktails had been tested and, unfortunately for me, the one that seemed to work best when I was sitting in bed caused my blood pressure to dip too low if I tried to stand up. One evening in hospital I regained consciousness on the floor with a bleeding face and a small corner of the bedside unit missing. I'd only been out for a couple of seconds but it doesn't take even a couple of seconds to fall. High blood pressure is a killer. So is low blood pressure.

I'd been prescribed five different types of pill. They were acting in harmony to keep my blood pressure within a healthy window and they were working well. In the early days I'd get a light-headed feeling if I stood up suddenly but I'd have enough warning to sit down or grab on to something if I felt it was going to get worse. But when you lose weight or get fitter – two things that were happening to me on a daily basis – your blood pressure naturally lowers. And so when I stood up beside that bridge I'd passed out, only for a second, but it was one second too long. If I'd fallen in any other direction except towards the metal railing I'd have smashed my head into the pavement or fallen into the road.

I needed a solution. The only one was to self-medicate and take less pills. I reduced my daily intake to four and hoped the situation didn't repeat itself when I was even slimmer and fitter. I made a mental note not to stand up quickly in future but for the rest of the day that scared, lonely feeling hung around like a fart in a lift.

To call Quessigny a one-horse town is to oversell it. It's home to just over a hundred folk. Despite having no shops of its own it does boast a town hall, although it's only marginally larger than a phone box. If you've business with the local government you'd better be snappy because the town hall only opens for one hour each week, from quarter to seven until quarter to eight on a Monday evening. Now that's a job I could manage.

My cousin Sarah's family moved to France when she was seven. She now lived in tiny Quessigny with her French husband Cyril and their two kids. I hadn't seen Sarah in over twenty years and she was going to celebrate this fact by poisoning me with a hideous sausage.

I sat at the dinner table with Sarah and her daughter Mila. Cyril emerged from the kitchen and put a dish containing four andouillettes in the centre of the table. Good, I thought, just one each. I didn't really want to be overfaced with more than one poo sausage. He then picked up a pair of tongs and plopped two of the huge, crispy, misshapen buggers on to my plate.

"Eh?" I said, hoping he'd miscalculated.

"Sarah and Mila are having something else. We've got two each," said Cyril.

"Oh goodie." Damn.

"Yak!" said Sarah, pulling an I've-just-eaten-dog-shit face. "They're disgusting. I don't know how you can." I didn't know if I could either.

Andouillette is supposedly an acquired taste and Sarah clearly wasn't planning to acquire it. She wasn't alone. All reviews I'd read online seemed to agree with her. And yet some Frenchies loved them so much they'd formed the AAAAA, the *Association Amicale des Amateurs d'Andouillette Authentique* or The Friendly Club of Lovers of Authentic Andouillette. This tripe 'n' intestine combo was the Marmite of the sausage world.

Cyril had frazzed the sausages on the barbecue and served them with fried potatoes and andouillette's usual accompaniment, a rich mustard sauce. Richer the better to hide the taste, I suspected. He loaded that little lot on to my plate and smiled the smile of an executioner.

"Ready?" he said.

It was time to be brave. I jabbed a sausage with my fork, severed a piece with my knife and picked it up to look inside. Dear me. Most sausages have a uniform consistency but not andouillette. Inside I could see jumbled coils of thick pink organ wrapped around jumbled coils of thick, white cack.

Now the sausage was open, a distinctly unpleasant odour emanated from within. Into my mouth it went. I chewed and chewed. It was like eating a mouthful of thick rubber bands. The more I chewed, the more the taste in my mouth filled me with a memory. I'd once worked at a company that made monitoring devices for waste management sites. If they broke down they'd be shipped back to the company covered in dried sewer juice. They stank. That was the memory this taste evoked.

Without the mustard sauce the andouillette would have been inedible but with the sauce they were merely foul. I finished my first sausage and was making slow progress on the second. Cyril looked at me.

"You don't have to finish it if you don't want to."

I was about to play the martyr and, against what my stomach was telling me, finish the lot.

"No, no, I'll carry..." I started.

"I'm not finishing mine," he added.

"Yeah," I said, putting down my cutlery, "I think I'll stop here too." I'd eaten my last ever mouthful of andouillette. Thank Christ for that.

After an extremely comfortable couple of days with Sarah and Cyril, I pointed the bike towards capital number four with the knowledge that my load was lighter than the last time I was waving goodbye to relatives. Since setting off two and half weeks earlier I'd lost more than a stone. If I kept up this rate of weight loss then by September I'd consist only of anti-matter.

France had been treating me kindly. The sun continued to shine. I hadn't experienced any rain since Milton Keynes. The wind was still blowing in my face but you can't have everything. It was a day of gorgeous, flat riding through fields of vivid yellow rapeseed.

The traffic started to thicken as I inched ever closer to Paris and I ended up twenty miles from the centre in an overpriced dive called *Le Pavillon Bleu*. Its grubby rooms were perfumed with the scent of stale cigarettes. I was only there because the nearby campsite hadn't opened for the year. I'd also tried to chance it on a gypsy site. I asked a miserable, little bloke if I could camp there and he said no but if I liked I could rent a building. When I asked how much, he quoted me a price per month and that didn't really fit in with my plans. I'd had enough for the day and the dive was the only choice in town. I'm not alone in my opinion of this hotel by the way. One of its reviews on TripAdvisor is entitled "Help! Run away!"

Poor though the hotel was, it was conveniently located for the assault on Paris the next morning, lying as it does near the busy D10. To ride on the road itself would have been awful but it came with its own cycle path that continued all the way until I hit the Seine. The route passed the 2,300 rooms of the massive Palace of Versailles, France's fifth most popular attraction and proof that lopping off the heads of your royal family doesn't diminish tourist interest in their buildings. I'm just saying.

There was also time a little farther down the road for a little snigger when noticing that Barnet is twinned with the unfortunately named Parisian suburb of Chaville.

Sarah had warned me about traffic in Paris. It's bad enough in a car, she'd said, let alone on a bike. But it's usually easier to cycle in a city than it is to drive. An unknown city, especially one the size of Paris, is confusing. If you don't know which direction to go at a junction you simply stop the bike and work it out. You can't do that in a car. And far from being the machine-gun-toting bastards that Sarah had described, Parisian drivers seemed fine to me. One guy on a moped even flagged me down to tell me my bike stand was dangerously low and risked scraping the floor. Thank you, *monsieur*.

I got myself installed in a hotel and set off to explore the city on foot. It was only then I discovered I could no longer walk. Most cycle tourers don't like to wear rucksacks while cycling. They say it causes backache but it'd never bothered me. I'd worn a rucksack while cycling on my previous month-long tour without a problem and I was wearing one on this ride too. It was mostly a security decision. All my valuables were in either my bar bag or my rucksack. If I had to pop into a shop I could unclip the bar bag and have all my vitals with me. If someone stole the bike while I was inside all they'd get were a couple of bagfuls of rubbish food and some dirty clothes.

So far on this trip I'd had the odd niggle in my legs while cycling but these minor gripes disappeared within a day or two. But now, walking the streets of Paris, my right leg was going all weird and tingly and I had shooting pains in my lower spine. Was it connected to the rucksack? Only time would tell. All I knew for now was that I needed to sit down for a few minutes after every 100 metres of limping along. I soon got bored with that and so I sat down for lots of minutes. Beer in France is stupidly expensive and, as you might have guessed by now, I'm a cheap sod. I managed to find a tiny place in the middle of happy hour – actually happy four hours – where beer was just slightly more expensive than any normal, miserable hour in Britain. So I sat there and had a few and waited for my back to cure itself or become alcohol-numbed enough for me to be able to walk again.

The next morning I formed a plan. I decided to cure my backache by brute strength. I'd force myself to walk hundreds of miles around Paris. I saw the Palace of Luxembourg in the

6th *arrondissement* and Notre Dame in the 4th. From there I headed through the 3rd and the 11th to reach my main target for the day in the 20th, the Cemetery of Père-Lachaise.

The cemetery is massive, more like a city of the dead, the only graveyard I've visited with its own streets. And it's stuffed full of household names in enormous tombs. Buried here are musicians such as Rossini, Bizet and Chopin, writers like Balzac, Proust and Oscar Wilde and scientists, philosophers, politicians, actors and even a clown. But, possibly most famous of all, which is a bit sad given his illustrious co-corpses, is Jim Morrison's grave. Once upon a time his grave needed heavy security to prevent fans from removing bits of it. Today it looked unloved. Jim's star is fading more quickly than his grave-mates.

Afterwards I trudged back through the 11th and 12th arrondissements to my hotel home in the 13th. I'd walked nearly every street in Paris at least three times but it'd worked. There was no pain in my back. The same couldn't be said of my feet.

The route out of Paris was as easy as the ride in and the terrain to the east of town was mostly flat with only the occasional hill to test my legs. I'd set off late but wasn't planning on cycling far as there was a campsite on the outskirts of the city in Villevaude. Unfortunately it was the closest campsite to Euro Disney. I winced when I discovered how much it would cost to sleep in someone's field. I found a spot to pitch my tent and merrily constructed my little house, whistling while I worked. Feed the first pole through to the end of the thin tube of material across the top of the tent. Bend the pole and bung its end into the little, plastic cup. Same with the second pole. Just one more to go. Bend it and – cock! The tent pole snapped.

After a bit of rejigging I could make a usable two-pole tent but the bike could no longer live in its porch and there were now considerably more flappy bits than there should have been. I'd no idea how it'd cope with strong winds. Maybe during the next storm I'd wake up and find myself in a field several miles from my campsite.

This incident damaged my confidence a little. I'd spent a lot of money on the tent because it was my refuge. At the end of a long day in the saddle it was the closest thing I had to a home. Apart from my bike it was easily my largest investment. I'd thought it was unbreakable. I'd only ever used it 25 times. I've had disposable razors that have lasted longer than that.

At the next opportunity I'd get in touch with Hilleberg, the tent manufacturer, famous for excellent customer service, and see what could be done. For now I'd just have to carry on with my crippled tent. In a few days' time I'd be in Luxembourg. Unless of course there was a storm during the night in which case I might be there a lot sooner.

Two days later, in the sparkly Champagne region of France, I hit the town of Thierry Chateau in mid-afternoon and saw a sight that made me do a double take. Walking on the pavement with a drunken gait was a bloke in his fifties. On top of his head sat an enormous comedy hat, one of those Saint Patrick's Day jobbies made to promote Guinness, a floppy, black and white, felt glass of stout with bright green brim. Saint Patrick's Day had been five weeks earlier. Oh well, I thought, that's the Irish for you, but he wasn't Irish.

I cycled past him. A minute or two later I stopped for a rest. Saint Patrick approached me and spoke in a strong French accent.

"Cycle tour?" he asked.

"Oui, monsieur," I replied.

"Moi aussi." Really? That was a surprise. After all, he had

no bike.

"Oui?" I said, exercising the full power of a very limited vocabulary.

"Anglais?" he asked.

"Oui."

"Moi aussi."

I thought about this for a second.

"What? You're English?" I asked incredulously.

"Yes."

"Then why are we speaking French?"

"I dunno. You started it."

Andrew didn't look like a cyclist. A packet of loose tobacco bulged from his shirt pocket. He had a greying, two pronged beard, mad eyes and a leery smile. His faux French accent mutated into a strong Norfolk one. He muttered to himself under his breath between the parts of his answers I was supposed to hear. He was cycling from his home near Norwich to Sicily's Palermo on an electric bike towing a little trailer attached to the bike with the loosest, wobbliest fitting you could imagine. It was like the sort of handiwork I'd do and then have to pay someone to put right.

It had taken Andrew three weeks to get this far, 190 miles from Norwich to Newhaven and 160 miles from the French coast. He'd wasted a lot of time getting lost in Dieppe until the early hours of the morning when he'd been picked up by the police for cycling on a motorway. He decided he'd overnight it in the cop shop but the police got sick of him and told him to sod off. But why did he get so badly lost?

"I don't have any maps," he said.

"You have a satnav then?" I asked.

"No."

"Then how do you know which way you're going?"

"Before I set off I sat down with Google Earth and wrote down the names of all the towns I'll be passing through. I have a list."

"Is that going to work?"

"Dunno. I hope so."

It was far from foolproof. France has frequent *Route Barrée* signs blocking your way. He wouldn't know which alternative route to bring him back on course. Imagine a village he needed to hit wasn't signposted from the last place on his list or he took a wrong turn. Bonkers though his plan was, good luck to him. However far he got he'll have had an adventure. I just have visions of him still wandering around central Asia, offending the local Muslims with his pint-shaped hat, clutching his little list of town names and wondering where the hell Geneva is.

My final day in France had me arrive on the edge of Montmedy with weary legs and an enormous hill in front of me. You can probably guess where the campsite was located. With the bike in its easiest gear, where 43 revolutions of the pedals equals one revolution of the wheels, I nudged myself halfway up the hill to the campsite's welcoming open gates. With sweaty hands I pushed the bike inside but it was empty, bar a couple of workmen. They looked around, surprised.

"We're not open yet," said one of them.

"The first of May," said the other, tapping his watch for some reason.

Today was the 27th of April. I was too early.

"Is there anywhere else to stay?" I asked.

"Try the tourist office," the first said.

"Where's that?"

"At the top of the hill."

Back on the bike I climbed to the tourist office that lives inside the citadel on the summit. Apparently there was nowhere to camp nearby but sharing my predicament was a young Dutch cyclist. He too wanted cheap digs for him and his girlfriend who I'd passed on my way up. Since there were three of us the tourist office agreed to open up the *gite* a couple of hundred metres back down the hill. With two dormitories Joris and Joëlle took one and I the other. So there, in the shadow of the citadel, I had a private room, a fridge, a freezer and a fully equipped kitchen, all for a few quid.

Joris and Joëlle were both slim with pretty faces. They were cycling from their home town in the Netherlands to Timbuktu in Mali but only four or five days into their ride Joëlle had developed a knee problem that prevented her doing much more than a few miles per day.

That evening we cooked together. I made a salad while Joris cooked up vegetable couscous. They had an amazing collection of store cupboard ingredients. It was like Ready, Steady, Cook. All I had to offer was a jar of chilli powder, the saviour of many a bland dinner. We finished off with a selection of stinky cheeses and quite a lot of tasty Leffe beer.

Joris and Joëlle were both fizzing with energy. I was fizzing with Belgian beer. Topics of conversation varied greatly I believe – the Leffe prevents recall – but I definitely remember one about national stereotypes that I thought you'd be interested in, especially if you're British.

"I think we see the Dutch as laid back, easy going, tolerant types, you know, with your attitude to drugs and stuff," I said.

They smiled their cute, little elfin faces, nodding in agreement.

"What do the Dutch think of the British?"

"They're pale," offered Joëlle.

"And loud," said Joris.

"Really?" I asked. The pale one wasn't a surprise but I didn't know we were noisy.

"Too many tattoos," said Joëlle.

"Always in football shirts," said Joris.

"Anything else," I asked.

"Yes," finished Joëlle. "And you're ugly."

I wasn't sure if this last statement was continuing the British character assassination or aimed at me personally. I didn't care. I was full of Leffe. Joris and Joëlle were both lovely, France had been lovely. The world was lovely. And you, you're probably lovely too. Tomorrow would be Luxembourg and it'd also be lovely.

Chapter 4: Doing drugs

Capitals visited: 4
Total distance: 1,010 miles

I've read a handful of cycle touring books. There seems to be a rule that at least one chapter must begin with the author suffering from the previous night's excesses. Not here, despite all last night's beer. That's because, although brain haemorrhages are probably best avoided – I mean, I can't recommend one – there's been at least one positive change in me as a result of my illness. I've developed a superpower. Don't get excited. I can't fly or shoot lasers from my eyes. Before I was admitted to hospital it'd only take two or three pints to generate a fairly unpleasant headache the next morning. But since the bleed I've yet to find an amount of alcohol that causes a hangover. I'm not saying there isn't a limit. I just haven't found it yet. Unfortunately, it's hard to see how I can use this superpower to fight crime.

Although I woke up the next morning in a bright and breezy mood this was soon tempered when I looked outside and saw the weather. This still being France it was raining *chats et chiens*. I waved my ugly hand and smiled my ugly smile and bid farewell to Joris and Joëlle.

The first 25 miles from Montmedy bruised the border of Belgium but there wasn't much chance of seeing what the country had to offer, plastered as it was with thick mist. As I reached Luxembourg it was still raining but the sun had started to dissolve the cloud a little. It looked like another sunny spring afternoon lay in store.

Luxembourg City is only fifteen miles over the border. Once there I found a room and went to hunt for foodie possibilities in restaurants and shops but there was nothing native to Luxembourg I hadn't had before. On the way back to my room I noticed an Asian supermarket, always a safe bet if you want to try something odd. I was sorely tempted by the chickens' feet but it's probably not a good idea to eat them raw. In the end I opted for Basil Seed Drink. Back in my room I opened the can and glugged a mouthful. Its sickly sweetness oozed down my throat. It had a texture unlike any drink I'd ever had and so I poured the rest of the can into a glass. It looked like frog spawn, tiny spheres of jelly each with a black dot at its centre. It didn't taste too bad as long as you tried not to think of tadpoles in syrup.

People frequently rave about Paris or Rome but I'd never heard anyone even mention Luxembourg City and I don't know why. It's a little gem. Luxembourg City proves you don't need to be massive to be a great city. It has the same population as Blackburn – tiny in terms of European capitals – but the similarity ends there. By now I was seriously beginning to doubt whether anywhere in western Europe could rival my home town. Surely there'd be somewhere near Chernobyl.

Luxembourg's old and new worked in harmony, with the fortified walls gazing down upon the old town with its winding, slow-paced river, while efficient, uptight, modern Europe, with a European Parliament and shiny office blocks sits up on the hill counting its cash. You can guess which was the more attractive but the new stuff didn't look bad either. Unlike London and Paris the locals here seemed relaxed and happy without the swarms of tourists buzzing from one site to the next. There was just a handful of wandering visitors taking the occasional snap.

Luxembourg appealed in other ways too. It has an excellent cycle path network and almost city-wide WiFi. I say 'almost' because the only place it didn't seem to work was in my hotel room. It also has a shop that sells nothing but

Gummi Bears. This appealed to me although I've no idea why. There's also a tranquil, little park beneath the city's viaduct if you want to escape the noise but, to be honest, there isn't really any noise.

My time was up. Hilleberg, my tent's manufacturer, had lived up to their reputation for customer service and had posted a replacement tent pole to a friend of mine in Brussels. Tomorrow I'd turn north and head towards it. Farewell, Luxembourg City. It was a pleasure.

The Low Countries are the Netherlands and Belgium. Sometimes though, people include Luxembourg too. These people are clearly taking the piss and can't have ever been there. It felt like I'd done more hills on my day and a half cycling in Luxembourg than the eleven in France. But Luxembourg was all behind me. I was now cycling in the hills of southern Belgium. Whoever included Belgium in the Low Countries was also taking the piss.

Leg pain aside, lumpy landscapes make for good scenery and the day had been spent on quiet roads bathed in sunshine counting cow statues that had been painted in national colours for some unfathomable reason. I arrived at my bucolic campsite in Bertogne, ecstatic to be alive in such handsome surroundings. The place had everything a campsite needed. There was a tiny restaurant, a little bar and a gurgling stream. Nothing could upset this reverie.

It didn't take long. Setting up my tent, it happened again, another broken tent pole. It was worrying that the pole had popped without the exertion of any unnecessary force such as, say, a light breeze or a falling leaf. Merely being in situ, bent as required, it'd snapped like a Chipstick. My tent couldn't stand up with only its single remaining healthy pole. This meant I had to put on my repairman's hat. It looked very much like my cycle helmet.

The Hilleberg tent pole is a series of ten golden tubes connected by smaller silver inserts through which a long piece of elastic is fed and tied to caps at each end to hold the whole lot together. Luckily, because my knobbled tent could operate on just two poles, I could use the unbroken tubes from the two knackered poles and make a fully functioning one. I could keep bodging the tent's two poles for another eight snaps. After that, I'd have no more replacements and I'd be stuffed. However, the chances of eight snaps before reaching Brussels and collecting my new pole in two days' time seemed remote. Facebook comments suggested I was doing something wrong, that the broken poles were somehow my fault. After all, Hilleberg has a reputation for high quality, and I don't.

I made the repair. The elastic inside the tube was extremely worn, almost worn through. I'd got the tent off Ebay from a seller claiming it was almost new and had only been used a couple of times. Seeing the condition of the elastic I had my doubts. Maybe the two times he'd used it had been the 1980s and the 1990s.

The rain came down the instant my two-pole tent was finally standing in a state close to upright. I retired to the restaurant, watching through the window as the water poured on to my tent's roof, waiting for another pole to crack under its weight at any minute.

I ate a bowl of mushroom soup and a greasy schnitzel with chips and mayo while sinking a strong Belgian beer and trying not to think the worst. My budget wasn't miserly but there was no way it'd stretch to a hotel every evening. I looked at the bottle in my hand, a 8.5% Duvel. If the tent died for good maybe one solution would be to get so hideously drunk in each campsite restaurant that the owner would let me sleep it off under a table. At least hangovers wouldn't be a problem. I ordered another beer.

*

The last time I'd visited Brussels, back in 1990, the weather had been very English. I remember it as a miserable, grey, corporate world. The old buildings were grand but dour. The new were identical office blocks. But the Brussels I saw before me today was a different animal. Could this just be because the sun was shining?

With the help of a highly detailed city map I found a beautiful and beautifully quiet route into Brussels via leafy suburbs and cycle lanes although, in reality, lots of the routes claiming to be cycle paths were simply white lines painted on existing, badly broken up pavements. You made your choice. You could dodge the traffic or dodge the splintered paving stones.

I must have been only a mile or two from the centre before there was any serious traffic. Like any normal person arriving in Brussels I hunted out a tiny statue of a little boy having a wazz.

The Manneken Pis, the symbol of Brussels, apparently has hundreds of different outfits – a sort of urinating, bronze Barbie – including an Elvis one but today he was decked out in the attire of a medieval Japanese warrior for some reason.

My big problem was accommodation. Brussels was full – full of humans and full of fish. An international festival of seafood had taken all the rooms, even in the cheap hostels. I'd suspected this beforehand when, three days earlier, TripAdvisor's best deal was an eye-watering €230 per night and it was confirmed today by the tourist office. My only option was to cycle out of the city and hope there was space in a campsite an hour and a half away. But I'd already cycled for eight hours and my legs were done.

Just in case the campsite was full and I couldn't make it back into the city I contacted Brussels-based Jo, a fellow OU student, to see if I could pop around and pick up the replacement tent pole that Hilleberg had sent to her address. She'd become my on-tour postal depot. An investment company in the Isle of Man had chucked some money to *Blood Pressure UK* on the condition I got a few snaps wearing their cycling team's colours in front of various landmarks. Their name was *Capital International*, an obvious link to my trip. The cycling clothes had arrived at Jo's too.

Perhaps I looked like I was dying when I arrived at her house because Jo immediately said I could crash there if I didn't mind the floor. After the possibility of a long, fruitless ride on weary legs this was luxury.

The next morning I had a bike tour of the city centre, shaking my bones on its stupid cobbles, and met up for lunch with Jo and another OU student Mike. He was a serial OUer, starting a new degree as soon as he'd finished the last. He'd already collected a handful and was currently working towards an MA in Classical Studies. I told you it's addictive. Before heading to the restaurant, they took a few snaps of me in my sponsor's colours in front of the richly decorated town hall in Grand Place, the main square. I was having to breathe in. Despite sending me a 'Large', the sponsor's cycling top was way too small for a blubber like me. I celebrated this fact by ordering a massive *filet amercaine*, something I'd never tried before. A huge pile of raw mince shouldn't have tasted as good as it did.

By mid-afternoon we were done and I cycled off to my campsite in Grimbergen. I bet you can't guess what happened there. It wasn't the calamity the previous breakages had been. I had my new pole after all and its arrival had at least proved the problem hadn't been my fault. The new pole was a different design. Hilleberg had obviously recognized this flaw and fixed it a long time ago, another hint my Ebay seller had been telling porkies. Still, seven more breakages and I'd be down to two poles again. Seventeen more breakages and

I'd be homeless. I was currently averaging a tube snap every two days. It wasn't looking good.

From Grimbergen onwards the Low Countries earned their name. The terrain was flat, which meant less work for my legs but less too for my camera. After an eight mile heavily forested cycle path I left Belgium and emerged in Baarle-Hertog in the seventh country of the trip. I celebrated this fact by setting up the tent and breaking yet another pole.

It was amazing to see how many of the people cycling in the Netherlands were in their fifties, sixties and even seventies. I suspect it's all this exercise that makes the Dutch such a physically attractive bunch. A lot of money has been spent on their cycle path network. If the result is a nation of slim and healthy people maybe it's an investment the UK could consider rather than the laughable paths I'd seen there a few weeks earlier.

In Willige Langerak I had some unusual fellow campers. I was reading on a picnic bench. A flaky, fourteen-year-old, Juliet Lewis lookalike danced up to me and asked me what I was doing. She told me she didn't like cycling but preferred climbing – an unfortunate hobby for a Dutch girl – and then waltzed off again, spinning around with her arms out like a Whirling Dervish. Then two emaciated lads in their early twenties turned up on tiny, paint-splattered mopeds and took two hours to erect a marquee-sized tent. Their bikes towed trailers that carried a collection of large stuffed toys. I thought perhaps they were building a venue for a party but no one else turned up. In the morning the two lads and their Care Bears were gone.

So well planned are the cycle paths that I made my way slowly towards Amsterdam barely looking at the map. I cycled down the side of a canal past a shop selling clogs. I turned the corner to be confronted by a windmill. It was as though I'd wandered into some Disney reproduction of

Holland. Approaching Amsterdam the Disney effect was switched off. I was slightly taken aback to discover that Amsterdam has a skyline that hints at industry and commerce. I was expecting to find streets lined with dealers and hookers, not a real, live, working town. And the cycle paths that'd been so lovely throughout the rest of the land were suddenly terrifying.

I'd never seen such a contrast between a nation and its capital. You can't get much more laid back than rural Netherlands. Very little seems to get done. Some sizeable villages couldn't even be arsed to have shops. I'd spent the previous three days enjoying a life of ultimate pootling, perfectly flat landscapes, a sun continuing to shine against all probability and, while not breathtaking views, some damn pretty ones. I shared the bike paths with a handful of people who cycled beside me and chatted.

But today Amsterdam was mental. The town was heaving. It didn't help that I'd arrived during Friday afternoon's rush hour. But not just that. I'd done another Brussels, turning up on a silly day. On this occasion there was no fish festival but it was a national holiday instead. The bike lanes were stuffed full of people trying to go in all directions, zipping this way and that but now there were other cycle lane users to watch for. Mopeds are allowed to use them and pensioners' shopmobility machines turned the paths into a geriatric *Death Race 2000*. Imagine three groups of people, all travelling at different speeds, all trying to use single lane cycle paths at once.

I saw two accidents within minutes of arriving. Some old fella was sprawled on the floor, a victim of a hit and run or, more accurately, a hit and pedal. Then a young lad came off his bike. Being considerably more handsome than the old chap he got many more offers of help.

For a city of its size it was light on cars but that's no

surprise where the bicycle is king. Not everyone was pedalling though. Some were enjoying a backie. There were various ways of going about this. Climbing on the rack at the back of the bike you have two popular seating arrangements: one-leg-each-side or side-saddle. Occasionally I saw a more daredevil approach with the passenger stood on the rack as though part of a motorcycle display team.

The bikes themselves are invariably black, heavy monsters that seem to come from the 1920s. They clunk and creak but usually have a comfy-looking saddle, like a small sofa. No one has an expensive bike. Theft is a problem here. Each bike comes complete with a couple of feet of chain, not a normal bicycle lock but the sort of stuff you'd use if you were devising a live stage show that involved velociraptors.

Like Brussels, the town was full and so I was lucky to find a hotel but not that lucky. Getting to my bed was a challenge. I had the room right at the top of a very tall house. The stairs were steeper than the steps on a bunk bed and sloped to the left, making you feel like you'd already had too much space cake. Given the attention and effort required to get up or down them it was odd the hotel's manager had felt it necessary to put up a 'No Running!' sign.

Top of my afternoon's List of Things to Do was a visit to Amsterdam's famous Red Light District. To reach it from my hotel I had to cross the main shopping area, full of the same brands you see everywhere, but repeated more often than usual. It wouldn't be long before a Euro-wide trip like mine would be entirely pointless, each city being an identical copy of the one before, the inevitable result of globalisation.

Once I'd reached Porntown everything felt a little incongruous. Despite the quaint streets and the little canals the vibe was more Channel X. Smoking cafés replaced the bistros and suddenly I wasn't being sold shoes and jeans from the shop windows but female flesh, all pouty and winking in sparkly bikinis. Strangely, for every shop that offered gimp masks and whips there was a Chinese restaurant. It felt like a sunlit version of *Bladerunner*.

The prostitutes came in all shapes and sizes. Some were gorgeous but lots weren't and one or two seemed to be catering for blokes with a Popeye fetish. Those were the ones that seemed to come on to me most strongly. Obviously I looked like that type of bloke.

My team, Blackburn Rovers, were playing West Ham that afternoon and it was being shown in one of the Red Light District bars. This meant I didn't need to go to a porn theatre to see a bunch of pussies getting screwed. It was a must-win game if Rovers didn't want to get relegated, which I assumed was the case but wasn't always obvious when you watched them play. Our lads should have come here. At least they'd have been certain of scoring.

After the game I wandered back to my hotel, tired of Amsterdam. It all felt a bit mad. A beer bus – basically a drum of ale powered by a team of ten cyclists sat facing each other – came around the corner on two wheels, its hen party occupants screaming like Janet Leigh, before nearly hitting a tram.

I still had to find something new to eat. Joris and Joëlle, the two Dutchies with whom I'd shared the gite, had suggested *krokets* but only after I'd mentioned I was looking for the weird and disgusting rather than an actual recommendation. They were supposedly just like potato croquettes but with the potato replaced by horse meat. I'd searched the streets with no luck. In the end I gave up and decided to employ a fall-back position. If I couldn't find a kroket for my challenge I'd buy some drugs instead.

I needed to try something I'd never had before and I'd never had drugs. Well, there was one time on my 21st birthday when my then-girlfriend scored me some sort of 'special' cigarette. It was just a pity I'd already had a skinful of lager. I'd never smoked a cigarette in my life. One puff is all I had and then I spent the next hour and a half throwing up. Happy birthday to me! Later the same girlfriend decided we should try ecstasy. Fearing the bad press it'd received we decided for our first go to share a tablet just to be safe, like a regular Sid and Nancy. We took the pill but it did bugger all. That's not true actually. It cleared up my headache. So there you go. My entire drug experience was a night of hurling and twenty quid on half a paracetamol.

But this time I'd get it right. I was in Amsterdam, the drug capital of Europe, for God's sake. I located my man, approached nervously, putting on my shades as I shuffled towards the dealer – best to remain anonymous, I thought – and did it. A sizeable amount of cash changed hands. I now had it in my sweaty, little fist – 30 grams – well, 35 if you counted the wrappers and sticks. OK, I'd bought two marijuana lollipops. I was Howard Marks. I was Bob Marley. Alright, I was Kojak, but Kojak who was possessing.

I cycled out of town the next day still holding my stash. Fifty miles later I decided to order a snack in a café and what should appear on the menu? Only a bloody kroket. Fantastic! Drugs *and* shit food. My life was looking up. I ordered one but was disappointed because it really wasn't bad at all. It was a deep-fried, battered roll with a moist slurry centre containing some kind of unknown meat chunks, like a Findus Crispy Pancake. But maybe it had been a posh, bistro version. Only two hours later, in the down-at-heel snack bar of that evening's campsite, I found another kroket, not as good as the first but still very edible, just like Findus Crispy Pancakes aren't.

Back at my tent I realised I still had my drugs to try. I unwrapped them, wondering what haze-filled experience, what hallucinogenic fantasies were about to unfold. Would I wake up three days from now in a cold sweat, imagining dead babies crawling across the roof of my tent, hooked on lollipops after only one hit? I popped them, one after the other, into my eager mouth and sucked. And sucked. And waited. And waited. Nothing. Absolutely nothing. I may as well have powdered and snorted a Chupa Chup. Just say no, kids!

Chapter 5: Take my breath away

Capitals visited: 7
Total distance: 1,519 miles

The scenery east of Amsterdam was forgettable. It didn't improve in Germany. It wasn't as flat as a pancake, more like a deep pan pizza. The cycling may have been dull but, in the western part of Germany at least, each day usually finished on a high with a campsite next to a huge lake with a restaurant selling ice cold beers for me to chug in the sun. It wasn't all bad.

Germany still had plenty of cycle paths but without the numbered network of the Netherlands. Without this hand-holding device I fell foul of a very simple assumption, that different towns have different names. I was in a village called Alfhausen and needed to get to Neuenkirchen and, from there, find the road to Damme. That'd be simple enough, I thought. I followed the signs to Neuenkirchen and, nine miles later later, I arrived. Strangely none of the options on my map matched the options on the road signs and Damme was missing completely. This was odd because Damme was the largest town for quite some distance. So I asked a local.

"Do you know which is the road to Damme?"

"You need to go to Alfhausen," she said, pointing back the way I'd come.

"No," I said, "I've just come from there. I had to find Neuenkirchen."

"Ah, you've come to the wrong Neuenkirchen."

"Eh?"

"There are lots of them."

Looking at the map more closely she was right. There were four Neuenkirchens within fifteen miles of Alfhausen.

Being a postman around here must be a challenge.

Moving ever eastwards the road took me through Hanover. It looked like a pleasant city and I decided I'd stay the night and have a look around. Unfortunately it didn't work out like that. The man at the Tourist Office told me the city's hotels, hostels and even its cardboard boxes were all booked up.

"Why is it so busy?" I asked.

"I think it's because *Cats* is starting this weekend," he replied. I checked my watch to make sure it wasn't 1981.

I cycled out of town and decided that, in the absence of campsites and given the dearth of available accommodation, I'd stop at the first place that had a free bed. As it turned out, slightly suspiciously, the first place I passed – a Best Western – had room at the inn. After checking in, a quick look on TripAdvisor told me that Hanover was teeming with empty hotel rooms. Perhaps the Tourist Officer in Hanover couldn't be arsed to find out whether any hotels were available. More likely though, he'd decided I was an undesirable who, like Sylvester Stallone in *First Blood*, should be hounded out of town. I looked in the mirror. My beard had attained 'dirty tramp' status.

The next morning, getting changed into my cycling clothes, I gave the maid a chance to walk in on me wearing nothing but my socks, the poor girl. She squealed an apology and fled while I went to the bathroom and realised I'd made an error. The previous night, with my tent still damp from that morning's condensation, I'd hung it to dry over the shower curtain rail. Only now did I realise I'd inadvertently filled the room with about three thousand beetles, moths and other insects that had secreted themselves inside. I spent half an hour hunting down as many as I could. I think I got them all but if you find a ladybird in room 121 that's probably my fault.

Right on the border with former East Germany is Wolfsburg. If I'd passed this way a few decades earlier this city of 120,000 people wouldn't have been here at all. Arrival from the west offers an unusual experience. Route 188, a main road I followed for most of the fifty miles from Hanover, mutated without warning into a car park for a massive factory. Wolfsburg, also known as Autostadt or Car Town, is a planned city founded in 1938 to build Volkswagen Beetles and is still dominated by the German company. They sponsor Wolfsburg's football team, who won the Bundesliga in 2009. That's impressive for a new town. It's a bit like Welwyn Garden City winning the Premier League.

I found a campsite, put up my tent and immediately made two portly new friends, a middle-aged German couple. For some reason I looked like I needed feeding up and was plied with endless cakes and coffee. The bloke introduced himself as Ferienland. The constant smirk on his face made it hard to believe anything he was saying. As Ferienland means 'holiday country' I assumed he was joking with the stupid Englander but he insisted it was true and said it was merely a rare name. I wasn't sure about his wife's name either.

"Remember zat time we met ze Englander and told him we were called Ferienland and Reinhilda?"

"Ja, das war super!"

"Und I put laxative in all zose cakes?"

"Oh, Helmut, you are such a joker!"

I cycled back into town where a party was taking place with a DJ and wine tents. Without knowing it I'd got very lucky. Apparently such events don't happen very often around here. According to Wikipedia, when Wolfsburg won the Bundesliga in 2009, "a party was celebrated in the city centre with about 100,000 people and was a first in the history of the city". Even allowing for the stereotypical joylessness of the German character, waiting 71 years for your first knees-up seems a little glum.

The switch in the appearance from former West Germany to former East Germany just east of Wolfsburg was sudden and obvious. On the eastern side all the villages were a little more unkempt and the petrol stations that had supplied me with Lion Bars dried up. Cobbled roads weren't uncommon. But for all that the place became more interesting to look at. I felt I was travelling somewhere slightly exotic. This was strange really because the eastern towns had a more run-down, Blackburn feel to them. Everywhere seemed to have suffered a distinct lack of recent investment and the street uniform included different variations on the shell suit. Also like Blackburn every male over twelve looked like he could take my face off without weaponry.

I moved east, through Stendhal, Brandenburg and Potsdam, troughing at the ubiquitous kebab shops. Although attractive places in their own right these towns were merely the *amuse-bouche* for the main dish, Berlin, and pitta heaven. At the last count, the German capital had 331 kebab shops.

It was the 18th of May and my birthday. I was excited, not because I was expecting a party but because Nina was flying to Berlin to meet me. Strangely for a such a technically competent nation, Germany's campsites had been miserly with their internet facilities and so I left all the arrangements to her. Rather than a hotel Nina opted to rent an apartment in Kreuzberg, a former part of West Berlin that'd bordered the east. Depending upon the website you read, this district of Berlin is described as 'trendy', 'bohemian' or 'dodgy'. I'd mentioned to a German where I was going to stay and he pulled the sort of face someone might make if he'd found a turd in his glovebox.

The ride into the city was wonderful. The roads were busy but the cycle paths huge. I passed Spandau and rode through leafy Charlottenburg and Tiergarten, the largest park in

Berlin and former hunting ground for its royals. The sun illuminated the golden goddess of victory atop the 66 metre column of the Siegessäule. This was a victory for me too, my eighth capital. I cycled triumphantly through the Brandenburg Gate to be confronted by a tiny tit in a Darth Vader costume selling photo opportunities to tourists.

As I approached Kreuzberg the mood of the place seemed to darken. Having cycled through the spotlessly clean centre of town, Kreuzberg's graffiti and general shabbiness caused my mum's voice to appear in my head. She'd always assumed I'd get murdered somewhere on this trip. According to her, the smart money was on Albania or Romania but a rough part of Berlin would do equally well. She likes to worry. It's a hobby of hers.

Over the course of our time in Berlin those mean streets transformed into something else. Reichenberger Strasse, our street, is known in Berlin as a key location for the once near-annual May Day riots. Today all was calm. When you looked more closely the graffiti was the work of artists rather than vandals, an attempt to jazz up the post-war buildings rather than degrade them further.

Berlin quickly moved to the top of my list of favourite cities. It's an amazing place. I hadn't expected it to be. Cycling through northern Germany had been very ordinary, with uninspiring scenery and unexciting villages. It improved in former East Germany but Berlin is special. It's a chameleon. Whatever you want – smart and modern, or leafy and suburban, or down 'n' dirty – it's there. Kreuzberg may have been shabby but it was also quirky. It had mohicanned punks and dreadlocked hippies rubbing up against Turkish immigrants and young Berliners with their kids happily strapped to their pushbikes, everyone just getting on with life but thankfully at a pace much slower than London and Paris. Other districts were tidier but, in my opinion, duller as a result. But you can have Berlin any way you want.

In the Jewish Museum, as well as the usual sickening holocaust stories, there are some interesting spaces-as-art. One of them, the Exile Garden, is a perfectly symmetrical seven-by-seven grid of rectangular concrete towers topped with olive trees. The ground is cobbled and slightly sloping. While you wander between the blocks surrounded by all this precision you feel disorientated. You have to find your own interpretation. Never employ a German builder, perhaps. But it's probably something deeper.

And then there was the Stasi museum, housed in their old headquarters in former East Berlin, a massive complex of dozens of utilitarian tower blocks, a monument to time wasted in the name of overbearing control and suspicion of the populace. The museum housed a funky collection of espionage toys and bugging devices. There was a secret camera built into a watering can so that people could be spied upon at cemeteries or gardens or any other place where you could carry a large watering can without looking suspicious. Just cemeteries and gardens then. There was also an oil drum containing a similar photographic device designed to take pictures of people in parking lots. If they'd spent half as much effort dealing with their economy as they did spying on their own folk their communist dream might not have gone tits up.

Unlike some European capitals where a very ordinary meal can cost up to one kidney, eating out in Berlin could be ridiculously cheap. The range of restaurants is immense too. Just over the river in the neighbourhood of Friedrichshain, you could move from restaurant to next-door restaurant and eat your way around the world. In the space of four businesses you might open with an onion bhaji starter at the Indian, wash it down with a bowl of borscht in the Russian next door, chomp on a huge steak for main course in the Argentinian joint and finish up at the Korean restaurant with a bowl of cocker spaniel ice cream.

It's also a cheap place to drink. A lot of the mini-marts put a picnic bench or two on the pavement outside the shop. You could pop in, buy a beer from their fridge at normal shop prices and sit outside drinking and chatting to your mates. It seemed to be the way the locals in Kreuzberg socialised.

Berlin is a place where odd but likeable stuff just happened. I'd never seen a wedding party on pushbikes before, including the bride in full gown, but there they were cycling through Treptower Park. And I'd never seen a beach in the middle of a landlocked city but there it was on the banks of the river Spree, covered in deckchairs with a beach bar serving Spanish tapas.

The weird stuff didn't end there. Walking back to our apartment late one night we stumbled upon a seedy-looking bar that contained an assortment of odd bods: a barmaid who stroked my hand each time she returned change, a mad, outlandishly gay Irishman who rambled incoherently, a Thor-like creature with a big dog and a lone dancing female crazy. We sat in the shadows and observed. A group of three arrived and tempted people in off the street to tango with them. There wasn't any music, by the way.

Prague was calling. I hadn't been on my bike in a few days and something felt wrong. The back tyre was too squishy. I could've stopped as soon as I realised this and fixed the problem while still in the centre of a major city containing dozens of cycling shops but I didn't. That's because my policy is usually don't-worry-about-it-everything-will-be-alright.

Ten miles from the centre of Berlin, in the middle of suburbia, I decided it was time to pump up the back wheel. I'm not the greatest mechanic in the world but I know how to inflate an inner tube. So imagine my surprise when instead of a nice, rock-hard tyre I was left with a broken inner tube nozzle and an entirely deflated back tyre. I knew what had gone wrong. It was because I'm an idiot. The special insert needed for my inner tube valves had fallen off my bicycle pump adapter and I hadn't realised. Using the adapter without the insert I'd broken the valve. I looked around. I was in a massive residential area. I'd have to walk miles to find a bike shop. A bloke walked past. Merely for confirmation of my predicament I asked him where was the nearest bike shop. He didn't even break his stride.

"Behind that building," he said pointing, and kept on walking. I could have kissed him, which is probably why he was in such a hurry. I went around the building and found the bike shop. There were no other shops – no grocer's, no newsagent, no supermarket – just a bike shop in the middle of a load of apartment buildings. This incident made me realise how fortunate I'd been so far. I'd cycled nearly 2,000 miles without a bike malfunction. I wondered how long my good luck would last.

Two days south from Berlin is a cute, little village called Lübbenau. With its riverside marina and ancient city walls it's the sort of place where old people go for the day on a coach. After ten minutes they've seen everything there is to see and then spend the rest of the day in the pub forgetting that there's no toilet on the bus for the two hour journey home.

Lübbenau has some peculiar obsessions. For a start it has a cucumber museum. According to the local tourist website for the Spreewald region, Lübbenau's is in fact Germany's only cucumber museum, which, if I'm being honest, didn't come as much of a surprise. The website also says it "offers a small but comprehensive exhibition about growing cucumbers". Have they sold it to you yet? If not, their next statement will do: "The highlight of any visit is the original tasting Spreewald cucumbers fresh from the tap." The tap?

Unfortunately it was closed the day I was in town and so there'll always be a cucumber-shaped hole in my knowledge.

Lübbenau also had several shops with the same sign claiming to sell eighteen types of mustard and ten types of horseradish. They weren't talking about Dijon or anything as mundane as that either. Here you could buy a pot of, say, raspberry mustard although no one explained why you might want to do that.

I suppose I could have sampled some fruit-flavoured condiment for my International Eat Something Daft challenge but I was already doing fairly well in Germany on that front. In Berlin I'd had *sülze*, a dish of cubed pork snouts in sauce. It looked like the stuff that oozes out of the stomach of a road-kill cat. And then that morning I ate something I'd later had to google to discover what it actually was and I'm still not sure. The menu had said *grützpinkel*. I was especially attracted to the final two syllables because in my childhood home, and apparently in no other house in the world, the male member was known not as a 'winkie' or a 'winkle' but as a 'pinkle'. I asked the waitress what a grützpinkel was. She beamed slightly manically.

"It's a grütz sausage of course!" she replied, with a tone that implied only a complete div doesn't know that. So 'pinkel' meant 'sausage', which at least justified my parents' choice of willy word. Unfortunately I'd no idea what 'grütz' was. Minutes later they arrived, two great, fat, grey wangers, on a bed of spuds and sauerkraut. I tucked in. Or rather I tried to. My fork bounced off the first sausage's protective sheath. When I finally penetrated its rubbery outer the innards spilled out lazily revealing the contents of a baby's nappy. They tasted alright though, like a gooey black pudding.

After my pair of pinkles I decided to go for a beer. Inside the bar I noticed they'd taken their horseradish obsession in a much more agreeable direction. They were selling small, refrigerated bottles of horseradish schnapps. Obviously, I bought one and it was bloody magnificent. Imagine drinking a chilled shot of decent vodka and then being smacked in the face with a fistful of horseradish. It was like that. In a good way.

With its throngs of day trippers with nothing to do, its cucumber museum and its keenness for mustard, Lübbenau was refreshingly different. After the dreariness of the first half of Germany I hoped this oddness would continue. I wondered what I'd find in the next village as I headed southwards. My money was on Germany's only cabbage activity centre.

Whenever the sun shines in Germany and wherever there's water your biggest challenge is to avoid seeing naked fat people. As I cycled past rivers and lakes in the afternoon heat there were frequent FKK signs – *Freikörperkulture* or Free Body Culture – to indicate that clothes are surplus to requirement. Usually the beaches beneath these signs stood empty – it was a workday in late May after all – but I wasn't always so lucky. Beside one long thin lake dozens of nudesters were sunbathing. There must have been a minimum weight restriction at these places. Few of them could have described their body shape without using the word 'morbid'.

FKK is big in Germany but it's not as popular over the border. Switzerland banned naked hikers in 2009 after an onslaught of pink Germanic flesh descended upon them via the Alps. This only encouraged the unclothed Germans but when they started to be fined they refused to pay. Given the few available storage holes in a naked human body the coppers were probably relieved the hikers didn't get out their wallets.

One afternoon in Grosskoschen I found a lovely lakeside campsite. The flat grass around the camping area was dotted with picnic tables and a little way in the distance it descended steeply to the water's edge. I'd arrived early, dripping with sweat after yet another hot day. The lapping waves called to me, tempting me to cool off. I was alone, the campsite and the lake all mine. I set up the tent and changed from my cycling gear into nothing but a pair of shorts. With my cycling tan I looked a right mess. I had nutty brown forearms and a ghostly upper arm where biceps usually live on any normal bloke. My chunky legs looked like they belonged to an anaemic wearing American Tan stockings with the feet cut out. In cycling clothes I appeared healthily bronzed but beneath them I had the body of a veal calf.

I started towards the slope, looking forward to the swim. As I neared the top I saw for the first time a thin strip of sand by the lake. Oh nice, I thought, a little beach. Walking onward I saw some more sand and a tiny, red boat. Perhaps I'd have a little paddle in that. I reached the top of the hill and looked down upon the lake's shore in its entirety for the first time. An elderly, naked German couple stood on the beach, both the size of Düsseldorf, the male of which was bending over as though about to launch something at me from his arse. Fair enough, I didn't want to go swimming anyway. I walked back to the picnic tables near the tent and, with my back to them, boringly did some maths instead, dropping heavy plops of sweat on to my Kindle and cursing my squeamishness when it comes to hairy-arsed Aryans.

Chapter 6: Dancing and dumplings

**Capitals visited: 8
Total distance: 2,110 miles**

Beneath the sandstone ramparts of Königstein's huge hilltop fortress I boarded a packed, little boat to cross the river Elbe and take me within a few miles of my next border. Perhaps the Czech Republic would provide something to compare with Blackburn. Surely a former communist country could offer up something grim enough.

Just after the border the cycle path that'd shadowed the Elbe on the German side came to a sudden end, not with a Stop sign but with a concrete slope that fell into the water.

Back on the road, brothels and very little else lined the edge all the way into Děčín, my target for the day. The town looked run-down but with a room for a tenner and pints for less than a pound I could make allowances.

The tiny woman at the B&B explained the front door system to me. There was a key – just one, mind – hanging on a hook inside the front door. If I left the building, she said, I had to take it with me because the front door locks automatically. I asked what about the others staying there who might want to go out after me. She didn't understand. Maybe we had to take it in turns, the lucky key grabber being allowed out while the rest of us waited in our rooms until he or she returned. Or maybe everyone goes out keyless and waits around outside until the key bearer returns. Either way it wasn't a great system. That though wasn't my problem. I had the key and I was going out.

It was Saturday evening but the town was dead. The only restaurant I could find had a sign to say it was closed at the weekends, an interesting business model during a financial crisis. Eventually I found a bar and went inside. The waitress was a dark-haired, brooding twenty-year-old with a face that promised rain and thunder. She looked like she'd much rather be somewhere else, probably the same place the rest of the town had escaped to. She gave me a beer and I took it outside. Later she came to see if I wanted more. I asked her how you order another beer in Czech and just for a second a tiny smile crept across her face. I didn't know if I could trust her. Maybe the phrase she gave me meant "kick me in the head".

That was as much fun as Děčín could provide. I went back to the B&B expecting a crowd of weapon-wielding guests huddled by the front door but the house was as empty as the town. In my room, I watched Barcelona beat Manchester United in the Champions League. At least that cheered me up.

The next morning I left Děčín with a warning from the landlady that Czech drivers are extremely dangerous because they're all on drugs. That should make things interesting.

The heatwave continued. I'd expected next year to include the heatstroke months – a summer cycling through Italy, Greece and Turkey – not this year's spring in central Europe. To compensate, the wind decided to cool me down by blowing strongly in my face whichever direction I pointed.

The next couple of days were spent meandering through the Czech countryside, stopping at restaurants and bars at regular intervals to eat huge platefuls of hearty food washed down with cheap and tasty beer.

The Czechs don't make conversation easily but when they do it's usually honest. In the small town of Terecin I told a fellow customer about my bike ride and he replied simply with "What a silly animal!"

Before setting off I had a plan of trying to learn at least a smattering of every foreign tongue I came across. I'd gathered a few language courses and the idea was to plug myself into my MP3 player a few days before reaching a border to learn the basics. Thanks to Pimsleur my knowledge of Czech was up to six words.

I'd tried a few of Pimsleur's other language courses in the run up to the ride and they all followed the same structure. Basically you're an American male in a bar trying to chat up a native-speaking female. I think it's really designed for gigolos or international sex traffickers. In one lesson you ask the woman if she'd like to go for a drink at one o'clock. She declines. So you suggest two o'clock. She turns you down again. You continue to repeat the question for every hour of the day with her steadfastly refusing to budge. Get the message, creep. She's not interested. My American's behaviour was worrying. Our next role play might involve popping to a chemist's to buy some chloroform. I promised myself I wouldn't give up but it was difficult to motivate myself with all the other demands on my brain and, more crucially, the possibility of drinking beer in the sun. And I wasn't sure how relevant the phrases would be that were coming in later units. Given my American's behaviour so far, I figured my vocabulary would be limited to booking cheap hotel rooms by the hour and negotiating a decent price for Rohypnol.

I was looking forward to Prague. I'd been there about twelve years earlier and knew what a gorgeous place it was. I also had some people to meet but first I had to find somewhere to stay. Although accommodation in the Czech Republic so far had been cheap I doubted this would be the case in the capital and so I opted for some city camping. In the north of the town is a single road, Trojská, that contains a mass of campsites. For not much more than a fiver you can curl up inside your tent at a site with hot showers, free WiFi and a cheap on-site bar, all a minute's walk to a city centre tram line.

I set up the tent, had a quick shower and trammed it into town for an early evening adventure. With a million others I crossed the famous 15th century Charles Bridge, our sweaty mass of bodies watched from above by the thirty baroque statues perched on its walls. Hawkers sold paintings and bits of tourist tat. People begged with heads down and outstretched hands in poses deliberately twisted as if their lives weren't painful enough. A young, just-married couple was being photographed, the bride in a traditional gown and the groom dressed for some reason as a Blues Brother.

I popped into a restaurant and ordered my favourite Czech meal: pork, cabbage and dumplings. It might sound boring but it's magnificent. Normally I detest cabbage, that British-style, dark green blob of vegetable matter boiled until the last microgram of taste has leached into the water. Czech-style cabbage is white, packed with flavour and as sweet as the apples with which it's sometimes cooked. Sat there in food heaven with my laptop I arranged my social life for the next few days.

I met friend-of-a-friend Jamie later that evening, a fellow northerner also living his dream. He'd quit his office job and the UK seven years earlier and moved to Prague with his guitar. He was playing tonight in a music bar called *U Maleho Glena*, little bigger than a single car garage but with an electric atmosphere. Watching Jamie was a mixture of pleasure and pain, the pleasure from the sound he made and the pain from the knowledge I'd never be able to do that. I've been playing guitar for fifteen years and I'm still rubbish. I have the manual dexterity of Abu Hamza.

After the show I got talking to another guitarist, a teenager from Ukraine who was soon to begin a university course in Prague although with no idea in what subject. It was Prague that mattered, not the course topic. He looked like a fifteen-year-old Brian May. I tried to pump him for information.

"I'll be cycling to your capital in two years' time," I said to him.

He laughed in my face.

"That's stupid," he said. "Nobody does that."

"Why not?"

"The roads are terrible."

But sensing he'd dissed his own nation, he changed tack.

"Did you know that Kiev was once the centre of a massive empire?"

"No. When was that?"

"In the 10th century."

"Have they updated the roads since then?"

He laughed again. I waited for some confirmation but it never came. Still, that's a problem for another year.

Walking back through town I crossed Charles Bridge again. This time it was beautifully illuminated and totally deserted except for the statues that looked down like saintly assassins ready to pounce. There are travel moments when you're suddenly aware you're somewhere magical, when all those sticky miles through sometimes tedious landscapes melt away to reveal the reason you're doing these things. An empty Charles Bridge at half one in the morning was one of those moments.

The next morning I stood dripping at the top end of Prague's famous square beneath the statue that provides its name. Good King Wenceslas looked out on the beast of Steven, a pink, sweaty freak with brown hair and luminous blond eyebrows, a facial anomaly that kicks in upon their receiving the first photon of the year. I looked like a reverse Alistair Darling. Prague was hot today. I was meeting local OU student Sasha at the museum. Who'd have thought Prague would have more than one? At least sitting there for ages alone waiting for her not to turn up gave me a chance to cool down.

Eventually we each figured out where the other party was and arrived at the National Museum. Sasha was pale and pretty, a slight almost frail-looking twenty-something with sunglasses much too big for her tiny frame. When she removed them she revealed a worried face.

One of the museum's exhibitions was about Czech folk tales. It was interesting but made me aware that our own fairy stories are only powerful because we learnt them as children. To take on a new set of myths in your early forties doesn't possess the mystery. This applied too to the numerous statues of famous Czech politicians in the museum. Václav Havel aside, they were all unknown to me. It wasn't my history. I may as well have been looking at sculptures of great Mongolian pastry chefs. I didn't need the folk tales and the history. I could've found all that on the internet if I'd looked. What was special for me was to meet a local, someone who could show me the places that mattered to her, the ones not mentioned in the Rough Guide.

Sasha was good company but sometimes icily detached, rarely making eye contact but then occasionally laughing explosively at something I'd said that really didn't warrant it. After the museum we went to her favourite ice cream parlour. We sat in its garden and talked about the Czech language. Sasha explained there's a sound in Czech – the ř in Dvořak – that's impossible to make unless your tongue is perfectly formed.

"My brother's wasn't perfect," she said. "He had to have the skin beneath his tongue sliced away."

"Didn't he mind that?" I asked.

"He didn't complain," she replied. I don't suppose he could have.

In the garden we were accosted by a young American

wanting signatures to support his organisation's dream of planting a million trees in Prague.

"How many trees have you planted so far?" Sasha asked him.

"Five," he replied. It was a start.

"What sort of trees do you want to plant?" I asked. He thought for a minute, for too long really.

"Y'know, leafy ones." It's always nice to meet an expert.

Sasha was hard to decipher. She seemed sad, as though she wasn't being supported. Her family couldn't understand why she wanted to study. But it seemed clear to me. She was sick of menial jobs. She'd worked in the UK as a cleaner and au pair but she'd taken a fairly confrontational approach to her family employers. She thought their standards of cleanliness were appalling and she'd told them. Despite being in her twenties she'd played the part as a matriarchal housekeeper rather than the babysitter. She didn't tell me she was fired but it was implied. What she really wanted to be was a teacher.

Later Sasha took me to the quiet, peacock-filled Valdštejnská garden, an understated place that seemed to match her mood. She'd once come here with a university professor with whom she'd been madly in love. Ghosting through Prague with this enigmatic woman talking of lost romance I felt like I'd fallen into the pages of *An Unbearable Lightness Of Being*.

Sasha wanted kids but couldn't see how she could afford them without a better job. Perhaps her studies could save her. The recent lies from Nick Clegg were a worry though, managing to hike university fees threefold rather than abolish them altogether as promised. She doubted she could afford to continue. It was her only hope. If she persevered and got the degree maybe the rest – the job, the family – would fall into place. I hope she gets there.

After a visit to Franz Kafka's grave in the New Jewish Cemetery that involved my wearing a paper yarmulke in case the top of my head offended an omnipotent being, I strode over to the Lennon Wall, Prague's graffitied monument to love and peace. Nearby is the first love-lock bridge I'd experienced although I'd see many more in the months to come. Lovers write their initials on to a padlock, fasten it to the bridge's railings and cement the union by hurling its key into the water. The locks come in all sizes although it's considered bad form to use an easily removable combination lock, a bit like including within your marriage vows "with this doughnut I thee wed".

I've kept quiet about my tent for the last thousand miles but the poles had been silently snapping behind the scenes. It happened again in Prague. I woke up one morning, a full 36 hours after erecting the tent, to discover another victim during the night. The tent had had more breaks than Steve Davis. By now I could repair a cracked pole in a matter of seconds but at this rate I'd be out of spare pieces by the middle of next month.

And the tent wasn't my only malfunctioning piece of gear. Cycling out of Prague on a mercifully cool, grey morning was more than a little hairy. The triple-laned main roads felt like motorways without hard shoulders. Towards the outskirts of the city the roads' edges were badly broken up. The clasp mechanisms keeping my panniers fastened to the rack had started to work themselves loose as a result of the lumpy road's vibrations and there was no obvious way to re-tighten them. With Prague a few miles behind me I sped down a busy hill and hit a tarmac divot sending the left-hand pannier flying clean off the bike and into the middle of the road. Only the quick reactions of the driver behind prevented by stove, gas canisters and all my food from being crushed flat.

The route to Brno, the Czech Republic's second city,

involved five days of wondering why the roads of this country never follow the contours. If there's a river you have to cross it. Down a steep hill, up a steep hill, over and over again. I slept in unmemorable hotels in unmemorable villages maintaining the diet of tasty stodge and far too many beers. Before arriving in the Czech Republic I'd already lost over two stone but was now regaining weight as I gorged myself on piles of potato pancakes and barrels of bacon dumplings.

I was well into my third month on the road and happily lost in the project, enjoying almost every minute, and wondering what lay ahead in future countries. I was in my own world. I hadn't looked at the headlines for weeks. Happy though I was, people were worried about me. Emails informed me I was cycling through a deadly cucumber epidemic. It was news to me. From the tone of the BBC's hysterical reporting you'd have been better off adding polonium to your salad. Luckily, Czech chefs rarely feel a duty to offer anything green. Five a day? I was lucky if I'd had five a month. I was free of the E. coli affecting Europe but suspected I had a touch of scurvy.

I wondered how the curator at Lübbenau's cucumber museum was taking the news, his pride and joys denigrated by the press. It was a storm in a salad bowl. The media had once again turned an unfortunate story into something of apocalyptic proportions. Putting it into perspective, more people die in road accidents in the UK on any given weekend than eventually died in total throughout Europe from the entire E. coli outbreak. I was safe, from cucumbers if not the cars. I continued to cycle to Brno happy in my bubble.

I arrived in the city and headed to a themed hostel. Its first theme was that each room was named after a famous person or event connected to Brno. Mine was dedicated to Brno-born Kurt Gödel, the mathematician, which seemed appropriate. The hostel's second theme was daft miniature beds. Even

Ronnie Corbett would've had to adopt a foetal position.

Brno's centre was attractive although no rival for Prague. I saw its flower market and its cathedral, one that's impossible to photograph well being hemmed in on all sides by smaller buildings. But I curtailed my exploration. Those strange shooting pains in my legs had been with me ever since Paris, returning most times I went for a long walk but now I had a painful dodgy knee as well. It was odd that neither of these afflictions were present when cycling, only when walking. Perhaps I was morphing into a bikebot.

I met Cat in the centre of town next to the large, black dildo that is Brno's astronomical clock. She was from Preston, just up the road from Blackburn, and had read about my trip in a local paper. We went to a bar and met her friend Ed. Both he and Cat had moved to Brno to work as translators after recently graduating from Oxford where they'd studied Czech. It wasn't a very popular course. There were only three of them in the class.

After a meal of fried cheese and chips Ed went on his way while I accompanied Cat to her dance group. In a bid to integrate into Czech life she'd signed up to a folk dancing club. They were going to practise in a sports hall. I sat at the back and watched. It wasn't the most attractive dance I'd ever seen. It mostly involved the women pogoing up and down on the spot whilst the blokes whooped, whirled and slapped themselves. They were enjoying themselves though. The communal vodka helped.

Despite her degree, communication for Cat still posed difficulties. To her new Czech mates she'd introduced herself as the local word for 'cat' until she realised it was a euphemism for a sexy woman. A few weeks after joining the dance group she'd casually mentioned to one of the women where she was from. The woman replied, "Oh, we didn't know you were English. We just thought you were stupid."

*

It was drizzling when I crossed the border into Slovakia. The Czech towns I'd cycled through on the previous day had been increasingly shabby but descended a notch or two here, especially now everything was painted in fifty shades of grey. No one smiled. This was truest in Malacky, twenty miles from the border. It looked as depressing as Blackburn. Now I realised the flaw in my search. I couldn't know a place just by passing through it. Besides, looking for the worst place in Europe, or at least a place worse than Blackburn, was a bit negative. Perhaps I should focus on merely finding aspects of a place that are worse than their counterpart in Blackburn. That way I'd be finding a positive for my home town. For example, the hotel I later found looked worse than any I knew in Blackburn. Walking its endless, uniformly drab corridors was like playing *Wolfenstein 3-D* without the Nazis. So that's a yeah for Blackburn. On the other hand, the hotel's restaurant was cheap and maintained the calorific charge of the Czech Republic. A lunch of tasty smoked sausage and cabbage soup followed by pork goulash, sauerkraut and dumplings and two pints came to little more than a fiver. So that's a yeah for Malacky.

The next day would see me reach another capital, Bratislava, and my beard would attempt to take a life. Nina had cursed me. In her attempts to inject spirituality into my existence she'd often provided me with a must-see list of places in some of the capitals. There'd been an incongruous Buddhist temple in the red light district of Amsterdam and visiting Kafka's and Jim Morrison's graves had been her suggestion too. These occasions had infected me, and my beard had become thoroughly evil. Its length had also got seriously out of hand. Every time I looked in the mirror I'd grab the phone and immediately start calling the Sex Offenders' Hotline.

In Bratislava it went beyond this. While casually walking through the centre of the city, a young woman whizzing past on her bike glanced at me. I thought nothing of it, and then – thump! – I turned around and there she was, picking herself up off the floor, while a middle aged woman lay sprawled in the middle of the road. My beard did that. Distracted by the idea of Peter Sutcliffe walking unshackled around her home town the girl's only option was to try to terminate the life of a tourist.

I'd got lucky when I arrived in Bratislava. I turned up at the tourist office and asked for a cheap hotel and the nice lady behind the desk took one look at me and thought, "Where would Captain Birdseye like to stay?" She immediately offered me a boatel, a boat that's also a hotel. It was a rusty, old tub moored up on the Danube but the room was great and the staff were friendly. They probably thought I was the skipper.

While there I shaved off my deadly beard. I had an exam in two days' time in Vienna and didn't want to get busted for smuggling in anything illegal via my facial hair. A Snickers bar had fallen out of it just that morning. And I also didn't want to be responsible for risking anyone else's life. For now, Slovakia, you are safe.

Chapter 7: It means nothing to me

Capitals visited: 10
Total distance: 2,501 miles

After weeks travelling east into a strong headwind I turned the bike westward to face Vienna and on that day, that very day, the wind changed direction and blew with equal force from the west. An experienced cyclist might say, "Are you sure? Perhaps you're confusing a headwind with air resistance." But I wasn't. The grasses at the side of the road continued to bow down before me. I was king of the weeds.

Some people love to cycle on well-established routes. One of these is the EuroVelo 6 that, on its 2,270 mile journey from the Atlantic to the Black Sea, hugs the Danube between Bratislava and Vienna. As a result I was expecting better cycling today than any old route I'd just casually made up myself but I'd be disappointed. The path is boringly straight and runs parallel to the river, but the water itself is hidden from view by tall trees. It is also raised to give the wind a more effective chance of getting you. The distances on the signposts were all over the place. First it was 32 kilometres to Vienna. Five kilometres later it was 34, then 30 and then 38.5. If this is a typical EuroVelo route I couldn't recommend it. It was the dullest day's ride of the year.

In the mid-nineties, when I eventually escaped Blackburn, it was in Austria that I first emerged from my tunnel. After failing to get that job in Manchester I'd given my CV to an employment agency. They doubted they could help me. No one had ever asked for a technical author before. They'd never even had one on their books. But two weeks later they called and asked if I wanted a job in Austria. A company based in Graz, the country's handsome second city, had come looking for a technical author and I was the only thing they could offer. Now that I was living close to the geographic centre of Europe, there were loads of great cities all within a few hours' drive. And then there was Vienna.

I don't understand Vienna. It looks great, has magnificent architecture and rich tradition but it leaves me cold. It always did. I'd occasionally pop up there, often in an attempt to entertain visitors. They usually loved it but I didn't. I'm not entirely sure why. It might be the sex factor. There's a hell of a lot about Austrian culture that isn't very sexy. Oompah bands aren't sexy. Lederhosen aren't sexy. Neither Mozart, DJ Ötzi nor Hitler is sexy. And if your nation's only sex-related story in recent memory is Josef Fritzl's then perhaps you have an image problem. The rest of Austria, the rural bit, gets away with it. Oompah and leather kecks fit the countryside. But capital cities, the seat of a nation's power, should be a bit spunkier. Vienna though feels staid, stuck in an era where the height of edginess is to eat chocolate cake. Midge Ure had it right. It means nothing to me.

That said, I had an important mission. It was exam day. I went to the OU's office in a street right off Stephansplatz, home to the city's cathedral, covered from head to toe in scaffolding. There were only three of us sitting exams. It was like being kept back for detention.

I didn't need to make the three day detour to Graz but I still had a lot of friends there. The ride was increasingly hilly and hot but allowed me to eat some of my favourite Austrian food on the way. Oh, how I'd missed *leberknödelsuppe*, a baseball-sized liver dumpling floating in a warm bath of beef bouillon. It's delicious although visually it's very reminiscent of an overly full potty. Then there's *leberkäse*. Describing leberkäse without making you feel ill is quite difficult. It looks like a meat blancmange although it's all the bits that can't be sold as meat in their own right, ground to a paste and then baked like a cake. It's like Spam without the class. Its name literally translates as 'liver cheese' but the inclusion of 'liver' in its name is just to attract more punters. It doesn't contain anything as recognizable as liver. You have a great, wobbly, pink slice of it on a bun with a dollop of mustard and a good grating of fresh horseradish. It used to be my perfect hangover cure but now that hangovers were a thing of the past I'd have to find a new excuse.

Speaking of horseradish, you have to treat the fresh stuff with respect. It's not the mildly pungent creamy sauce you get with beef in Britain. A pinch of it can blow your nose clean off your face. On a visit an English friend ordered a plate of cold meats, which, as is normal here, was topped with a fistful of the freshest grated horseradish. I didn't warn her in time.

"Oh good," she said, "Mozzerella!"

She picked up a giant forkful and shovelled it into her gob. She couldn't understand what happened next. Cheese doesn't do that. She danced around with her eyes streaming, wafting her face and howling. She probably thought she was dying. I'm glad it happened though because, first, it serves as a warning to you but mostly because I laughed myself sick. Her nose has only recently grown back.

All the grease hiding in my leberkäse didn't help to overcome my first experience of 'bonking' on this trip. Bonking, if you don't know, is an all-consuming fatigue brought on by lack of fuel rather than anything sexual. The last two days' rides hadn't been much more than fifty miles apiece but after weeks of flattish cycling I suddenly had to contend with thousand metre climbs each day under a blistering sun and I was utterly pooped. The scenery was gorgeous but it's true you can't live on views alone. Feeling light-headed, I had to find calories fast but found myself in a *gasthof* desert. I asked a passer-by where the nearest place was. She pointed up another massive hill. I wanted to cry.

Eventually after many stops I made it to the top and walked inside to be greeted by a barmaid who clearly wasn't impressed with my purple, dripping head and grubby cycling clothes. It's the sort of reaction you get in Austria if you deviate from the norm in any way at all. They like convention. Still boiling, I decided to eat al fresco, opting for an enormous bowl of cheese soup plus the world's biggest schnitzel and chips all washed down with a pint of shandy. If she was unimpressed when I walked in you can imagine her disgust when she came outside a little later to see if I wanted anything else and found me asleep with my head on the table. Classy.

But I was worried. Looking at the map of my westward journey Austria just kept on getting more and more mountainous. The hills that'd worn me out recently were mere nipples compared to what was ahead. Some of the passes would take me close to 2000 metres. I expected to be woken on a daily basis with my face in a bowl of soup.

It was great to see my friends again and even better to find an Austrian dish I'd never tried. *Beuschel* is probably best translated as 'organ stew'. Traditionally, it was made with hearts, lungs, spleens and livers. Nowadays it can be a ghoulish pick 'n' mix of any of those things although to be authentic it should always include lungs. Mine did. It may have also included spleen but since I've no idea what spleen tastes like I couldn't be sure. The stew was a grey-brown sludge with slimy black bits – those were the lungs – and it was edible but I doubt I'd order it again unless I wanted an easy exit from a relationship with a vegan girlfriend.

I don't really understand why Graz isn't more famous than it is. When I'd gone there for my interview back in the days when you booked flights by visiting a travel agency the woman at Thomas Cook had never heard of the place. It was the European City of Culture in 2003, which brought a temporary spike in visitors. It's also the capital of Styria. You might not have heard of Styria either but you would've done if Bram Stoker had stuck to his original plan. It was going to be the home of his vampire until he discovered Vlad's story. He made the right choice in relocating him to Romania. It's not very spooky around here unless you're terrified of fat men in lederhosen, which you probably should be.

The old favourites were still in Graz. The Uhrturm – a clock with its hands on the wrong way and the symbol of the city – sat on top of the Schlossberg, the tree-covered hill in the centre of town. But new features had appeared since I was last here. City of Culture status brought new investment. A partially open-air, glass and steel café was now fixed in the centre of the fast flowing river Mur that divides the city. The bridge over it had become home to another collection of love-locks. I wondered how often the diners below had a key lobbed into their beuschel. And the new art museum was open. It blends architecturally into the Italianate feel of the city about as seamlessly as The Gherkin would in a Scottish hamlet. It's enormous, futuristic and deep blue, a plastic, alien internal organ covered in thick, severed arteries plopped awkwardly in Graz's traditional streets.

Graz and Styria may be unknown but this doesn't mean the region can't be up its own arse when it comes to some of the stuff it produces. I'm no wine expert and my palate can comfortably take the cheapest of plonks but I can't manage *schilcher*. A lot of Styrians are bizarrely proud of it. It's basically a very expensive bottle of vinegar masquerading as quality rosé. I've heard it described by an elderly Austrian as "so sour it can suck your shirt through your arse." Just to prove a point, a mate of mine successfully topped up his car battery with some. And just as no sparkling wine produced outside the Champagne region is allowed to use its name, schilcher has similar protection although I'm fairly sure no one has ever challenged this.

One nice thing about telling people you're trying to eat weird shit is they start searching for it on your behalf. I cycled out of Graz with a gift from my friend Nem, chocolate from Zotter, a local company that adds unusual ingredients. She got me one bar flavoured with balsamic vinegar and another with celeriac. She'd tried to get the bacon, cheese or fish varieties but they'd sold out. Seriously.

After a week or so surrounded by people it took me a few days to get used to the solitude again, even with good friend Damian accompanying me for the first day and a half out of Graz. We got lucky and stumbled across two different annual town parties in the space of a few hours, in Köflach and Judenburg, where the excellent local beer made the far from excellent local music bearable. We'd earned the celebrations. In between the two parties we'd climbed to the high point of the ride so far – the Gaberl pass – at 1,551 metres and, despite being the end of June, it was a chilly, teeth-chattering descent. The views down were spectacular, with shafts of sunlight picking out distant villages. Austria is magnificent.

The ride westwards followed the river Mur, through the gorgeous, little village of Murau, home to one of Austria's most popular beers, until Tamsweg when the road went north to Radstadt over a 1,700 metre pass. I was in proper ski country now – the resort of Schladming was just down the road – and my legs were feeling it. On the way I got talking to a German cycling couple in their seventies. She used an electric bike because of her dodgy heart but his was a normal road model. There's no age limit for this sort of thing.

After swapping maps with a team of Swedes and Macedonians coming in the opposite direction over the 1,276 metre Thurn Pass, I freewheeled for ten miles down the other side into Kitzbühel and spent a very English afternoon with British OU student Louise. Her beautiful, wooden Alpine home was conveniently placed at the top of a steep, little hill but I was instantly met with a giant trayful of home-made cakes. Wimbledon played on the telly in the background and there was a pot of real English tea.

Austrians usually prefer fruit tea and this was the only pain relief on offer during childbirth to a friend of mine in an Austrian hospital. Since homeopathy is entirely mainstream here the tea was probably as useful a medication as she was likely to get.

July had arrived and Austria was saving its toughest climb till last. The assault would take place from the small town of Zams. Sitting as it was in a bowl of mountains there was only one sensible way out of this place and that was the way I'd come in. If I wanted to continue west I either had to go over a 1800 metre pass or burrow through an eight mile tunnel, and I wasn't allowed in the tunnel.

I'd been energized to make this final climb by the most incongruous gasthof in the country. On the outside it was typically Austrian, all timber and pretty, little flowers spilling from the balconies but this place was run by a Chinese family and supplied chow meins alongside their schnitzels. Their Eat-All-You-Want buffet was delicious although I'd caution you to read the labels on the serving dishes carefully. Garlic sauce and battered bananas isn't a winning combination.

Full of noodles I set off towards the Arlberg pass. The first fifteen miles with its 500 metres of ascent were fine. I was barely climbing but drowning in the sort of scenery that made Julie Andrew's whirl. Once I reached St. Anton the pass put on its serious hat and became steep and relentless. In the heat of early afternoon I stopped every few hundred metres for a breather. Finally, reaching the top at 1,800 metres, I celebrated with an expensive frankfurter and an Almdudler, the fizzy, sweet pop some claim is the national drink of Austria if you forget about beer and schnapps and ropey wine.

What followed was a magnificent freewheel with the chilly summer air at the summit warming gradually as I approached my twelfth country, Liechtenstein. Would it be a land of excitement and mystery? No, it wouldn't.

Chapter 8: A marmot for dinner

Capitals visited: 11
Total distance: 3,139 miles

I once knew a coach driver. His role often took him and a busload of punters through the heart of Europe. For novelty value he'd drive through Liechtenstein and its capital, Vaduz. He'd announce to his passengers that he was going to park up for half an hour to give them a chance to look around the city. That's not long enough, the mob would shout back in unison. But it was. Ten minutes after disembarking, a queue would appear outside the coach. Ten minutes is about nine minutes too long in Vaduz.

Removing the border controls in Schengen Europe makes the whole place feel like the edges of individual nations are blurring, becoming one unit working together. I know that's an idea that repulses a lot of Brits but I think it's amazing. A handful of decades ago we were blowing the crap out of each other. Now, the richer nations help the poorer ones. Having to produce my passport for the first time since leaving the UK to enter Liechtenstein made me feel like I'd moved back into the land of the suspicious and uncooperative.

I was hoping Liechtenstein would be another Luxembourg, a place that didn't draw the masses but hid something worth finding. But whereas Luxembourg was lovely, Liechtenstein wasn't anything at all. The good views it possesses belong to Austria and Switzerland on either side of it. The capital, Vaduz, has the population of a Port Vale versus Grimsby match on a wet Saturday in February and with even less to entertain you. Let me illustrate this with an example: Liechtenstein's biggest tourist draw is a denture factory. It could've been so much more. Actually, no, it couldn't. It could've been a little bit more. There's an attractive castle up on the hill over Vaduz. Unfortunately, the royal family live up there, gurning smugly from on high and refusing us proles a look inside. We have to be content with the gnashers emporium while they lounge around on thrones, gargling Dom Pérignon and smoking €500 notes. Except they don't use the euro. They use the Swiss franc. And their border is patrolled by Swiss border guards. Basically, Liechtenstein is a canton of Switzerland. Twenty minutes was all I lasted and then I was in my third country of the day, not a pointless pretend Switzerland but the real one.

The next morning I woke up on a campsite in Buchs. It'd been raining overnight. Normally I'd leave the tent to dry in the morning sun before packing it away but today I had people to meet. I shook the tent gently to remove the excess water and this most tender of tremblings caused yet another pole to snap. I was down to my last few. I couldn't believe this tent. I'd known more robust meringues. Once again, Hilleberg's customer service came to the rescue. After a quick email they promised to send two more of the improved poles. My tent would be better than new.

If you arrange to meet someone off a train at eight in the morning in the UK you know it's going to be twenty past before the heaving beast finally wheezes into the station. Or maybe quarter to nine. Or perhaps tea time the next day. Not in Switzerland. The timetable said eight and so eight it was. Welsh Elli quickly appeared followed by daughters Andie, Flurina and Aisha, and Swiss hubby Pädi, all five on bikes. Both Elli and Pädi were OU veterans but there'd be no studying today. All six of us were off on a ride together down the bank of the Rhine. The cycle lane was flat all the way but the total distance was over thirty miles. Little Aisha, who was only a dot, managed the whole way with only a little towing from Dad towards the end.

Elli and family ended their ride after a picnic on the shore of gorgeous Lake Constance in the town of Rorschach. (Ironically, when viewed from above, Rorschach looks like a giant ink blot.) But my cycling day wasn't over yet. In order not to cheat on my continuous tour of Europe I'd refused the car ride back to their house and still had another fifteen miles and a few hundred metres of ascent to reach Elli's village. To make the climb easier, Elli had loaded all but my toolkit into her car. Without the usual load I floated up the steep hill to Oberbüren, revelling in the thought that for the first time in years I was properly fit. That's what cycling 3,000 miles will do for you.

Elli had told me her house was difficult to find and so we'd arranged to meet halfway down the hill into her village. They'd flag me down, she said. I found the hill and freewheeled down it, waiting for friendly faces to leap out at me. They didn't. I got to the crossroads at the bottom of the hill and tried to text Elli to see where she was but I had no credit on my phone. For reasons known only to Orange this phone had never let me top up abroad and so I waited to see if they'd show up. Twenty minutes later I was still waiting. It was getting dark and I'd no idea where Elli lived. Normally this wouldn't have been a problem. I would go and find a campsite and make a new approach the next day but unfortunately Elli had all my gear.

To make matters worse I was also supposed to be on a train the next morning to Zurich to meet Nina before flying on to Nottingham for an Open University residential course. Elli was supposed to look after my bike. I couldn't just abandon it here, and even if I did I'd have no clothes, no computer, no course materials and only the money in my stunt wallet rather than the real stash at the bottom of the rucksack.

I cycled back up the hill just in case I'd arrived there more quickly than they'd expected but no one was about. So I cycled back down the hill to the crossroads through which I suspected they'd have to pass if they were out looking for me. The freewheeling didn't seem as much fun this time. I suddenly remembered I had an old SIM card in my wallet, a UK one, with hardly any credit on it but with perhaps just enough to get a message out. Luckily, it did. There was a small detail they hadn't given me about Oberbüren. There are actually two hills into the village and I should have taken the second one. We met up and I followed them down a lane to their farmhouse, tucking up my bike for a fortnight's holiday in one of Elli's sheds.

I knew something very special awaited me upon arrival. Elli took my hunt for original food to a new level. Not only did she unearth a species I'd never had before but a new order. Until that day I'd never eaten any kind of rodent but here in a pot was a pasta sauce made with dark and gamey marmot meat. It had taken her two days to prepare because the taste of marmot fat is reputedly so disgusting that it has to be completely removed before cooking the meat. This was especially laborious because marmots are chubby, little buggers.

In case you're wondering, the Swiss don't actually eat marmots. Elli works for an environmental agency involved in the monitoring of pollutants found in fish and wild animals. Once an animal has been tested and deemed clean it's sometimes frozen so it can be eaten at a later date. Better not to waste them. The salmon they test find their way on to dinner plates quickly. I think the marmot had been hanging around the freezer for a while.

Elli's house was a rustic paradise, full of animals and surrounded by an orchard and a ramshackle vegetable garden growing an entire supermarket of produce. Sam, a huge, affectionate dog, bounded around. He'd developed a knack of stealing the chickens' eggs and burying them until they became properly rotten before digging them up for a tasty treat. Inside the house the children's projects, collages and papier maché animals filled the place.

After a very comfortable night's sleep Elli drove me to the local station and I caught a train that arrived at exactly the timetabled second and glided me effortlessly into Zurich.

I'm fairly certain Nina and I spent our first night in Zurich in a brothel. The hotel advertised itself as being located in the red light district but it undersells itself. It's attached to a 'night club', a euphemism for cat house. On the wall outside was a flesh collage, a pornucopia of available girls, some clad in bits of underwear, others less so. After a little exploration of our hotel we found a connecting door linking the hotel to the club next door. We should have known something was up at reception when they asked how many hours we'd be staying.

Downstairs in the hotel was a supposedly English pub but in reality it was as English as Saint George. They'd tried a little too hard to make it the genuine British experience, with the usual theme of expensive beer, but they'd overshot even the UK's daft prices and were charging nine quid a pint.

Switzerland, and Zurich in particular, wasn't entirely what I'd expected. I hadn't associated Switzerland with prostitutes and red light districts. In my head it's more of a cuckoo clock, melted cheese and Nazi gold-type of place. What I had expected though was expense and it didn't disappoint there. Usually a pizza and a kebab in a poky café sat on plastic garden furniture is the dining choice of the hard-up. Not here. Add a plate of chips and a couple of cans and the whole lot came to forty Swiss francs, about thirty quid. The same meal up the road in Berlin wouldn't have come to a tenner. In Switzerland if you want a cheap meal and can't be arsed to cook then you just have to pretend you've already eaten. Even the bins are padlocked to prevent you from helping yourself to someone's mouldy old leftovers.

And it wasn't just restaurants. In the supermarket an entry level, scrawny chicken started at eight quid. Or maybe it was a quail. The sort of full-size chicken you'd buy back home cost twelve here. I thought I'd found some fish that compared favourably to prices in Spain until I realised it was for 100 grams and not a kilo.

The trolleys had a strange additional feature: a magnifying glass on the side. Nina hadn't really looked too closely and had taken it to be a side mirror to allow safer navigation around the supermarket aisles. It wasn't such a silly idea. You can imagine the Swiss doing that, indicating to go into the Cheese section and then pulling out slowly. But the magnifying glass was useful. It enabled me to see the piece of meat I could afford to buy.

Zurich is a handsome city, on the shore of a lake of the same name, and it has some interesting attractions. We visited the Kunsthaus. That's an art gallery, by the way, and not the Swiss parliament as you might have guessed. We had a pleasant afternoon examining its Picassos, van Goghs and Rodins and getting told off by the staff for various misdemeanours. Nina was in a playful mood. We shouldn't have taken those felt tips with us.

More unusual was the Moulagenmuseum containing hundreds of wax recreations of hideously disfiguring diseases and skin conditions. Although it'd appeal to those fascinated by the macabre the museum is in the medical university and is a genuine educational tool. Speaking of tools, it was heavy on syphilitic genitalia, great swollen penises and a particularly unattractive, oozing vagina that seemed to be developing its own collection of painful-looking raspberries. This was powerful anti-porn. I can now diagnose most types of sexually transmitted disease. Well, it's something for the

CV, isn't it? By the time we emerged from the horror show we both felt pretty queasy. Since neither of us felt like eating, that at least solved the problem of the supermarket prices for a while.

After a week of maths in Nottingham I was back in Swissland. Two shiny new poles from Hilleberg were waiting for me. I stayed the night once again in Oberbüren, breakfasted on another new food – instant donkey milk – although I can't remember why it exists as a product and cycled out of town accompanied by Elli and the girls for a couple of miles before waving goodbye to them. And to my helmet that I'd accidentally left on a hook in her shed. It didn't matter. I'd only worn it once, on the first day. I hate helmets. I was only carrying it because they're compulsory in Spain. Sort of.

I'd been expecting Switzerland to provide dreamy, Alpine scenery like Austria's but my route going from east to west wasn't taking me through the most spectacular areas. Still, Lucerne was attractive even if it's an identical carbon copy of Zurich with the addition of a mountain.

The further west I went in Switzerland the easier people seemed to smile. It's not what I'd expect from an even partly Germanic people. Those five years I'd lived in Graz were spent smiling at people only to receive endless frosty glares. Don't misunderstand me. Mine weren't leery, you-fancy-some smirks but casual, top-o'-the-morning beamers. I asked a German friend what she'd think if a stranger smiled at her.

"I'd just think he was mental," she said.

Switzerland improved the farther west I went. One Zurich-dwelling friend had described Bern as 'a toilet' but I liked it. It had a bit of atmosphere missing from Zurich. I still couldn't afford to breathe there but you can't have it all. In Bern came the first real test of my new poles. One evening a storm with cherry-sized hailstones pummelled the tent and all remained solid. My house was going to be alright. Thank you, Hilleberg.

When it comes down to it I'm not sure why anyone visits Switzerland. It has nothing its neighbours don't and the prices are double. But if you want to meet friendly people or stay in a country where you probably won't get stabbed in the face I suppose it's not to be entirely discounted. If you're simply ticking off another country or capital then you, and I, will just have to accept we're going to pay for the pleasure.

If proximity to France improved Switzerland the next ten days would be fun as I re-crossed Gaul, only this time during a lovely, toasty time of year, and headed for Andorra and the Iberian peninsula beyond. A physical challenge lay ahead first though as I slogged up the shallow but long climbs over the lush hills of Jura. What followed was one of the most glorious days of the trip so far. After a ten mile climb I had a delicious fifteen mile downhill section through densely wooded hills. I put some music on my MP3 player and sang my head off as I let go of the pedals. The road twisted smoothly left to right and back again. It felt more like skiing than cycling.

Once clear of the Jura hills and its ramshackle villages France became a little more industrialised. Campsites are scattered liberally about France but I hadn't seen a sign for hours. The weather was warm and it would've been a shame to waste money on a hotel on such a pleasant evening. Surely there was a campsite somewhere.

I was feeling lucky. I picked a village called Heyrieux at random and cycled into its centre. Usually you'll know soon enough if there's a site. There'll be signs right on the edge of town. But here there was nothing. I carried on cycling and reached the village centre before seeing a single, tiny sign about the size of a playing card. Yes, there was a site, a couple of miles out of the village in the general direction of

Nowhere. I pedalled the short distance and arrived at a knackered collection of neglected caravans surrounding a crumbling farm. There didn't appear to be a reception and so I knocked on the door of the main building.

I stumbled into a French film. Stripped to the waist and lighting a Gitane as he emerged, thirty-year-old Julian was followed sheepishly by a Tahitian girl wearing only a short silk dressing gown pulled tightly around her slight frame. He'd obviously just unplugged himself to answer the door. She, understandably, seemed quite miffed when he asked where I'd come from and a conversation began.

"Sit down, sit down!" he demanded, pointing to a picnic table. He ordered his lover to get me a beer. "He's just cycled from England," he repeated.

Julian wasn't the owner. That was a guy called Walter, of whereabouts unknown, who, in our combined and clumsy Franglais, I worked out was a giant of a man with a huge moustache. He was also, according to Julian, a psychotic peasant. Julian seemed a little scared of him.

We chatted over beer and it turned out Julian had a Spanish traveller father. As a result of his dad's wanderings, Julian hadn't learnt to read until he was twenty. His first love – not the Tahitian, she was just something casual – was horses but there wasn't much work around. He'd have talked all evening but I still hadn't determined whether I had a bed for the night. Perhaps Walter would just order me off his land or scythe me in two. Everyone else staying here was a permanent tenant. It was unusual for anyone like me to turn up. Maybe they should get a bigger sign.

Politely refusing another beer so I could sort out my bed Julian and I did a quick tour of the site and found Walter. Yes, he was tall and had a large moustache but he was no peasant. When Julian told him I was English, Walter said in his native tongue that he supposed this meant I didn't speak any

French. My French is terrible but I gave him a sentence or two and that seemed to win him over. Julian was uncomfortable in his presence and scarpered, leaving me alone with the psycho. Not only was I allowed to stay on the site but Walter also told me the safest route south and stole a folding chair from one of the other residents for me to use. Walter was alright.

I set up the tent and sat down on my new folding chair to do a little work in the evening sun. Almost immediately, Julian reappeared with a beer in hand and another in his pocket that he'd smuggled out of the house for me. The conversation resumed. I could imagine Miss Tahiti storming around the bedroom, sexually frustrated, cursing him. It was amazing how much we managed to get across to each other despite our linguistic differences. He couldn't understand that I didn't want kids.

"Is that because you like men?" he asked. No, it's because I don't want kids.

In the morning, while still dozing, a car pulled up outside my tent, footsteps approached and I heard a paper bag hit the entrance flap. Was this Walter's parting gift, a bag of French dog poo? I looked in the bag and saw something brown. It was a *pain au chocolat*. Some psycho.

From Heyrieux I continued, southwards down the Rhône's grape-covered valley in the sticky, early August heat before hanging a right just north of Orange. I trundled south-west, camping beside the famous castle in Carcassonne, filling in the gaps from a school trip I'd avoided when I was thirteen. I'd hated talking French then and didn't want to spend a week's holiday doing it. Nowadays I enjoyed the dickishness of trying.

As I approached Andorra, the landscape tilted and swelled. I knew my last day in France would be tough but my legs felt strong. I pumped up the first slope to 800 metres, the weather perfect, overcast and cool. The climb continued to 1,450 metres but I lost most of that before ending the day back at 1,000 metres in a rapidly chilling tent in a campsite on the slopes of the Pyrenees. It'd been a long day with lots of climbing but there'd be much more tomorrow when I'd tackle the highest climb of the entire ride.

Chapter 9: God loves me

Capitals visited: 13
Total distance: 4,076 miles

It might have been the 10th of August but at 1,000 metres and half six in the morning it was freezing. The outside of the tent was frozen. I set off wearing my fleece for the first time on the trip. The bike felt heavy, a combination of the wet tent and weary legs from yesterday's climbing. I soon warmed up, overheated and shed the fleece.

I climbed and climbed. The traffic was heavy as the southern half of France popped over the border for cheap booze but it wasn't going fast and, these being French and Spanish drivers, everyone gave me a width berth. The gradient remained steady, quickly gaining height. Eventually, after thirteen miles and a thousand metres of ascent, I reached Pas de la Casa, the scruffy resort town just over Andorra's border. I refuelled with a couple of pain au chocolats to go with the pain in my legs.

I might have reached Andorra but I still had more hills to climb. Before I could reach my fourteenth capital, Andorra la Vella, there were another four miles and four hundred metres to do. Bike signs every kilometre told me the gradient but I didn't need them to tell me it was getting steeper. The sky was a perfect clear blue and as I reached the top of the Envalira Pass at 2,407 metres a panorama of gritty beauty revealed itself, a parched landscape bounded by tall, grey peaks. I was over the hill and I felt it.

It was time for my reward, an eighteen mile descent during which I'd lose 1,400 metres. I wanted to savour this. I trundled rather than screamed down. For an hour I whirled from side to side on the switchbacks, drinking in the vistas.

The air temperature rose with each passing minute, from a cool blast at the top to a hair dryer in the face towards the bottom. It was the finest hour I'd ever spent on a bicycle.

There wasn't a single tourer on either side of the hill, only Tour de France types with their luggage-less, helium-filled bikes, something that gave me a level of smugness usually only achieved by Tory MPs. Cycle tourists crossing the Pyrenees rarely go this way, taking the easier options east or west but if I wanted to see Andorra la Vella there was no other way to go.

Andorra itself is absolutely stunning – scenery overload – and Andorra la Vella is a bustling, little city situated in a natural bowl with the Pyrenees on all sides. I'd only been expecting three houses and a dog.

I like it when I turn up somewhere new and I have someone to meet. On this trip I'd met some great people but one of my favourites was Clare. At 65 years old she was one of those people about whom younger folk say, "I hope I've got half her energy when I'm her age" without realising that even now they don't possess a quarter of it. She fizzed with the vitality of a busload of schoolkids with firecrackers in their pants.

One of the things Clare regularly does is visit the sick Brits in hospital here who haven't yet learned the local language. They suddenly find themselves in an alien world, unwell and without the words to describe what's wrong with them. She offers her support and interpreting skills. Today, she had a friend to visit and took me along for a look around the clean, modern hospital.

"This is Steven," she said to her friend. "He's just cycled over Envalira today. Can you imagine that?" I smiled like a tool.

"Yes, I can," her friend replied. "My brother does it every year when he comes to see us." My smugness withered. "He's seventy," she added. My smugness died.

Clare drove me to her house on the outskirts of the city, perched on a hillside with dramatic views of the valley below. The large windows in her living room framed the mountain views outside. At home was her husband, a sprightly if now slightly deaf Edward, thirty years her senior, an Uncle Albert lookalike. His look matched his passion. He'd started sailing at six years old and only stopped in his early nineties. In all that time, unlike Uncle Albert, he'd only lost one boat when, engineless, she'd hit rocks off the coast of Ireland and he'd had to swim for it. He'd been around the world more times than the moon. I love sailing. I wanted to suck the knowledge out of his head with a straw but it wouldn't have helped his hearing.

Clare and Edward's courtship had been an interesting one. In his late forties, bachelor Edward was interviewed by a UK newspaper about his seafaring. He lamented the fact his lifestyle hadn't been amenable to snaring himself a wife. Tempted by adventure, eighteen-year-old Clare wrote to him and offered herself up. Their first date was a 7,000 mile drive from the UK to Singapore to retrieve Edward's boat. If your relationship can survive that it's probably going to work out. They were still married nearly fifty years later.

To leave Andorra and cross the border into Spain I had more height to lose and was expecting more joyous freewheeling but the wind was against me, as it would be the whole way across the Iberian peninsula, and so I had to pedal just to go downhill. To make matters worse, the thermostat had been turned up on the Spanish side of the Pyrenees.

The journey westwards became hot and monotonous. Although the terrain was only gently undulating it was still a challenge to do seventy miles in the 36°C heat. The sun was drying me up. It'd started in France but was more of a problem now. My lips were cracking. I resorted to the high protection lip balm I'd bought in the Pyrenees. Thick, white lipstick may look cool on a handsome ski instructor. On me, I morphed into a New Romantic. Spanish men seemed particularly uncomfortable with my new look.

I approached my first big city in Spain, Zaragoza, a place I knew absolutely nothing about. From the smoking stacks visible from the hills around, it didn't look too promising but, upon descending, things picked up. After negotiating the suburbs, there suddenly loomed a magnificent mosque-like church standing on the banks of the river Ebro. The building would play a pivotal role in this evening's events.

I cycled to the centre and found a bed at the Hotel Sauce, a Carry On name if ever there was one, and popped out for a wander. Oh Lordy, what was going on? Pope Benedict was due to visit Madrid and thousands of Christian teens had descended upon Spain. Unfortunately they appeared to have ended up in the wrong city. The streets were teeming with kids from all nations, parading around with banners and t-shirts and testosterone. Some were even dressed in robes and these were, let's not forget, teenagers.

I continued to explore. It turned out that the big churchy, mosquey thing I'd seen earlier was the Basilica of Our Lady of the Pillar, a cathedral. It was here in 40AD that the Mother of God had supposedly appeared to Saint James and given him a small wooden statue of herself, although that seems more than a tad unlikely. I didn't even know the Creator had a mum. This cathedral was the centre of a massive international youth Godathon.

In the same square as the cathedral was an equally impressive water feature, a cascading irregular shape. Its juices eventually end in a trough that could easily accommodate a dozen or so people. The Christians were in there today. With the wheelchairs gathered around the fountain it was clear some well-meaning types had intended to get the crippled walking again with the power of tap water. When that hadn't worked they'd resorted to baptisms. Once they'd realised that this was Spain and everyone was already baptised it basically turned into a wet t-shirt competition with the blokes dunking the girls and then getting semi monk-ons and looking all guilty about what they'd own up to at their next confession. I was hoping they'd chuck a few fitter girls into the fountain instead but I couldn't see any. Don't sexy women believe in God?

I went for a Chinese, the quickest meal I've ever had. At one point I had three courses on my table at once. Maybe the Spanish prefer it this way, to have your multi-course Chinese meal served like a selection of tapas, but it's probably just a way to get punters in and out more quickly. After what felt like five minutes I went back outside to see how the revival was going on.

The square's floodlit stage now contained a dozen seated Vatican types. At regular intervals a squadron of believers would get up and deliver a monotone piece, while around 2,000 teens sat enrapt. What were they getting out of it? What about nightclubs and cider and feeling up girls in the park?

After a couple of hours a Christian-themed concert started up. It was odd to see them all there, lighting candles and swaying like alcoholics. They weren't doing anyone any harm though. Back in Britain, kids of a similar age were trashing the place in the riots that swept the country.

The only route westwards out of Zaragoza was a motorway. This was often a problem in Spain. Rather than build a brand new motorway, an existing A-road would be widened and converted, which meant there was no longer an A-road. Cyclists and those on mopeds or horseback are then without a road on which they can legally travel. Even had I not been on the hard shoulder I may still have been illegal due to my lack of a hat. Spain's helmet laws are daft. You're supposed to wear a helmet in all cases except three. First, you're exempt if you're cycling within a town, which is odd because that's where the cars tend to be. Second, you're exempt if you're cycling uphill, although I'm not sure what you do once you reach the top. Stay there or push the bike down presumably. Third, you're exempt if it's hot. This is Spain. It's always bloody hot.

With a hurricane in my face the flat road felt like a steep hill. I managed less than thirty miles in four hours, which is rubbish. Eventually I rolled into Tarazona, a town that hosts one of the most bizarre parties anywhere. Unfortunately I was a fortnight too early. Towards the end of August the town takes to the street. The *cipotegato*, a local youth elected for the event, dressed in a green, yellow and red harlequin outfit, has to leg it through town to the central square while being pelted with tomatoes. If he manages to get there he's raised up on a central plinth that towers above the masses below. If he doesn't, presumably they bury him where he falls.

It seems like a bit of fun but has a darker history, based as it is on a old local tradition that isn't a million miles away from The Running Man. A prisoner would be released and given a stick. If he could make it out of town he was free but the townsfolk stoned him as he fled. Lovely.

I was now entering one of Spain and Europe's least populated regions, the desolate area around the city of Soria in the community of Castile and León. Halfway through August it wasn't far from desert. I'd taken to cycling only until lunchtime. If I still wasn't where I wanted to be, I'd find a shady tree and have a siesta, finishing off as things cooled marginally in the evening.

My sun cream was useless. I'd apply it half an hour before

leaving in the morning but within five minutes of setting off it was dripping off my face, stinging my eyes and leaving me exposed. I was painfully red. My bleached eyebrows now looked radioactive. Long, straggly, sweat-matted hair completed this vision of beauty.

I edged my way across the furnace that was northern Spain. I'd decided not to bother with Madrid this year. It'd be much more appealing at the beginning of next year in the cool of the spring rather than the heat of summer. I skirted the capital, making a city tour of its north and west, and arrived in Segovia. Not all the Christians who'd descended upon Spain had mistakenly gone to Zaragoza. Some had got lost in Segovia instead. While in town I was accosted by three young South American girls who wanted to tell me that God loves me. That's nice, I thought, that He's singled me out. But they didn't mean it like that. He loves everyone, the slag. We had a theological discussion during which I said I didn't think we needed God to explain the universe. Science has had a good stab at that. Anyway, we all got on. Belief obviously made them happy. I had no use for it. No one was converted but we all walked away with a respectful understanding of each other. No crusades were launched. No one was stoned to death.

Half an hour later I came across another bunch of young Christians, all singing and waving flags. As they marched through the main square, one of lads made eye contact and came over. Brilliant, I thought. He explained that he was nineteen and from New Zealand and had once found happiness in girls and beer and surfing – which sounds pretty ideal to me – but God had shown him this was wrong, the tool, and that there was another way.

"God loves you," he finished.

"Right," I said, "First of all, thanks, but I'm not really interested in this story. What I *am* interested in is why

Christians keep coming up to me in particular and telling me that God loves me?"

He thought for a second and said, "Because you look a bit red and sunburnt and like you might be homeless and living on the streets."

I looked like a hobo. He wandered off before I could ask him why he chose to approach desperate people who might sign up to the Lord in return for a bowl of soup rather than the sinners in their Porsches.

Tramps generally don't do restaurants but I love Chinese food, especially at Spanish prices, and I decided to discover whether, unlike their compatriots in Zaragoza, the joint in Segovia understood the concept of separate courses. Unfortunately, the dishes were fired from the kitchen even more quickly. Thirty seconds after my soup arrived the spring rolls turned up, with the rice and main course being delivered one minute later.

My meal looked like it was going to last fifteen minutes, if that. I reckon if you're going to pay for a meal in a restaurant it should last at least an hour and half. And so, if only to amuse myself, I decided it would do. The food was gone but I sat there and waited. The staff glared at me like I was shitting on their favourite beige rug. I got out my little notebook in which I write stuff down. It was red. You might even say that it was a Little Red Book.

Eventually, after half an hour of glaring, I decided to go for dessert. Unfortunately the lead and only Spanish-speaking member of staff had popped out for some reason, leaving a dopey woman in charge. I asked, in Spanish, if she had any ice cream.

"You want bill?" she replied.
"No, ice cream, please" I repeated.
"Bill?"
"No, ice cream."

"Bill?"

I checked with the restaurant's only other occupied table, a young Spanish woman spoon-feeding her boyfriend who had both his hands bandaged. Was I pronouncing 'ice cream' correctly in Spanish? Yes, I was. Eventually the waitress brought the menu and I pointed to a picture of what I wanted.

"And a brandy?" I added.

"The bill?"

"No. A soddin' brandy."

"The bill?"

I walked to the bar, grabbed the bottle myself and handed it to her. She was only small. She couldn't have reached it anyway.

The road to the Portuguese border took me through other attractive Spanish cities, Ávila, Plasencia and one of Europe's best preserved medieval old towns in Cáceres, the location of many a film. The ride also allowed me to witness my first ever pensioner punch-up. In the village of Zarzuela del Monte I was tucking into a lunchtime snack when a commotion broke out down the road. A tiny but solid old woman dressed in black was slapping and kicking a slightly younger, marginally taller old man. Her problem seemed to be his lack of cojones, a fact she continually repeated. She was really going for it, slapping him in the face and punching his paunch. I continued eating. In my head my non-intervention was down to cultural sensitivity – maybe this was normal around these parts – but really I didn't want that little bruiser to turn on me. The old bloke looked like he'd had enough of her and was just about to lamp her when another geriatric stormed in and broke them up. You can't pay for that sort of entertainment. The old people of today, eh?

The weather stayed hot. The heat made me a little

homesick and for a minute I thought perhaps Blackburn had an advantage over Spain with a temperature more suited to long distance cycling but one day of Lancashire rain would have reversed that decision.

Unsurprisingly, very little changed on the Portuguese side of the border except the houses and towns were a little more run-down. I twirled on winding country lanes, climbing high to look down on sugar cube villages before tumbling back to the bottom of the hill. On the bigger roads the verges were smaller than Spain's and the trucks came closer but not scarily so.

Spain's motorway conversion policy may have been annoying but Portugal's was even worse. It didn't even bother to upgrade its A-roads to motorways. It simply designated some bits of them with an IP number giving them motorway status, meaning faster traffic, minimal to zero hard shoulders and no bikes allowed. These roads though are the veins of the country and to get anywhere while avoiding them adds a lot of distance. On my first day in Portugal the A-road I was on morphed into an IP. The traffic was terrifying. I nearly cacked myself. I got off at the next turn-off and had a lie down.

As Portuguese was the last new tongue of the year I tried to pick up a bit using a language course. I didn't put in much effort as I'd been told the Portuguese understand Spanish. Having spent a few years on the south coast of Spain I thought I'd be able to muddle through. Written down the two languages are similar but it's an unusual accent. It sounds like Sean Connery speaking Russian.

On the outskirts of Lisbon a car stopped in front of me and dumped out a prostitute wearing the tiniest white shorts. She took up her position at the side of the road. With a slightly overcast sky the temperatures were perfect for cycling although there was still the ever present wind in my face. I was looking forward to hitting the western edge of Europe so

I could turn around and have it behind me for a change.

Portugal does its best to confuse the traveller. A roundabout with five exits and no signs isn't ideal. Instead I went off a bearing from the compass on my handlebars and, almost inevitably, ended up on a motorway, a real one this time with a proper hard shoulder rather than an upgraded death road. I put my head down and pedalled like a demon.

With a pumping heart I pulled off at the first exit into the city and quickly discovered that the centre of Lisbon isn't really designed for cycling. If a road isn't cobbled then it's potholed and many of its streets are so steep it feels like you're cycling up a wall.

With my next residential course deadline in only a few days I couldn't afford to hang around. That afternoon I hoofed it around the city, knowing I'd have to be on my way in the morning.

The only road out of Lisbon in the direction I needed was a bridge and it was off limits to cyclists. My only option was a ferry to the other side of the river Tagus. The boat spat me out in Almada for my onward journey. Unfortunately, the road was blocked by police and ambulances. Some poor sod, with face covered, was being carried off a bus. It didn't look good. Either that or he'd found a great way to dodge his fare.

The death theme continued. A few hours later, on a busy main road, a beautiful baby stork landed not far in front of me. It was the purest white, graceful and sleek, and then ten seconds later it was stork pâté as it managed an aborted take-off quite spectacularly into the bumper of a speeding car coming in the opposite direction. There were blood and feathers everywhere. It was like a massacre in Danny La Rue's dressing room.

I was facing eastwards again. The wind I'd expected to be on my back remained in my face despite turning nearly one hundred and eighty degrees. The Wind God hates me.

On the first of September I was back in Spain. I'd entered the last week of this year's ride. I'd had an amazing few months but my body was ready to stop. I felt fit and lean and I'd lost over three stone since I'd started but there was an underlying tiredness. Since the 25th of July I'd cycled around 2,200 miles. In all that time I'd only had two rest days and there wouldn't be another until the end.

The bike was also feeling a bit ragged. Mechanically it'd been nearly perfect, with only that inner tube malfunction on the edge of Berlin and one other puncture in Austria. But its dense foam handlebar grips had been dissolved by my sweaty mitts and were only held together with duct tape. The saddle was also falling apart. Repairs would be needed over the winter.

Sweaty mitts wouldn't be an issue as I approached Seville. The cloud was low and rain looked imminent. My plan was to zip around the edge of Seville and head for Gibraltar. My map didn't match the roads on the ground. Negotiating Seville was only possible with a compass. Every roundabout tried to lure me on to another motorway. I eventually popped out the other side of the city and it started to monsoon. Luckily ahead was a petrol station and I hid under its forecourt canopy until the worst was over. While waiting, a bloke shuffled past and showed me a card trick. I was impressed until he divulged his Magic Circle secrets and owned up to having a trick pack of cards that enabled him to scam punters. He wasn't interested in scamming me. I still looked like a tramp. He just wanted to hide from the rain.

It was already early afternoon. After an hour the rain slowed and I figured I'd better get going. My route involved a short river crossing. On the other side, in the super-flat, featureless swamps that lie to the south east of Seville the rain restarted with double force. With nowhere to shelter and a strong gusty wind accompanying the rain I couldn't have been wetter if I'd cycled into the river. I was blown about and drenched and for a few minutes at least I went slightly mad. I cackled like a maniac. How lucky had I been with weather this year? I'd had plenty of rain in the UK but elsewhere I'd probably only had five days of light rain in total. It was only fair I'd get my six month's quota on a single day in one of Europe's driest countries.

Ah, Gibraltar. I'm not a fan. I was offered a job there in the late nineties but turned it down when I saw the tiny colony. One of the interviewers told me how Franco had built the huge petrochemical plant in nearby Algeciras to cover Gibraltar in smelly fumes. He said El Generalisimo had got his sums wrong and the wind took the stench in the opposite direction but if that's true it doesn't explain why the place stinks whenever I've visited. My interview coincided with Gibraltar National Day, which culminated in an outdoor event attended by a sea of people all wearing red t-shirts containing siege-mentality slogans like "We will never surrender". It can't be great to feel you're perpetually at war with your neighbours.

The main drag through the centre of town sees a sprinkling of old British chain stores alongside dozens of supposed duty free off licenses and dodgy electronics shops. I found it odd that a pint of lager in duty-free Gibraltar was nearly twice as much as one in next-door, non-duty-free Spain.

Still, life here was better than it had been. If you wanted to travel from Gibraltar to Spain before the border re-opened in the 1980s you first had to fly back to the UK. No planes or boats were allowed to land in Spain if they'd set off from or visited Gibraltar. At least now you could easily escape.

The plan was to sneak in and out. I didn't need to stay

there and get ripped off by British-priced hotels when the ones in La Linea, the Spanish border town, cost around a third. Although I wouldn't be there for long I felt it'd be cheating to visit Gibraltar and not cycle up The Rock. Since leaving the UK I hadn't had to push my bike up a hill. I suspected today might be different.

I left the town below and started climbing. It was steep and very, very hot. A young woman sat at the roadside, looked at me and started laughing.

"This is fun," I said sarcastically.

"Really?" she asked.

"No."

"Then why are you doing it?"

"I need a photograph," I said.

"What of?"

"A monkey."

"Why not just buy a postcard?"

It was an option but a postcard wouldn't have a picture of a monkey sat on my bike and that's what I really wanted. I came to the cash desk that collects money from tourists who want to drive this road. The price list had the costs for cars, motorbikes and coaches but the man had no pricing policy for cyclists and he let me and my luggage in for free with a big "you're a dick" smile.

The town grew smaller beneath me. The Straits were littered with oil tankers and container vessels. I stopped every now and again for a breather but so far I hadn't had to push. I'd need to go higher if I wanted to see a monkey. Up and up I went. I passed a group of tourists on foot and received an "Olé!" And then it was Monkey City with Barbary apes scampering around, clambering on the walls and trying to mug the holidaymakers.

I set my bait. I rested my bike against the wall and stepped back. Within a few seconds, a cheeky chimp had climbed on top of my tent, strapped to the bike rack. I got my photo. Then he got bored with posing and starting trying to dig into my bags. He got a finger inside. I shooed him off but he wouldn't budge. I had to make a lunge at him before he tore my stuff to pieces. Watch those little sods. They'll have you.

I was quite proud of getting to the top of The Rock without needing to push. It turned out to be more difficult going down. With the steep descents and all the weight on the bike my brakes weren't up to the job. They squealed and squawked and refused to slow me down. I got off and pushed. Oh, the irony!

Having spent a while down here, frequent car rides along the N-340 – lovingly known as The Road of Death because of its horrendous statistics – convinced me that to cycle the coast route from Gibraltar to this year's end in Nerja would be extremely unpleasant and possibly suicidal. The traffic is always thick and fast and thanks to the heavy tourist development there's little in the way of scenery to take your mind off your impending doom. To avoid this I headed inland, which added on a few extra miles but more crucially around 3,000 additional metres of ascent, half a Kilimanjaro just to bypass a scary road. The bonus was the scenery. The limestone peaks of the Sierra de las Nieves rise close to 2,000 metres through which ancient rivers have cut deep gorges, like the one in Ronda where one side threw to their deaths the other during the civil war.

And then I was over the mountains and back by the sea only 25 miles from Nerja. Normally I'd have finished the ride rather than spend an extra night in a hotel so close to the end but the next day my mate Boz would accompany me on this leg's last day. I was feeling good. Nothing could stop me from completing the first year now. I could walk it from here.

I celebrated with a few mojitos. All was well with the world. The first year was as good as done. That night I slipped into a deep coma-like sleep, happily drunk in the knowledge that tomorrow was the shortest of cycling days and then I could have my first rest day in a month.

Boz arrived at the allotted time and we pootled along the coast road – it's still the N-340 but quieter east of Málaga – at the pace of a tortoise with a gamy leg, talking crap to each other. We trundled into Nerja. Boz took a photo of me standing heroically, or cockishly depending on your view, beside the five foot high letters of the Nerja sign on the edge of town and then we hit the bars on the beach front. He insisted on telling absolutely everyone what I'd done, which decreased in embarrassment with the increase in alcohol. The day descended into liver abuse and memory loss. I've a collection of photos that I find very difficult to explain.

More than 5,700 miles from the Isle of Man I'd visited 16 capitals and had proven to myself I could study and cycle at the same time. Yes, I'd deliberately chosen the easier and less politically exciting countries for the first year and the next two years' rides would be more difficult – hotter or hillier or with a dodgier infrastructure or all three – as well as nearly fifty per cent farther but this idea, the best idea I'd ever had, was working.

YEAR TWO

Chapter 10: The brains in Spain

Capitals visited: 16
Total distance: 5,728 miles

It was March and I was back in Spain having a very strange conversation. He was dressed in a beige linen jacket and sporting a floppy straw hat. All the whites of his eyes were blood red.

"I wrote to the Queen about it," he added. I was in a bar trying to check my email. He'd come up to me and started yacking about some paranoid nonsense. Apparently, all the politicians were out to get us. He didn't mean rob us. He meant kill us. I hadn't really been listening until he mentioned the Queen's involvement. I closed the lid of my netbook.

"And what did she say?"

"She said she'd passed my letter on to the relevant authorities for processing." That'd be the bin then.

"Really?"

"The politicians are terrified of me. I've written to loads of them."

"And what did they say to your accusations?"

"Nothing. No one replied."

"Then how do you know they're terrified?"

He looked at me like I was a chump. "Dur. Because they didn't reply."

"If you've stumbled upon a nationwide conspiracy to kill us all, is it a good idea to write to the conspirators and tell them you know about it?"

He stopped talking, looked worried for a moment and then changed the subject.

"Crop circles," he said. Oh lord.

"Go on."

"What do you think?"

"Well, they're not made by aliens if that's what you mean. It's just a couple of dicks messing around in a field."

"No, it's not aliens. They're made by humans." Wow, I wasn't expecting that. "And yet," he continued, "no one has ever seen them being made."

"That's 'cos it's dark."

"No. People watch the fields. They see nothing. And then the next morning there's a crop circle. How's that possible?"

"Because people don't actually watch the fields?"

"No. They do. It's because of magnetic fields or ley lines or something like that. The people making the circles get...special powers."

"What sort of special powers? What, they become invisible or something?"

"Yes." Amazing. I'd have thought if you'd the ability to become invisible you probably wouldn't toss around in a wheat field at midnight up to your knees in cow pats. No, surely you'd be something productive like hiding mouse traps in Piers Morgan's cultery drawer.

"Isn't it more likely that the reason they can make circles in the dark is because they got themselves some infra-red goggles off Ebay?"

"No, there's absolutely no evidence for that." Ah, evidence. I didn't realise we needed any of that.

It'd been fun but I'd had enough. "Right, I'm off," I said.

"Where are you going?"

"A long way away."

Since the end of last year's ride I'd been a busy bee. I'd visited Majorca for an OU astronomy course involving very little sleep but lots of nerdy things like asteroid tracking and the spectral analysis of distant stars. Then came the maths exam for the course I'd studied while cycling. But the big job had been to write the 20,000 word dissertation for my philosophy MA. I could tell you all about it but I don't think you'd appreciate it.

Other educational news hadn't been quite so promising. Nick Clegg's deceit had meant ditching my degree in Physical Science. The OU had promised to maintain course fees at the old rates for existing students but only for one degree. I couldn't afford to pay for the second at the new prices.

I retrieved my bike from Boz's hillside storage depot and took it in for a service. I knew it needed a new saddle and handlebar grips and probably a new chain but the shop assistant gave me a long list of other things that needed fixing. She chuckled and told me that for only thirty euros more she could sell me a brand new bike. How I laughed.

Because I didn't know what opportunities would present themselves on the road the last task before leaving was to eat something in Spain I'd never had before. With access to a kitchen I figured I'd treat Nina to a delicious dinner of fried testicles. I learned the correct word I needed – *criadillas* – but I also learned not to approach the butchers' counter and ask, "Do you have testicles?" In one, the bloke looked positively crestfallen. In the other, she really wasn't amused. "Do you sell testicles?" was probably the better way but I still got funny looks and, in any case, they didn't have any.

Instead I scoured the supermarket shelves for odd stuff and found a packet of pigs' brains. I was surprised how small they were but perhaps they'd only been special constables. There's something macabre about eating a brain – it's difficult not to feel like a zombie – but the secret was apparently in the preparation. I downloaded a brain How-To and went to work. The result was an inedible, snot-like mess. We managed a mouthful each but the brains in Spain went mostly down the drain.

So, at the end of March, this year's adventure began. Leaving behind my friends in Nerja I pedalled out of town and suddenly felt very alone. At least this year I wasn't starting as a lard arse. I'd managed to keep off most of the weight I'd lost last year and so hopefully there wouldn't be too much initial pain. But the route north from Nerja to Madrid meant unavoidable hills and on the first day, after six months off the bike, there was a climb of 1,300 metres.

The road to the Zafarraya pass twists through olive groves and scattered fincas and in mid-spring is speckled pink, white, yellow and blue with wild flowers. The pass itself, a huge rocky gateway, welcomes you into the province of Granada. The steep climb was torture. It may have been early in the year but the temperatures were already approaching 30ºC. Eventually I arrived in Alhama de Granada. I hadn't cycled much farther than forty miles from Nerja but it'd taken me all day.

I found a cheap *pension* and went out to get provisions. Once again I'd arrived somewhere on a fiesta day – in Spain most days are fiesta days – and everything was closed. In the end I had to settle for a sandwich from the pension's bar and a couple of pints. I was in bed and asleep by nine o'clock before the fiesta outside had even begun. All hail the party animal!

I meandered northwards towards Madrid, climbing to reach delightful Montefrío with its church sat on top of a huge, rocky outcrop, and Moorish Priego de Córdoba as well as forgettable towns like scruffy Montoro and industrial Puertollano. In those first four days I cycled over half an Everest. There's nothing like breaking your legs in gently.

Under a grey sky, the next day had me cycle into a tiny arsetown called Malagón and a David Cronenberg movie. Despite only having 8,000 residents the town was a sprawling, crumbling mess. If Malagón were twinned with something, that thing would be plague.

The visit started with a fat budgerigar on my head. Unable to find a hotel I wandered into a desolate-looking bar advertising itself in six foot tall painted letters as a *hostal*. As I entered its equally bleak interior the four blokes inside were scuttling around trying to recapture a bird. Before its colourful feathers could be wrestled back into its minuscule cage it flapped around and landed in the nest-like hair on my bonce. But no one was finding a home here today. As it turned out this place hadn't been a hostal for years, as the barman told me wearily, although I can't imagine he'd had to explain this fact very often. Minus the bird I kept on looking.

The one-star hotel I eventually found was alright, clean enough although the tap water shared its colour with the urine of someone dangerously dehydrated. In its small lobby was a huge painting of a deer being ripped apart by a gang of dogs. Maybe for balance or for the deer lovers out there, at least one of the dogs had been given a right good hoofing. He lay in the corner painfully bleeding to death.

Malagón felt odd. Wherever I walked I attracted the suspicious stares of absolutely everyone, like I'd stumbled on to a town with a dirty secret to hide. In the streets there was little to entertain me and I found myself back at the hotel and its bar. I ordered a beer and was offered a free tapa. I surveyed the options. They had some strange mini aubergines, green and the size of a ping-pong ball. I'd seen them here in the supermarkets but had never tried one and so it was the obvious choice. The aubergine was pickled, which gave it a nice tartness, but was stuffed with olives and twigs, something else I'd never eaten before.

Time passed. Outside the hotel bar window, on a grim bit of park land, the young mothers of the town smoked while their kids fought for the slide. Like a lot of the back-of-beyond towns I'd seen on this trip, and like Blackburn too, many of the mums in Malagón seemed to be in their early teens. There's not much else to do, I suppose. But time didn't work properly here. I'd been in this bar for at least two hours and yet the clock has moved on only twenty minutes. Maybe these young mums were actually in their early forties.

Also like Blackburn, most people looked ill. Blackburnians have an excuse for their pallor, what with sunlight being unable to penetrate the thick blanket of rain cloud that hangs permanently above it, but Malagón sits in the southern half of sunny Spain. Perhaps the town had been a dumping ground for several train loads of government, experiment-gone-wrong guinea pigs.

An old man stood next to me at the bar. I smiled at him. For no apparent reason his face started to bleed, a large streak of blood from near his left eye ran down the length of his cheek. He scuttled off holding a tissue to his wound. Perhaps it was a stigmata. It was Easter after all. Or maybe I'd caused the bleeding, a sort of low level Scanner. I avoided the gaze of the other bloke in the bar in case I made his head explode. Malagón gave me the creeps.

I was relieved to cycle away in the morning and today's destination couldn't have contrasted more with Malagón if it'd been located on the surface of Mars. The route there once again gave me no alternative but a motorway. Barrelling down a curved hill I turned the corner and saw a police car sat in the hard shoulder accompanied by another car. I slammed on my brakes and waited. After a couple of minutes the coppers finished ruining someone's day and drove off. I had a good reason for being there but I wasn't sure my Spanish was good enough to convince them.

Toledo was magnificent with its massive cathedral and stunning ancient centre. Once the capital of Spain, and much grander than Madrid, it was the first major city to be reconquered by the Christians after capture by the Moors. It was also famous for La Convivencia, the happy co-existence of Christians, Jews and Muslims. No one eyed me suspiciously or bled when I looked at them.

Toledo is famous for its steel. In many ways it's the Sheffield of Spain except that, as I said, it was stunning. And all this steel probably accounted for the sword and armour shops that it had. Maybe I'm no Alan Sugar but I would've thought, in the 21st century, in a country of forty odd million people, Spain could probably support at most one sword and armour shop, maybe two if there was a bout of extreme civil disobedience. But Toledo had hundreds of them. I know they're aimed at tourists but I'm pretty sure you'd struggle to get any of their swords through customs. Or maybe RyanAir lets you book in a two-handed broadsword for an extra charge.

Throughout Spain I'd been looking for a decent map of Madrid. My large countrywide one of Spain gave up close to large cities and just displayed the motorways. Often there's a secret way to sneak into a city and that's always a more pleasant experience. In Toledo I found a map that gave me hope. Even with this decent map it was clear the Madrid road system was designed in an unusual way. Someone with a nasal infection had sneezed on to a piece of A3 and a committee had said, "Yep, looks good. Let's build it!" There were thick, angry streaks of red, chunky strands of yellow dribble and thread-like splatters of white. They all came together to make a city that looked almost impossible to penetrate on a bicycle. Madrid was protected with a titanium hymen of motorways and dual carriageways.

The ride out of Toledo was easy enough but I knew that to avoid the motorways I had to resort to the smaller tracks that appeared merely as thin black lines on my map. I was expecting tarmac or gravel at worst but the route following a dry river bed was first sand, then deep sand and then very deep sand. I pushed the bike, the wheels useless in the powder. I disappeared further into the countryside. The sun was out again. It felt more like Kenya than central Spain. Desert wasn't one of the obstacles I'd envisaged on my way to Madrid.

Once through the Sahara, I got lost in little villages, incoherent in industrial estates, hazy in horrible housing projects and mystified in massive business parks. But finally, without ever having to use a motorway, I found the hotel I'd booked in Fuenlabrada and had to keep the bike in my room because the guy on reception didn't trust the security of his own garage.

Capital city suburbs aren't the most exciting of places and so I googled Fuenlabrada to see if it threw up anything interesting. It did. The first thing was that, almost 28 years ago to the day, Chelsea's striker Ferdinand Torres was born there. Even better, the previous summer, another local Torres – Father Andres Garcia Torres – was removed from his priestly role for allegedly engaging in homosexual behaviour. The fun part of this story is that he actually offered to have the width of his anus measured to prove no one had been up there. He should take comfort in the fact that at least he's scored more recently than Ferdinand.

The assault of Madrid proper took place the following morning. Although not entirely free of its motorway force field, the next day involved an early morning leap from suburb to suburb, inching ever closer to the centre. To begin with everything went well. I was basically heading north. My compass was great for that kind of navigation but then it started to act bizarrely, confused by local magnetic fields. I turned a right-hand corner and it suddenly shifted to tell me I was now facing south. So I turned around 180 degrees and I was still apparently and impossibly pointing south. I cycled in circles for a bit until I completely lost my sense of direction.

I'd no idea in which direction was the centre. All I could be certain of was it was ten miles away. For all I knew it could have been ten miles upwards. And then I saw, like a motorised Buddha, a fat man in a car. I cycled up to his sagely window. He called upon the wisdom of ages and prophesied that if I turned left and then left again I'd find the Road To Madrid. And he was right.

It was too early to check in to our hotel so I sat in a café and waited for Nina to arrive. My bike was leant against the wall outside so that I could see it from inside the caff. As I sat there eating my breakfast roll I noticed something blue on the back tyre and went outside to check. The expensive, almost unpuncturable Swalbe Marathon Plus tyre had worn right down to its blue interior. Carrying a chubby sod and thirty kilos of luggage 6,000 miles wasn't bad but it made me realise how shoddy my bike preparations had been. A little later, when I removed my panniers, I saw the rack had cracked. Luckily there was a bike shop up the road but this was a sign.

The day we had together in Madrid was full of food and wine and loveliness, seeing sights and exploring the city. We discovered a weird, little Far Eastern food emporium. In case I stumbled upon a country with no original food of its own I bought a strange, squishy, black, shrink-wrapped hard-boiled egg to carry with me as an insurance policy.

As a capital city Madrid is a bit of a disappointment. Barcelona and Seville are both grander, more colourful and jazzier so I wasn't overly sad to leave the place the following morning and head towards the Pyrenees for the second time on this trip. The route eastwards out of town was much easier than the route in and included a special highlight when I accidentally wandered into what could only have been a secret government base. Well, I say accidentally. I saw the PROHIBIDO signs but it seemed like the right way to me. It wasn't. It was a centre for phytogenetics, which basically involves stitching pigs' heads on to the bodies of human infants. Probably.

On the outskirts of Guadalajara I came across a young Spanish cyclist called Diego. We had a chat.

"You speak good English," I said.

"Yes, I studied it in North Wales for three months."

"Nice. Did you like it?"

"No, I hated it. It rained every day." Oh well. That's Wales for you.

Two days later I was cycling through the spectacular gorges of the Alto Tajo National Park. I'd come this way in the opposite direction in 2009 and so was aware of a hotel in the town of Molina de Aragón with a restaurant providing a good *menú del día* for not very much. On my previous visit to the hotel's restaurant I'd stumbled across a foodie first with *morteruelo*, a sort of Spanish meat porridge. It's hard to describe accurately and so it's probably best to explain how I think it's made. Imagine two Weetabix in a bowl. Add lashings of hot milk and leave until the 'bix have gone soggy. Then stir in a tin of dog food. It tasted better than it sounds but then again it'd have to.

Tonight was a different sort of treat. A menú del día is a fixed price meal where you have a choice of three or so options for each of the three courses. Normally you also get bread and a drink, often a glass of wine or a small beer. The food is usually plain but well-cooked and filling, which was true today. What was unusual about today's menú was that rather than a single glass of wine it came with an entire bottle of red. I wasn't sure whether I was allowed to drink it all or just be civilised and fill my glass once. I noticed another guy eating alone, watching the telly that's in all but the smartest Spanish restaurants. His wine glass was nearly empty. I kept watching. And then he definitely refilled his glass. That was my cue. I ate and I drank and I finished the lot and then looked again as the Spanish fella got up to leave. His bottle was still half full. So I suppose I'll never know whether I breached Spanish restaurant etiquette but when a tasty three course meal with a bottle of wine comes to eight quid I was past caring.

I moved north-east, towards the river Ebro. While it's only the second longest river in Spain it has the greatest water flow of any of the Spanish *rios*. As a comparison, the longest river in the UK, the Severn, is less than half the Ebro's length and discharges only one-seventh of the Ebro's water.

I stopped for the night in a strange town called Caspe. Despite being in the north-west of Spain and not far from Catalonia it felt like Morocco. There hardly seemed to be a Spaniard there. Many of Caspe's shops had their names and advertisements written in Arabic script. I'd slipped into a Muslim world. This wouldn't have been a problem except that I was looking for wine.

I went back to my pension empty-handed and was having a beer in its little bar instead when three English blokes walked in. Capitals aside, I've tended to avoid tourist places on this trip and so meeting Brits by accident hadn't happened before. They were discussing their day's fishing. I hadn't realised Caspe is on the banks of a reservoir created by damming the Ebro and has some of Europe's best angling. We got talking. They were from Southampton and all in their late thirties or early forties, roughly my age. Mark was six foot four and built to match, physically imposing. Simon and Steve were shorter and slighter. These guys were serious anglers, there for a few days, hunting the massive carp and catfish in the reservoir. They'd first been here five years ago and as part of their haul they'd landed a catfish weighing 63 kilograms. That's ten stone for Cod's sake!

But that was five years ago. This time the fishing wasn't so good. This was a shame given the reason they'd returned. Mark was ill. At 39 he had an inoperable brain tumour. He'd been diagnosed several years earlier, he'd had chemo and the cancer had been in remission but now it'd started to grow again. He worked as a carpenter and had recently blacked out on the roof of the building. There'd almost been the need to get a rescue helicopter to winch him to safety. As a result of this – for his own good, he admitted – Mark had lost his licence and couldn't do his work any longer. He said that, as he'd been self-employed forever and as he wasn't actually disabled, he couldn't claim anything at all. He was stuck. No work, no benefits, no money. Although he seemed perfectly healthy on the outside Mark only had a few months left. Simon and Steve had paid for his fishing holiday. They wanted to make these last months special. All Mark said he wanted was to watch his kids grow up.

Since being dammed in several places the Ebro isn't working like it used to do. In the 20th century, as a result of its barriers, 29% less water flows between its banks, and its sediment load, responsible for keeping its delta healthy, has been reduced by 99%, with the silt stuck behind its dams. The river Ebro was dying and Mark was dying. But, in reality, we're all dying. We should remind ourselves of that on a daily basis, appreciate we're still around and try to squeeze as much as possible into what's left. If you ever had plans to catch a fish, now's the time to go fishing.

Chapter 11: The maggots go down

Capitals visited: 17
Total distance: 6,770 miles

The previous night had been cold, camping in Ripoll in the high foothills of the Pyrenees, the only idiot on the entire site so early in the year. Snow was forecast but didn't come. The long climb up the mountain the next morning defrosted my limbs and the prospect of a return to the land of pâtisseries raised my spirits. The pass at 1,500 metres was well above the snow line and icicles quickly established themselves in my beard on the descent with a strong, bitter headwind as I freewheeled into France.

Wearing all the clothes I carried I abandoned the ride in Amélie-les-Bains-Palalda, a well-touristed spa town and found a hotel room in which to warm up. Unfortunately the heating didn't work. If my hotel couldn't remove the chills then hopefully a restaurant would. I'd burnt a lot of calories today and deserved two meals, kicking off with a huge warm salad of ham, goat's cheese and pears followed by a rustic pizza covered in potatoes and cream. The French owner told me her family had once lived in Salford. Lowry wouldn't have had any matchstick men to paint if she'd set up shop there.

The next few days were spent weaving through the towns of France's south-west – Perpignan, Beziers, Narbonne and Montpelier – refuelling on pastries and cheap wine.

The south-east of France is home to my dad's relatives, his sister Liz and husband Mike. The distracting thing about my aunt is that she looks just like my dad and has exactly the same mannerisms. It's like seeing him in a dress. And the last time I saw him in a dress was on a package holiday in

Majorca when I was 15. He'd volunteered for a part in the cabaret, which involved his dressing as a woman and doing the can-can. All was well until he kicked a little too strenuously and a testicle flopped from his underpants and swayed heavily as he continued to kick for a couple more minutes. Memories like that don't fade quickly.

It'd been fifteen years since I'd last been to Vence to visit Liz and Mike but little had changed. Liz was still a great cook and Mike was still driving her crazy. Their relationship is similar to that of Inspector Clouseau and Chief Inspector Dreyfus, Mike acting like a hyperactive six-year-old despite being in his seventies and Liz desperately reaching for the fags while telling him to shut up.

From Liz and Mike's I trundled down the hill to the coast and the nearby swanky city of Nice. Tell people you've been to Nice and, believing themselves to be the first person ever to think of it, they'll immediately reply with "That's nice." Always. I promise. Try it.

A cycle path along the Promenade des Anglais guarded me from speeding Porsches and, heading eastwards along the Côte d'Azur, the longer tunnels had escape roads to prevent me from becoming another Grace Kelly statistic. I arrived on the outskirts of Monaco, only a mile or so from its centre. I entered a tunnel and it was immediately obvious this principality isn't an ordinary sort of place. Most countries build tunnels as a necessity, to burrow through a pesky mountain that's in the way, and even then they keep them as small as possible to reduce costs. Not in Monaco. Today's tunnel was merely a bypass, and a bypass that contained roundabouts. Roundabouts in a tunnel? That's mental. The bypass did its job a little too well and spat me out on the other side of the country making me miss Monaco entirely. I heaved the bike around and found another way in.

I cycled around for a while looking for the casino as a nice location for my official photograph to prove I'd visited capital number eighteen but I couldn't find it. I've never really understood why casinos are associated with wealth, exotic cocktails and sophistication while betting shops are associated with poverty, alcoholism and tiny biros. At heart they're both the same, although admittedly it's hard to imagine James Bond in a bookie's. Even Monte Carlo's casino is just a collection of slot machines and spinning wheels. It's Blackpool's Golden Mile in an Armani suit.

Bugger the casino. I found a lovely location for my photo, the new breakwater on the harbour. It was also time for my Eat Something Silly challenge. Surveying all the opulence before me, speedboats the size of houses, the million dollar apartments, the Pradas and Versaces, I reached into my bag, took out a packet of maggots and ate them.

You might consider this to be cheating but I saw it as a contingency plan. I assumed there'd be a few countries on this trip, the ones I could cycle through in ten minutes, in which it'd be difficult to find something I'd never eaten before. Dean, a friend from Nerja, had given me a packet of BBQ-flavoured maggots for just this type of occasion. They're deep fried rather than live – I'm not a monster – and so I ate them, took my photograph and cycled out of Monaco to visit my cousin Vicky, who lived just the other side.

Vicky had arranged for me to be interviewed by a young and enthusiastic puppy dog of a bloke from Monaco's tiny TV station. He wanted to film me for their daily news show. We met at the harbour again. With beard and straggly hair I looked like a disciple of Jesus, surrounded by all the things that'd get my boss yacking on about camels and eyes of needles. With a camera stuffed in my face the puppy dog began the interview. There was local pride in his questions. He was clearly a servant of Monaco.

"And what do you do in each capital?" he asked.

"Well, one thing I like to do is eat something I've never tried before. In France I had an andouillette and in Switzerland I even ate a marmot."

"And what did you eat in Monaco?" he beamed, probably imagining my munching down caviar or oysters or a big bag of diamonds.

Oh dear. Could I be honest? Had I really cycled 7,000 miles to arrive in his magnificent Monaco and eat a handful of maggots? Is there anything less associated with Monaco than maggots? If someone has such pride, far be it from me to piss on his chips, or his frogs' legs, or whatever Monaco's national dish is.

"I had *barbajuan*," I replied. Luckily, the evening before, Vicky had sourced a Monegasque pastry, stuffed with *bette*, which is a special leaf apparently but, to all intents and purposes, is spinach. It was a cop out answer. I'd eaten spinach in pastry before but diplomacy states sometimes it's better to lie than to admit to a fondness for invertebrates. Besides, maybe a non-maggot-loving billionaire watching this on the box would be intrigued by my ride and sponsor me a million pounds. Or pay squillions for the film rights. Yes, of course. That's exactly how you become a billionaire, by giving away tons of money to an insect-eating tit.

Monaco was an important marker on my trip. Of the eighteen capitals I'd visited so far on this ride I'd already seen eleven of them in a past life and the new ones were often dots like Saint Helier, Andorra la Vella and pointless Vaduz. This was about to change. I'd seen very few of my remaining 32 capitals. This year alone would offer brand new, mouth-watering experiences like Rome, Ankara, Sofia, Sarajevo and Belgrade. And despite not being a capital I was also planning to sneak Istanbul into the mix. There were also dodgy countries like Albania and Kosovo. And it'd all start from here. I offered Vicky a final chance to try what remained of my maggots – she once again refused, the young fool – and I bid farewell, following the coast road into Italy under a shining sun.

I've read on cycling forums about how dangerous Italy is to cycle. One bloke had visited northern Italy with his wife and endured so many near death experiences on their first day that they'd packed up and immediately left. It was true the traffic was a little closer than it'd been in Spain and France but it was no worse than the UK. Not yet anyway.

The next evening I found myself hosting a beach party. Admittedly, not many people came. Actually, it was just me, sat on a beach near Savona with a picnic of bread, cheese and salami, and a bottle of red wine but I had a great time. The event was to celebrate passing my philosophy MA. I felt the wine was justified. After all, Aristotle was a bugger for the bottle.

I thought it was appropriate the party should have a philosophical theme and so, as the sun went down, I sat there reading Schopenhauer, famous for being a gloom-monger but today talking about happiness. Much of what he wrote makes a lot of sense and could have saved bookshelves of self-help manuals written in the 150 years since. Happiness, he said, isn't something we find. It comes from within. We generate it. If we're too dependent on others or on possessions for our happiness then one day these might be taken away and the foundations of our happiness crumble. (Some philosophers have taken this a little too far. Epictetus suggested men should marry unloveably ugly wives so we wouldn't miss them when they left or died.) It was especially pleasant to read these wise words under a reddening sky with the wine and the Mediterranean lapping a couple of metres from my feet.

Then the fishermen turned up. I'd seen this before in Spain, blokes fishing from the beach. Although I'd never watched them closely, in all the times I'd passed them I'd never seen anyone catch a fish. I'd never seen anyone get as much as a bite. I'd be sitting here for a couple of hours so this would be a chance to see how many fish they catch in a session. I watched and I waited.

I also kept reading. Schopenhauer continued that only those pursuing intellectual goals and who hide themselves away from society – since other humans cannot offer us anything – can be truly happy. There is, he said, no happiness in friends, partners, sex, wine, games, sport, travel or any sensual pleasure. OK, maybe he wasn't so wise after all.

An hour passed by and the fisherman had had no luck. But then they noticed a small patch of sea boiling with fish, grabbing at a swarm of flies on the surface. One of them skilfully launched his weight, hook and bait to just the other side of the shoal and, reeling in, trawled his tackle right through the middle of them. He did this three times and all he managed to do was lose his bait each time. The fishermen didn't seem too bothered by this. Perhaps catching fish wasn't even the purpose of the exercise. Perhaps it was just a chance for each of them to get out of the house and spend some time with his pals. They left the beach shortly afterwards, chatting and laughing.

Philosophers often get a bit up themselves, especially when it comes to what makes us happy. Failing to catch fish with friends, drinking wine on a beach at sunset or cycling thousands of miles are all things that Schopenhauer would've said can't create true joy. What a chump.

I'd be meeting Nina in Rome for my birthday, three weeks away. This meant I'd more time than I needed to get there and so I decided on a city tour of northern Italy. It'd been pretty cycling with the sparkling Mediterranean on my right for a few days but after my beach party I turned inland and headed towards Milan, the rolling Piedmont hills feeling like a shabby version of rural Austria. The sun went in and stayed there and the rain came down.

Close to Pavia the road system did everything it could to get me on to a motorway, with the white, non-motorway signs also pointing me in that direction. In the end it tricked me and I did a couple of miles on the hard shoulder. A police car travelling in my direction gave me a toot but didn't stop. Once you're on such a road there's little else you can do but carry on to the next exit but this wouldn't be my last time on an Italian motorway.

Towards Milan the rain got worse so I hid in a café. A woman approached me and assumed I was German. When I put her right she simply said "Chelsea" and walked off. The rain wasn't going to stop so I figured I had to go for it. I passed another cyclist coming towards me. She had a Lidl's carrier bag over her head as a rain hood, those crazy, fashion-conscious Italians.

Entry into Milan offered my first experience of Italian cobbles. Here they were big and placed at 45 degrees to the road. On the face of it this seemed like a good idea. Neither cyclists riding down the road, nor pram-pushing mums crossing perpendicularly, would slip between the cracks. The problem was that also set in the cobbles were tram tracks. If you're on a bike and want to cross a tram track without jamming your wheel and causing expensive dental work you need to turn your front wheel at an angle to it but then your wheel gets jammed in the cracks between the cobbles and you still need a dentist. It was safer to push.

Once in Milan the heavy rain made the city difficult to enjoy. I ducked from shelter to shelter but the heavy greyness hanging in the air managed to make even Milan's cathedral look weary.

Two days later I was in a lift, taking my left pannier, my slightly heavier right pannier, my bar bag, my tent and my rucksack down from the third floor of a rickety hotel in Piacenza. The lift doors closed, I selected the ground floor but nothing happened. Not sure what to do next I stabbed the buttons on the control panel repeatedly. Eerily, the lift began to sink very slowly, seemingly without power. I quickly remembered my How To Survive Anything book's advice of spreading yourself on the floor if a lift starts to plummet. I didn't want to chance getting splattered. When the lift got close to the second floor I prised open the door, jumped the last bit and escaped. It wasn't easy with all the bags. Fun times!

The day improved. There was a morning tour of the beautifully serene cobbled centre of Piacenza followed by a pleasant ride in gorgeous sunshine to Parma. In the evening I met up with Italian OU student Silvia. She'd told me she wanted me to experience some of the food for which Parma is famous. In true Italian style it was an offer I couldn't refuse.

I met Silvia and her daughter, Valentina, in Parma's Garibaldi Piazza. As an aperitif we went for a prosecco and then wandered over an old Roman bridge to the classy Antica Cereria restaurant. Along the way we were joined by Valentina's younger sister, Zoe, who'd borrowed her sibling's bicycle to reach us in time. It suddenly hit home what I was doing and how the OU had helped to make it happen. It was amazing that I could get on my silly, little bike and cycle halfway across the continent of Europe, continuing to study, and meet up with such wonderfully kind people.

And then there was the food. The meal began with a pile of prosciutto, pancetta and the richest salami followed by two types of pasta, herb and ricotta stuffed ravioli and tagliatelle covered with crispy little bacony bits. There's probably a more technical term for those. Main course was parmesan-stuffed brisket with fried potatoes and rosemary, all lubricated by a rich, creamy red Lambrusco. This was much better than my usual camping stove noodles. I was loving Italy. And then we finished up and went into the dark street outside. What had been Valentina's bike was now simply a broken bicycle lock dangling from an iron railing.

I left Parma full of food and headed towards Modena, the home of many an Italian sports car manufacturer but surely it should be more famous for generating the world's most famous Ghostbuster, Gabrielle Amorth, Roman Catholic priest and lifelong president of the International Association of Exorcists. He claims to have performed 70,000 exorcisms, which over his lifetime works out at around eight per day, possibly feasible if he'd sat in an office and had the demons come to him but if you were really possessed – Linda Blair possessed – you surely wouldn't catch the bus to his place to have Caspar removed. According to Amorth, the secret to being a successful exorcist to be "completely detached from monetary concerns, profoundly humble and treasure obscurity", as he obscurely wrote in his book on the subject, just before doing the Sunday Telegraph interview, or the one on telly with Anthony Head. That kind of obscurity.

I cycled around Modena looking for ghosts. Perhaps Amorth was inspired as a lad by the sheer quantity of ghouls in his neighbourhood. The only ones I could find were in the photo collection at the base of Modena's lovely Ghirlandina Tower, a tribute to the young blokes killed fighting the Nazis.

The city tour continued eastwards towards Bologna. The road was boringly straight but light on traffic and the driving wasn't anything like as bad as I'd been led to believe. I arrived in Bologna through teams of prostitutes and its narrow, car-filled streets made it less appealing than the other Italian towns I'd recently seen. With Milan's rain a distant memory and the sun firmly reinstalled I headed out of town and found a campsite. Lying outside the tent with a cold beer I was listening to an Italian language course when a bloke pulled up with a caravan and asked for my help.

"*Che posso fare?*" I asked using a phrase I'd learned a couple of minutes earlier, as though I knew what I was doing.

Julio wanted me to help push his caravan into place. He couldn't manage it alone. Ten minutes later, as a thank you, he came out with a bottle of cold prosecco and shared it with me, which seemed very generous bearing in mind how little I'd done. We guzzled the bottle in about five minutes.

Inside his caravan was his massive hound Vincenti, the size of a small horse. Julio let him off his leash but Vincenti got drunk on freedom and legged it. The recapture took half an hour. After that Vincenti remained tied up and seemed to regret his escape bid.

A little later, sat outside my tent, I could hear Julio talking about me on his phone. He brought it over and asked me to say something in English.

"Hello!" I said.

"Welcome to Italy," said a woman on the other end.

"Thank you. Who are you?" I asked, but she shyly refused to answer and was quickly replaced by a bloke who didn't speak English. I passed the phone back to Julio and that was that. It's not a great story but you can't fault the Italians when it comes to friendliness.

The ride continued, taking me near the coast, to Ravenna with its stylish shoppers loaded with bags from the town's upmarket stores, and then to the coast proper, to Cesenatico, a sort of Italian Southend. And then not far from Cesena I crossed the Rubicon, which wasn't as dramatic as I'd imagined. But that didn't matter because I could now see the towering rock that is San Marino or, to give it its full title, the Most Serene Republic of San Marino.

The most serene person in San Marino must be the centre forward of their national football team, stood up front the whole game fairly certain he's never going to get a kick. San Marino are officially the worst team in the whole world, right at the bottom of FIFA's rankings. Since their inception in 1986 it took fourteen years before they won a game. They do, however, hold two world records. The first is that they were on the receiving end of the largest thumping in national footballing history when Germany battered them 13-0. And what can the other record be? One more of humiliation perhaps? No, they scored the fastest ever goal in World Cup competition, after only eight seconds. Against Liechtenstein perhaps? Or the Faroe Islands maybe? No, against England. Perhaps not one of our better days.

San Marino apparently has no naturally level ground. If two Sanmarineses serenely want to play, say, a game of Subbuteo they must take their felt pitch and little plastic fellas to Italy for want of a large enough flat surface. And I know this is absolutely true and not something I've made up because I cycled up to the town of San Marino that sits atop the 750 metre hill in the middle of this tiny country and didn't see a single person playing Subbuteo.

That hill took some cycling but the views were worth the effort. Perhaps for reaching the top I'd earned some star appeal and that's why a Japanese girl wanted to take my photo. I humbly accepted. A little later an Italian bloke waved his camera at me. I posed again but his impression changed to one that said, "C'mon, you dick, just take a photo of me and the wife."

I needed something to eat. For some reason I'd imagined San Marino would spell the demise of my black, shrink-wrapped Chinese egg but it wasn't to be. I managed to assemble an entire meal of things new to my palate. For main course I had a couple of *piadinas*, which were simply San

Marino's answer to panini and which I suspect I should have cooked first. This was followed by utterly foul San Marino coffee yoghurt. This motley collection was flushed down the neck hole with Hell Bier. Its name almost makes sense in German but this is an Italian lager and so I reckoned they'd opted for that moniker just to annoy the Catholics.

I'd enjoyed my day in San Marino and although the food was rank at least the beer from Hell was acceptable but things weren't over yet. My campsite had, for the first time on this trip, a television room – more of a shed really – and it also had Italian Sky TV. Normally this wouldn't interest me but today there was an important football match. That evening Blackburn Rovers were playing Wigan and we had to win to avoid being relegated from football's top flight to a division no one watches or cares about.

We'd had a bad time of it recently. Eighteen months earlier we were sitting pretty in the middle of the Premier League with a decent manager, Sam Allardyce. We weren't ever going to break into the top six but neither would we be relegated. But then Blackburn sold out to Venky's, a sort of Calcutta Fried Chicken, who had so little clue about what they were doing it made you wonder whether they knew Blackburn Rovers was a football club at all. Within minutes Allardyce was gone, replaced by Steve Kean, a man whose post match interviews did strange things to the English language. Sentences would start and sentences would end but nothing joined them in the middle except a sort of jabbering. Under his control, if that's the right word, Blackburn slipped down the league like a drunk on a bobsleigh track, only narrowly avoiding relegation right at the end of the previous season.

Sat in that shed watching the game was an exercise in positivity. At kick off I was in a great mood, reflecting on what I'd achieved so far since I'd started cycling, on the distance, on the MA, on the friendship of the dozens of people I'd met and the experiences I'd had. I was high on the endorphins from today's monster climb and yet ninety painful minutes later, after watching that shower of shite, the joy was gone. If I'd started the game feeling anything less than ecstatic I'd probably have been found in the morning swinging from the light fitting with a television power cable for a noose. We were awful. Desperate to win we'd managed a single attempt on target. And so to end a lovely day I watched Blackburn descend into the Championship thereby destroying the last thing the town still had going for it, its membership of the world's most prestigious football league. Maybe San Marino weren't the worst team in the whole world after all.

Chapter 12: Drinking holy water

Capitals visited: 19
Total distance: 7,774 miles

For a town on top of a huge hill offering views for miles around, San Marino was unusually difficult to escape. All routes tried to send me back up the mountain or to Rimini, and I didn't want to go to Rimini. In the end I had to concede and start climbing again. An hour and a half after setting off I was back where I'd started.

Not far from San Marino is Tuscany. After the flat, sometimes uninspiring landscapes that stretch from Milan to Cesanatico, Italy began to reveal its majesty. The route to the village of Santa Sofia had me sweatily inching my way up steep mountain roads, peering down on emerald green pastures framed by dark forests on the weirdly folded rock beyond. On top of one hill I found a party of German cyclists. We had a chat about our respective journeys. The pack leader called me a "fiery dog". Is that good or bad?

Apart from my day in Surrey I'd only experienced total friendliness from the people I'd met but the Italians took this to a new extreme. In Spain you get smiles but very few questions, in France you get smiles and quite a few questions but in Italy they stopped their cars to talk to me.

The next day I climbed pass after pass and in the evening, via what felt like a back door into town, I trundled into Florence. I found a campsite on a hillside on the other side of the Arno, looking down on the city of the Medici. Michelangelo Piazza, a viewing platform for the city, was next door and I arrived just in time to see the setting sun bathe the city in gold. This was too special a place to cycle right through and so with time to kill before Rome I awarded myself a day off the bike.

The next morning's sun was baking the inside of the tent by seven o'clock and so I got up early, walked down the hill to town, crossed the Ponte Vecchio and almost had the streets of Florence to myself. I wandered aimlessly, down dark, cobbled lanes that suddenly exploded into brilliantly sunlit piazzas playing host to a cathedral or a church or some other architectural wonder. As the morning passed, the streets thickened with tourists but they couldn't diminish its splendour.

The Italian city tour continued onwards to Arezzo and Perugia and the weather was heating up. By midday I'd only stop the bike if I was in the shade of a tree. Until now all the cyclists I'd met on the road had been male and so it was great to have a chat with Franny, a Mexican student living in Perugia. She'd just finished a geography MA that focussed on landslides. Apparently Italy has a lot of them. That was news to me.

I was hoping the scale of my map was the reason why just up ahead near Todi my only option seemed to be a motorway. Surely there'd be a back road to avoid this but there wasn't. I'd only need to do a mile or so and the traffic surely couldn't have been much worse that the dual carriageway I was currently on. I sneaked on and it was empty. Two hundred metres from the exit I heard a car approach from behind. It pulled up ahead of me and a policeman got out. I held up my hand and said there'd been no alternative and I was leaving at the next junction. It's a bit daft to be thrown off a perfectly safe, quiet motorway with a giant shoulder on to an A-road with lots of traffic travelling at almost the same speed and hardly any shoulder at all.

Ten minutes after my run-in with the law I met Shane, a lean, lycra-clad Irishman. He was a WWOOFer, a member of the scheme that places volunteers on small organic farms all around the world. Workers don't get paid but receive free food and lodgings. It's a great way to see the country in which the farm is based. Shane worked the land in the mornings and the rest of the day was his. Off he went on his bike to discover wherever he happened to be living. He'd moved around Italy from farm to farm, staying a few months in each. He'd seen Italy from the inside, by living and working with Italian families.

His life had always been bikes. He'd been a cycle courier in London for years, darting in between cars, annoying taxi drivers and getting parcels to places more quickly than engines could manage.

"Wasn't there a high mortality rate?" I asked.

"Ah, no. Only two or three of my friends died," he replied without irony. Thinking about this for a second, he continued, "That's quite high, isn't it?"

After years of cycling the streets of the capital he'd had enough. He was earning lots of money but felt he was just giving it all away. Life in London was too expensive and so he changed things around. Now he earned nothing, but spent nothing and had plenty of free time to indulge his passion.

Having spent a lot of time in their company, Shane found the Italians, or maybe the rural Italians, very conservative. One of the ways this manifested itself is a belief that only certain sauces are allowed to go with certain shapes of pasta and that it's sacrilege to mix the wrong pasta and sauce. It does seem odd that, even in the tiniest village supermarket, there are shelves and shelves devoted to pasta and it's all essentially the same stuff: egg, flour and water. Maybe only Italians can understand the Pasta Laws. The next day this conservatism was demonstrated at a campsite shop I'd popped into to buy something for dinner.

"This pasta is nice," said the young shop assistant. "It goes really well with tomato and bacon."

Thinking of Shane, I laughed to myself. "OK. I'll have some of that."

"Do you have any bacon?" she asked.

"I have salami."

She tutted. "Ah, but that's not bacon."

Yes, I'm sure the pasta would be an absolute abomination with salami. I bought the pasta and, over my little camping stove, made a sauce. Not only did I use salami instead of bacon, I even added some bloody sardines. It was lovely. Sod off Pasta Laws!

Unlike the previous year my tent had behaved itself impeccably but hadn't really been challenged this time around. A gentle shower and a light breeze were all it'd had to handle. Tonight I found a campsite miles from anywhere. It was little more than a farmer's field and a food-less bar that closed at tea time. It looked like it'd be an early night. At seven o'clock the wind got up and it started to rain, thick splashes that increased in size and frequency until it sounded like someone was machine-gunning the canvas. After a couple of hours the roar of the bullets was joined by thunderous explosions and lightning filling the tent with brilliant flashes. The wind began to howl. The capacity of my tent was halved as its thin walls bellowed inwards with each gust. So much for an early night.

Sleep would be difficult with the racket outside but I was warm inside my sleeping bag. I'd just ride it out. By midnight the wind was a hurricane and suddenly, while lying there snugly and smugly, half of the tent collapsed. If unsecured, even a strong tent like this one would be ripped apart by winds this wild and so I'd have to go outside and fix it. I got dressed, slipped on my trainers – the only footwear I had with me – and unzipped the tent door. It was like the end of the world out there. The previously parched farmer's field had been replaced with chocolate-flavoured Angel Delight. Its gloopy hold threatened to suck the shoes from my feet. The soft ground and the strong winds had loosened the pegs. I traipsed around and fixed the tent as best as I could. My trainers were now twice their original size, covered in a thick, brown batter. Cold and wet I climbed back into the tent and my sleeping bag. Half an hour later I was warm again but I lay there awake listening to the weather. Despite the crashing I started to doze off when, around three in the morning, my phone jolted me back to consciousness with two texts from Orange welcoming me to Italy. I'd only been here three weeks. I switched off the phone, retracted my head into my sleeping bag like a tortoise and didn't sleep a wink. I love camping, me.

Today was a big day. I was about to do something I wouldn't manage on any other day of this entire trip. I'd tick off two capitals within minutes of each other, my twentieth and twenty-first. Getting lost looking for a campsite in the north of the city I had no real idea where I was and then suddenly I arrived at the Vatican City with its parade of enmarbled holy blokes looking down on the tourist hoard from the roof of Saint Peter's Basilica. At least I now knew where I was. A different campsite, one to the west of the city, now seemed the better option. But if all roads lead to Rome there must be just as many leaving. I chose the wrong one and got lost again. Back out of the city I tried to find another way in. It took me two hours and several terrifying excursions on busy dual carriageways before I found the site. It would've taken fifteen minutes if I'd cycled there directly.

Most visitors to Rome get their city info from guide books and the internet but I was privy to insider information. The friendly Birreria Marconi, a pub with an Italian name and Irish staff, was the meeting point for three OU students who lived in Rome. First came Giovanni, an Italian banker, studying so he could make a career change and no longer be one of the bad guys. Next was a very smiley Christine, a Canadian, who until recently had been the Italian correspondent for an English-language Iranian TV station, a job description that takes a few seconds to process. Later in the afternoon, tour guide Elaine, another Canadian, arrived. I jokingly asked her, given the huge population difference between the USA and Canada and that I'd now met three Canadians on this trip and no Americans, could it be possible she was pretending to be Canadian to avoid America's unpopularity? No, of course this wasn't true but she said there's a company in the States that sell Canada Kits to help American backpackers disguise themselves as their less militarily aggressive neighbours. Between them, Giovanni, Christine and Elaine circled their own highlights of Rome on my city map and these sites became my targets over the next few days.

Waiting for a bus to take me back to the campsite I appreciated the beauty of cycling. A murmur ran through the crowd at the bus stop. They started to look at their watches and wander off. What had they heard? The bus was late and I felt powerless. Here I was, in a strange city, barely speaking Italian and with no knowledge of its transport links. If the bus didn't show up, all other options would be slow or expensive. On my bike I'd just point it at something and pedal. I'd get there. I'm not a control freak but relinquishing my ability to get myself to where I want when I want made me feel unsettled. A bus eventually turned up half an hour later. When I got back to the campsite I wanted to kiss my bike but refrained, not wanting to undermine the master-slave relationship we'd developed.

I was looking forward to the next morning. My campsite was in the west and Pigneto, the district of Rome in which

Nina had booked us a place to stay, was in the east. I was going to cycle right across the very centre of Rome. After the warnings about Italian driving surely this would be the biggest test of its dangers.

The ride was exhilarating, the traffic dense but, as a result, slow moving. The turn of each corner found me on a new piazza or boulevard, ancient buildings, some crumbling, some pristine, lined the route. Rather than being a wallflower, I imagined I was a Vespa buzzing through the traffic, cycling in very visible parts of the road rather than crawling along its edges. At no time did I ever feel in danger. It wasn't the exhilaration of that hour's descent in Andorra but it was a different sort of fun.

After the success of locating ourselves in Berlin's funky grungeland, Kreuzberg, Nina had attempted to do the same in Rome. Despite sounding like the worst idea ever for an ice cream, Pigneto is famous as the location for a number of 1960s Passolini films. It also recently featured on the cover of a Morrissey album although he's basically lying on some railway tracks and, to be honest, he could just have easily shot it in Manchester, the big ponce. At least in the UK he'd have been in no danger of getting run over by a train. Like Kreuzberg, Pigneto is working class and almost entirely devoid of tourists. In fact, it falls just off the edge of the official city centre map and so, to all intents and purposes, doesn't actually exist. Pigneto's main thoroughfare, with its graffiti-covered walls enhancing an already colourful daily market, morphs at night into a student-filled street party with more bars than Strangeways and a similar police presence. But this was real Rome, where the smiles weren't attempts to sell you something and where the beer didn't cost six euros a pint as it did in the tourist traps closer to the centre.

Our first day was a typical tourist fortnight. We saw the Colosseum, the Vatican, the Pantheon, the Trevi Fountain and absolutely everything else Rome has to offer. In total we walked 367 miles. This allowed us to take it easy for the rest of our stay, absorbing our base, eating far too much pizza and waiting for feet to grow back on to our bloodied stumps.

Ah, the pizza. When you think of interesting toppings you don't immediately think of tubers but the best one I ever had was a potato and rosemary pizza in San Lorenzo, the student area of town. Although I'd never eaten a potato and rosemary pizza before it hardly counted as a new food. No matter, I had the rest of my days in Italy to find something weird but the Vatican City had to provide something right now. Finding something original in Popeland was always going to be a problem. The papal-faced lollipops that comedian Stewart Lee talks about were either an invention of his or are no more. I always had my black Chinese Egg of Doom to fall back on just in case but surely there'd be something. And then we saw it. A roadside fountain spewed forth what, given its location, could only be – ta-daah! – holy water. So I drank some and I saw the light but then again it was a sunny afternoon.

Holy water is a difficult concept. I can understand the instant at which the water might become holy, such as after a blessing or, of course, when piped through a Vatican fountain but when, if ever, does it stop being holy? What happens if holy water touches non-holy water? Does it all become infected with the spirit of the Lord? If so, surely by now all the water in the world is holy and there's no need for priests. Or is the holiness diluted and the combined liquid only, say, partially pious water? We need answers.

After a harrowing day on a busy dual carriageway, I met Francesco in the town of Latina, south of Rome. On an old bike he arrived, a slim, elegant, grey-haired man in his sixties. I followed him around a maze of suburban streets to his house where he introduced me to his wife Leandra and his enormous husky called Husky.

If there was ever a poster child for the concept of life-long learning it was Francesco. He was an epidemiologist studying patterns of disease around Latina. As well as his medical degree he had an MSc in tropical diseases and was currently working towards an OU degree in mathematics so that he could later take another, more maths-based MSc. He spoke English fluently, Italian obviously, but also French, Russian and German. He was currently studying Spanish and Portuguese. During our time together he talked knowledgeably about music, films, architecture, history and geology. He was also utterly charming. The word polymath was designed for him.

Francesco and Leandra showed me unbelievable kindness. After a late lunch of mozzarella and tomatoes they took me to the mountaintop village of Circeo, named after the witch who seduced Odysseus and turned his crew into pigs. The view from the mountain summit was the most impressive thing I'd seen so far this year. At a height of more than 500 metres, on a rock that juts abruptly from a huge coastal plain, you feel you're looking out of an aeroplane window. Later we drove to another gorgeous village, the 14th century Sermoneta, where they fed me local specialities in a tiny trattoria. That night, in their spare room, I slept the sleep of a lucky man.

Loaded with more mozzarella, apples and cake, the next day I began my crawl down the shin of Italy towards Naples and ended up camping inside a volcano in Pozzuoli. The town's name is derived from the Latin verb meaning 'to stink' because of the sulphurous stench leaking from the crater. Solfatara hadn't erupted since 1198 but the caldera, in which the campsite was located, had puddles of boiling mud and spurting fumaroles. An army of school children was being led around the site. Their tour guide got the kid's teacher to stand near one of the larger smoke vents so she looked like she was burning to death. The kids loved that bit.

"Burn the witch!" they shouted, probably.

It was only a bit of fun. No harm was done except her clothes would now reek of bad eggs for the rest of the day. But I couldn't help thinking that, had this been the UK, a man with the words health and safety in his job title would've taken a very dim view of it all.

But maybe we should have been more concerned. Not far down the road was Pompeii and we all know what happened there. To reach it I had to cross Naples. The entire sea front road was temporarily closed to cars making it the perfect route for me. The hillside above was crowded with tall apartment blocks but with an interesting air of grunginess about the place, a city-sized version of Pigneto.

On the other side of town the traffic returned as did the cobbles. These weren't the thoughtfully laid large cobbles of Milan but lumpy little sods, smaller than house bricks. Yes, they're uncomfortable to cycle on but they must also shake cars to pieces too. And they're bloody noisy even when a car drives on them slowly, and this is Italy so nobody does.

It can't be easy being an Italian driver. For one thing, it must be difficult to control a car with a mechanism that only lets it move forward if a mobile phone is pressed to the driver's ear. It was in Naples I learned how Italians, or at least southern Italians, really drive. Parked cars pull out and then, within a few metres, pull back in again, or they pull out of a side street and within a metre or two park up. They hop around the entire town like this. I estimated it would take the average Neapolitan at least three months to get across the city. But then I realised what they're doing. They're shopping. It can't be cool in Italy to walk anywhere and so rather than park up properly and visit each shop on foot as in other countries, here they just double-park outside each and every shop they need to use. I've no idea how they cope in shopping malls. It must be a nightmare getting a Fiat up those escalators.

The cobbles ended but they'd taken their toll. A strange clicking sound appeared to be coming from the pedal crank. In true optimist style I decided it'd probably go away if I ignored it and eventually it did.

That afternoon I rolled into a campsite only a denarius's throw from the ancient city of Pompeii. I hoped there'd be no repeat of what happened there in AD 79. Even with the new and improved poles the tent wouldn't have been much protection. I'd always wondered how the people of Pompeii were caught so unawares by Vesuvius but now at least I have a theory. In every Italian city, attached to one lamp post per mile, is a clock. Without exception the clock is always wrong. And not five minutes wrong. We're talking hours wrong. Perhaps it's always been like this. Someone probably predicted the eruption for six pm, their clocks told them it was now only three and they had hours before they had to get moving.

After a wander around the ruins of Pompeii I decided to try to eat something I'd never had before. I'd been recommended *arancini* by Vicky in Monaco but she wouldn't eat maggots so what did she know? I don't know if my supermarket arancini was a bad example but the tasteless rock of congealed rice required more saliva than I could muster. It took several beers to wash it down so it wasn't all bad news.

From Pompeii the roads got quieter and after a long and glorious coastal ride that climbed and fell I ended up in the village of Castellabate. I found Camping Marvelosa, a name grander than its scruffy little sign, but it promised a bar and a mini-market and along with a bit of grass I needed little else. Reception was a wooden booth but it was empty so I wandered inside. Curiously, apart from one dilapidated,

1970s-style motor home, the entire site appeared lifeless. Where was the bar? The mini-market? Other campers? In the far corner were a couple of rudimentary bungalows and then some trees. Perhaps the bar was lost in the forest. I went for a look. Suddenly a barking dog sprang from the house shortly followed by its owner, a trim but muscled, short-haired fella in a white vest.

"Are you open?" I asked, a question that should probably worry any businessman.

"Yes, of course," he replied with a grin.

"Great. Where's the mini-market?"

"Just tell me what you want and I'll go and get it for you."

I suppose this system works like a mini-market but it's not a mini-market, is it? Anyway, the price was cheap enough and though the toilets and showers were skanky I decided to stay. I set up my tent and cycled back out of the site, found a real supermarket and got some grub for dinner.

Shortly after my evening meal, it started. I assumed at first the campsite was near a large hotel, maybe a specialist one catering for the tone deaf. At disturbingly loud levels the sound of karaoke flooded the air. But there was no hotel. The din was emanating from one of the bungalows in the corner of the site. I listened for a bit, unable not to. The singer crooned in flat Italian and at the end of each tune he thanked an imaginary audience. Sometimes he introduced the songs too, like a real singer. After half an hour of this, and with no let up likely, I went to investigate. Inside the bungalow were Nico – the campsite owner I'd met earlier – his long-haired mate Gino, and Kika, the little, white dog that had tried to eat me. Despite the run-down look of the campsite their living room was like a NASA control centre, deep with computers, screens, mixing desks and a loudspeaker the size of a wendy house. On the wall was a clock showing twenty past eight. Wow, I thought, an Italian clock that works. I was impressed.

"Do you want a beer?" asked Nico.

"That'd be great."

Nico leapt out of the front door.

"Where's he gone?" I asked Gino.

"To get your beer." I heard the sound of a car roar off from the gravel outside. Nico was a man of his word. His minimarket had sprung into action. He was only gone a few minutes and once home again the karaoke could restart. His enormous flat screen was full of little Skype faces watching him perform, friends from around the world, keeping a safe distance and with the ability to turn down the volume when necessary. He cranked up something I'd never heard before and started to sing, dancing around like he was on X Factor. He finished and I gave him a little round of applause but it was clear that in return for the beer I had to sing too.

"Who's your favourite artist?" Nico asked.

"Radiohead."

He looked through his collection of karaoke tracks.

"There's no Radiohead."

"Ah, damn," I said. "Never mind." Ha!

"It doesn't matter. We can get something from YouTube." Bugger. And he did. A microphone was thrust into my paw and I had to choose from a shortlist. I went for the wonderfully miserable *No Surprises*. I play this at home on guitar and so I knew I could manage it with my limited vocal range. They seemed diplomatically impressed but what the thousands of others who could also hear it thought we'll never know. Their beer and encouragement got me in the mood and I got bolder with later choices. We took it in turns to murder songs. My *Karma Police* was just about acceptable, my Bublé's *Haven't Met You Yet* began the descent especially with that sodding key change near the end and I apologise to the population of southern Italy for what I did to Coldplay's *Viva la Vida*. I'd been there a couple of hours and, great lads though Nico and Gino were, I needed some sleep. What time was it, I wondered. I looked at the clock. Ah, it was still twenty past eight.

For the first time since the Channel I crossed a sea, on my way to Sicily. From Messina I headed south, the east coast road gorgeous and lightly trafficked in the late May sunshine. Just before Taormina a beautiful island, half the size of a football pitch and worthy of a Bounty ad joined the beach by an isthmus. Holidaymakers paddled in the warm, blue sea.

Two days later I arrived at the ferry port of Catania, the harbour from which the ferry to Malta leaves. Except that it doesn't, because you have to get on a bus – something the Virtu Ferries website was strangely silent about – which then, in theory, drives south for an hour and a half to the real port of Pozzallo. I wasn't on that bus because there was no room for my bike despite there being plenty for the four boxed up, metre and a half wide, flat screen tellies loaded by a friend of the driver. It's who you know.

At seven o'clock in the evening, suddenly realising I wasn't going to Malta after all, I needed somewhere to stay in Catania, I legged it out of town to the only place my map showed a camping symbol. What the symbol didn't say was that Campeggio Europeo was The Worst Campsite In The Whole World. I arrived at the site to be greeted by the surly, middle-aged owner who openly mocked by admittedly sad attempts at Italian. That's OK, I thought as I smiled at him, he's morbidly obese. He'll be dead soon.

I pitched my tent and then set out to find the site's bar or restaurant or mini-market for which there were numerous signs. The directions led me all around the campsite in a big circle until I ended up back at my tent. There was no bar or restaurant or mini-market and I was miles from any shop. Oddly, for a site lacking any entertainment at all, it was full of eighteen-year-olds. I noticed another sign during my circuit of the site. It said "Attention to the ground. Danger of depression!" No kidding. Luckily, there were holiday homes next to the site and an amiable but deaf, old bloke with admirable capitalist spirit had set up a table and a fridge selling crisps and beer. I happily bought some of each. It was a pity though he hadn't bothered to plug in the fridge. Back at the site a visit to the lav showed the sort of conditions you'd expect to find in the cell of a prisoner making a dirty protest, shit all over the walls and vomit on the floor. Lovely. You really should go there.

I had a long way to go tomorrow – the unplanned-for ninety miles to Pozzallo to catch the ferry – and so I decided I'd get going by six-thirty. I had my warm beer and crisps and settled down for an early night. At ten o'clock the music started. I can't blame the site for this but I'd managed to pitch my tent in the ideal spot to attend the Rizla Original Cucaracha Beach Party attended by world famous DJs like Monika Kruse. No, me neither. On the other side of the slender fence behind my tent was the dirt track giving cars access to the event and so at least they drowned out the music. At three in the morning the fireworks started. At four o'clock, as party-goers started to leave, the car alarms kicked in. I managed to grab an hour of sleep around five-ish.

During the night I'd warmed myself with the thought of a noisy early morning departure as revenge on the bleary-eyed youngsters but obviously the buggers were still partying when I woke up. I cycled off, half-comatose, to the sound of cool teenagers jigging to crap like Imagination and naff seventies disco. Monika Kruse is available for weddings and eighteenths.

I cycled and cycled. Approaching Syracuse I was taken unawares when my nice, normal A-road suddenly and without warning turned into a motorway. I kept going planning to escape at the first exit but around the next corner sat a police car on the hard shoulder. The policeman saw me and pretended to be angry for a bit. How distraught could he have been? He fights the Mafia, for Christ's sake. Compared to organised crime, what's a dick on a pushbike? Faced with an apology and a smile he decided not to fine me and in the end gave me a police escort off the motorway.

Finally I made it to Pozzallo. With a few hours to wait for the ferry I settled down for a nap on a wall inside the port, resting my head on my rucksack. A citrus-arsed port official moved me on, presumably mistaking me for a tramp getting his head down for the night. The way I looked I could hardly blame him, my hair shoulder length, my beard bushy and ninety miles in the hot sun probably hadn't done too many favours for my body odour.

The modern ferry eventually left Sicily at half nine in the evening. A large screen in the lounge showed the view from the bow, the contrast turned right up so we could make out indistinct shapes in the darkness. A single harbour light blazed like the sun. As we approached, Valletta was in the middle of a firework display to celebrate the Queen's 60th year of being head of the world's richest family on benefits. Watching the blasts and explosions on the high contrast TV screen we appeared to be arriving in Fallujah.

Turning up on a bike in a strange and pitch black port close to midnight isn't a great idea but luckily I'd booked a hotel and memorized the Google map to get there in the shortest time. What Google Maps hadn't told me was the route I had chosen was predominantly steep steps, even more unpleasant on a heavily panniered bike. By the time I arrived in reception I was sweating more heavily than after cycling that day's ninety miles in the mid-afternoon heat. I looked a mess. The friendly bloke on reception waived all need to check-in properly – that could wait until tomorrow – and I removed my sweat and stench from his nostrils – possibly the real reason for the hasty entry procedure – and de-tramped myself with a shave and a long, hot bath.

Here I was in Valletta, capital 22 and the second most southerly of my trip and it wasn't what I was expecting. I'd suspected it might be another half-English, half-local, worst-of-both-worlds craphole like Gibraltar but it wasn't. Valletta is fairly magnificent. It had a wonderful atmosphere, the buildings tall and grand though their splendour faded and dusty. Walking around its regular grid of streets at any time other than high noon provided shade and there always seemed to be a cooling breeze coming from somewhere. And it felt exotic. The Maltese language is still spoken by 200,000 of the island's inhabitants. It's the only official EU language that's Semitic and the only Semitic language written in the Latin script. It's stuffed full of Zs, Js, and Qs, funky double-barred Hs and a scattering of diacritical marks on letters that don't normally wear them. But the exoticism is tempered with old-fashioned English shops. Hairdressers' displays offered 1960s styles and underwear outlets advertised girdles. I didn't think women still wore girdles. If Doctor Who landed here, it'd take him a minute or two to work out in which decade he was.

In my short time there I went looking for something odd to eat. I was disappointed when the restaurant offering a rabbit burger on its menu outside couldn't deliver the goods. Another Maltese possibility was Widow's Soup. I've never eaten a widow so I was tempted but a little research told me it was just a poor man's vegetable soup.

While on my quest I discovered a snack bar with an unusual concept. Some tourist restaurants bypass linguistic difficulties with photo menus. This café in Valletta had gone one better and pre-prepared their entire menu, placing it behind a glass counter so you could really see what you were getting. The problem was they'd obviously made most of this stuff days ago. The chips were wilted and the salad brown and limp, all garnished with dried up bits of cucumber. It's not a strategy that's going to catch on.

I didn't want to leave Valletta. I wanted to cycle around the entire island, to see the villages as well as the tiny capital, but I had to keep moving if I was going to finish this long year in time for exams and revision.

For the next five days I retraced my steps, cycling back up the east coast of Sicily, past the pale purple Mount Etna in the distance and returning to mainland Italy and up its leg. It's never as interesting cycling the way you've already been but if I had to do one stretch again it would've been this one. Italy's a great place to cycle.

From Sapri I headed inland. A boat in Bari was waiting to ferry me to Greece and to get there I once again had to cross the spine of Italy. As I topped a high hill on the way to Potenza, a group of tourists taking in the view shouted me a *Rispetto!* I punched the air triumphantly, inducing an embarrassing wobble. I'm like the Fonz, I am.

The next day, accompanied once again by that familiar clicking noise from the bike, I was back on the east coast in the warmth and breeziness of Bari. My six and a half week tour of Italy was over. Of all the countries I'd visited so far it'd easily been my favourite. Its mountains are majestic, its coastline spectacular, its carb-heavy food perfect for refuelling and its people the friendliest I'd ever met. *Rispetto, Italia!*

Chapter 13: The world's worst philosophy tour

Capitals visited: 22
Total distance: 9,452 miles

The ferry dumped me at lunchtime on the scorching tarmac of Patras on the north-west coast of the Peloponnese. I was back on the same latitude as Sicily again and the journey south had raised the temperature by more than I was expecting. It was still only early June. If it was this hot now I didn't want to imagine what it'd be like in Turkey at the end of July.

Greece can be difficult unless you know their alphabet. Knowledge of the language wasn't necessary for restaurants here – along the coast they catered for tourists – but some of the road signs to smaller places were only in the Greek alphabet. My map used our own and I needed to translate between the two. Despite the difficulty it's great to see someone giving the language a go even if they get it wrong. I went for a walk in the hills and ended up following a Brit. As each Greek passed in the opposite direction he barked a lusty "Good day!" At least that's what he thought. Good day is *kalimera* but he greeted them with *kalamari*, the equivalent of wishing his fellow walkers a hearty "Squid!"

This was an interesting time to be cycling around Greece if a mostly depressing time to be Greek. Most conversations, once we'd got past the pleasantries, delved into Greece's financial woes. As well as the crisis the whole of Europe had suffered, Greece had additional problems of its own.

At a campsite in Korinthos, I met Peter, its owner. The site could've accommodated hundreds of campers and came with its own lovely stretch of beach. Unfortunately, there weren't many of us staying there.

"Usually we're busy right now," Peter said, "but this year we've never had more than eleven people on any given day."

Peter was born in London and his family moved back here when he was six. He admitted the Greek people hadn't been blameless. In recent decades, they'd been offered easy ways out of paying tax and they'd taken them. Would it have been different anywhere else? Probably not. He argued it was the job of solid government to ensure there aren't easy ways out.

When I came to Greece in the nineties there were hundreds of houses with flat roofs and metal poles at each corner suggesting an additional floor was planned. You only paid tax once your house was finished. The owners had no intention of adding another storey but, with poles in place for an imaginary floor, they could argue tax wasn't due. Only now was this being addressed. At last the countryside had stopped looking like an army of cube-shaped hedgehogs with partial alopecia.

But as well as obvious fixes the tax situation had gone into overdrive. Peter calculated between 70% and 80% of his income now went to the government. Additional ad hoc payments were also regularly announced that all businesses had to pay, even those with few campers.

The Greeks were angry and saw Germany as the bogeyman inflicting the pain. Peter claimed he couldn't drive his BMW around Athens for fear of reprisals. That said, he was wearing a T-shirt that included a German flag and so maybe he liked to live dangerously. He was seriously considering moving back to the UK but he loved it here and the prospect of British weather filled him with dread. Besides, to move back he'd need to sell up and his business was hardly an attractive proposition during this climate.

I set off early the next morning with Athens as my goal. I

crossed the Corinth canal on the motorway, the only option as far as I could tell. By nine o'clock it was baking hot. The sun bounced off the Megara Gulf, blinding me even in shades. By midday I was on the outskirts of the city hiding from the heat, munching a ham and cheese sandwich at a petrol station while a salivating dog stared me out until I gave him a bit of my butty.

I entered town via Piraeus and fought through Athens' thick traffic. In the centre, in Omonia Square, I stopped to buy a map. An eight-year-old policeman came over to chat. When I told him what I was doing he called over a couple of his mates and phoned up another copper who was a cyclist. Before long I was surrounded by five policemen. At least no one was going to steal my bike. They were in no hurry to leave.

"Are you busy today?" I asked, after about fifteen minutes. He didn't notice the sarcasm in my voice.

"We're always busy."

We carried on chatting for another ten minutes.

"Where are you staying?" one of them asked.

"A place down Archarnon," I replied.

He pulled his face. Nina had obviously done it again. Eventually they let me go before they could do me for wasting police time and I cycled to the apartment Nina had found. I'd visited Athens a couple of times before, as a springboard to the islands, not staying more than a night because I always thought it a noisy, grimy sort of place. I'd never been to this part of town. Down the long Archarnon road it was an ethnic diversity wonderland with supermarkets of every nationality. Had you been kidnapped and released here you'd have trouble guessing which country you were in.

Inside the apartment I met Eleni, its owner. The conversation quickly moved on to the usual tales of woe about the Greek economy. Eleni was a little powerhouse of energy and jigged about as she told her story. The political parties that'd been in power for years, the ones that'd co-won the recent election, were utterly corrupt, she said. Defence Minister Akis Tsochatzopoulos had personally creamed off tens of millions in a dodgy submarine deal. He was now in prison. Other frauds abounded.

The election alternatives were a communist party wanting to escape the euro entirely or a neo-Nazi party offering their own unpleasant solution. The options didn't seem great. Unlike Peter, Eleni wasn't quite so forgiving of Joe Public's reluctance to pay his due. While the government made it easy to avoid tax, some actively stole from the lax system, she said, inventing relatives whose pensions they claimed.

From previous visits, I couldn't remember any beggars, or women with babies huddled in dirty corners, or old men passed out in the street. They were here now. Eleni described how, years earlier, millions of immigrants had got themselves smuggled into Greece to find work, of which there'd been plenty. Now there was none. But these people had no papers and couldn't leave, and no one was helping them to go, even though they wanted to. They were trapped in a country with no money and no ability to make money. Like Peter, Eleni wanted out. She'd set her sights on Thailand but also like Peter she'd have to sell up first and no one was buying.

Around eight, with the sky darkening, I hoofed it across town to meet Nina at the airport. On the way I once again passed through Omonia Square. A political demonstration was being held, the place heaving with thousands on this sweaty June evening, a speaker barking commands from a brightly lit central stage. I squeezed through the crowds as they chanted in unison. I'd no idea if this was a communist or neo-Nazi rally or someone else entirely. I didn't want to know. I wanted to get out of there. Any crowd hanging on the word of a single man with a microphone and thinking as one is dangerous. I kept on pushing my way through. A man standing on a wall grabbed my hand and raised it in the air to indicate my support for their cause, annoyed that I hadn't yet been assimilated. I snatched my hand back and carried on. I felt like a salmon swimming upstream. I reached the edge of the square and the crowd thinned out and eventually was gone. Thinking back, maybe it wasn't a political rally at all. Maybe the speaker had just been the MC for a Demis Roussos gig.

Athens may not have appealed on previous visits but I'd studied philosophy since then and so perhaps now I'd see a different side of Athens, the Athens of old, the Athens that gave us the earliest superheroes of thought. I put together a philosophy tour. In my tour group, apart from me as guide, was Nina and absolutely no one else. This, as it turned out, was just as well.

Our first destination was the garden of Epicurus. Despite giving his name to an adjective suggesting excess and gorging – two swans and a koala bear for breakfast, that type of thing – his own diet couldn't have been more different. He shut himself away in his Athenian garden with his friends, wrote more books than Barbara Cartland and ate little other than bread and cheese but this simple life made him happy. Chasing wealth was for fools, he thought. Chasing Epicurus's garden was also for fools. The first problem was that it didn't exist any longer. The internet gives clues to its former location, perhaps in the grounds of Saint George's church. As a memento of our inaugural tour we found the church and I took a snap. Tour item one completed! An hour later, when I checked the map properly, I realised it wasn't even the right bloody church. Saint George's wasn't the one in the scruffy bit of park with a woman taking a piss around the back. No, it was the nicer one we passed later that I hadn't photographed.

It was this sort of half-arsed planning that was to plague the rest of my first ever guided tour.

Next up was Plato's Academy, one of the first schools of philosophy. Unlike Epicurus's garden this still exists although Athens seems strangely reluctant to tell anyone where it is. After trudging out through a dilapidated industrial estate and walking for what seemed like hours in the midday heat – mainly because it was hours – we didn't find it. A quick google once we got back to the apartment told us we'd walked right past it and then a few miles further. Signposts are for the weak, not the Greek, obviously.

Stop number three on our tour was more successful. Possibly. This was a visit to Aristotle's Lyceum, a metro ride across town from the school of Plato, Aristotle's former teacher. We found a site that had some ruins in the spot where the internet said the Lyceum was and that'd have to do. There were no signs or labels, just a big metal fence behind which may have been the site of a great philosophical school. Or maybe not. But at least we saw something.

The next day – yes, softies, this was a multi-day tour! – was Socrates Day. The plan was to find the Ancient Agora in which Ol' Pug Face used to annoy people and then find the prison in which he was forced to drink hemlock as punishment. Both of these locations are below the Acropolis, an area rich in sites and again poor in signage. We quickly gave up trying to find the prison but we had a higher goal, the Ancient Agora. It was famous. It was massive. It was incredibly well-preserved. It was, er, shut. It wasn't usually closed on Sundays but it was today, just this one Sunday in probably four or five years of Sundays, because it was election day. My philosophy tour was cursed.

And with that, my philosophy tour finally ended. Nina and I retired to a taverna for a huge kebab and enough beers to ensure we talked bollocks, albeit philosophically. If you and your friends would like to participate in any future philosophical excursions I might run, please contact me. All trips will include a pre-tour lecture in how to handle disappointment stoically.

I was back on the road. On one of the evenings in Athens the wind had got up and practically destroyed the awning on the terrace, ripping it down and bending its metal poles, and the wind had never gone away. It was strong and right on the nose. This was good for its cooling factor but meant I had to push the bike up some of the hills.

It wasn't until I'd arrived there that I realised Thiva is actually ancient Thebes, the home of Oepidus, he who'd blinded himself after realising he'd married and shagged his own mum. His self-mutilation seemed an extreme reaction. After all, his mum had already hung herself. He was single again. If he hadn't stuck pins in his eyes he could've had a pop at his sister.

The wind continued and to get me over the dusty hills I needed constant refuelling with flaky cheese and spinach filo pies. I needed liquid too. I stopped at a garage operated today by two ten-year-old kids but they had no water. A bloke sitting on his verandah across the road asked me if I needed something and invited me over. His missus brought out a large, ice cold bottle and gave it to me. There are kind people everywhere.

On the slow climb up the hill before Lamia I saw my first wild tortoise. He crawled painfully across the hot tarmac wearing an expression that said, "Billions of years of evolution and this is how it ends." A little later one of his cousins lay dead in the road, its back cracked open by the weight of a car.

From the top of the hill I could see Lamia in the distance. I hadn't realised how high I'd climbed. I screamed down the other side. At the bottom was a garage. I needed more water. I tried to go in but the door was locked. I could see two middle-aged women inside along with six kids under the age of eight. One of the women came to the door, unlocked it, let me in and locked it again. This was the entry and exit procedure for every customer. Either someone was paranoid or Lamia was rough.

Later I found a campsite but its main gate was locked. I assumed the site was closed but suddenly a woman on a shopmobility scooter appeared from nowhere. Just like the garage, she unlocked the gates, let me in and locked them again. I set up my tent and decided to pop out to buy some food. All the gates out of the campsite, including those to the beach, were locked. I was trapped. I hunted for a way out, which set two dogs barking wildly. Scooter woman turned up again. She let me out but I had to go through the same procedure to get back in. What was it with this place?

It was nearing the end of June. The weather had been getting hotter and hotter. For today the AccuWeather website had scarily replaced its sun symbol with a burning match and predicted 38°C. That wasn't good, especially as I had a 1,000 metre climb, passing near Mount Olympus. The hill went up and up, getting steeper as it reached the summit. It didn't help that I'd discovered the source of the bike's clicking sound, one of my pedals. Over these last few days it'd started getting stuck, not revolving as it should have done, throwing my foot off. This would happen several times and then, with a heavy clunk, it would right itself. I'd have to get it sorted soon.

At the top of the hill I celebrated with a herd of cows and a glorious view of the snow-capped summit surrounded by countryside of pure, lush green. The gods were sitting up there deciding which beautiful nymph to seduce next. Greek gods are much more fun than their Abrahamic brethren. I also celebrated a big milestone, my ten thousandth. The party was a twenty mile freewheel down the other side to Katerini.

The town offered some creative graffiti: "Merry Crisis and a Happy New Fear". I was having a fear on my own. I discovered I'd got a disappointingly low mark in one of this year's maths assignments. I'd been on a downward slide of late and I'd no idea why. Whenever I did the practice exercises I got nearly everything right but assignment scores were very average indeed. The problem I had was that all my tutor's comments were being sent home. I wouldn't know what I was doing wrong until I finished for the year. I'd discovered a drawback to studying on the road.

As I was nearing my exit from Greece, Sean Conway was cycling in from Turkey. We met not far from Asprovalta. Sean was one of nine cyclists who'd set off from London on 18th February that year to race 18,000 miles around the world and attempt to claim the record for the fastest time. The existing record was an amazing 106 days. Unfortunately, Sean's attempt was scuppered when a truck ploughed into the back of him at 55 miles an hour in America. He spent a couple of weeks in hospital and then, lacking enough insurance, another week being kindly looked after at the home of one of the hospital's medical staff. With such a delay the record was out of reach but he decided to finish his trip anyway.

The existing world record had been completed as a supported tour, in other words with help from a team and a car to carry the cyclist's gear and keep him refuelled. Sean's attempt was self-supported, which made it even more challenging. I couldn't believe how little he had with him. I've carried more than that on a ride to the pub. Compared to his, my bike looked like something with advanced elephantiasis. Hanging from this handlebars, his sleeping bag looked more like a tea bag.

"Smallest sleeping bag in the world!" he said. "And the smallest ground mat."

Yes, that little bag included a mat as well, although it only fitted his back and ignored his legs. He was wild-camping most nights, setting up a sheet from the top of his bike wherever he was when darkness fell and sleeping beneath it.

Although I massively admire Sean's athleticism it's not the way I'd like to see the world. Every day he cycled from before dawn till after dusk. Now the competition was over he could slow down a little but he was still pushing it. Since the accident he hadn't done a day of less than 100 miles whereas I hadn't done a day over 100. With such a punishing schedule there's little time to see the sights, to rest for a snooze on a pretty hillside or to chat to the people you cycle past. I'm sure our conversation would've been a lot shorter, or non-existent, had the record still been within reach.

Mike Hall, one of the guys who set off with him, won the race and the record, slashing the time to just 91 days, an average of nearly two hundred miles per day. Sean still hankered for a record of his own. (Coincidentally our paths will cross again in over a year's time shortly before he gains one. You might even have seen him on the telly as a result.) Sean could have achieved a record much more easily. Surely he was in with a chance of World's Most Ridiculous Beard. His enormous, ginger fuzzbox was about a foot long. It looked like it was on a piece of elastic.

I stayed the next night in Nea Kavali and popped into town to get a beer. There I saw a pitiful sight. An old man in a dusty brown jacket slowly cycled past me and down the road on a squeaking, creaking pushbike. He got slower and slower and then just keeled over in the middle of the road. It was like he'd given up and decided to die there and then. A man ran out of his shop to help him up. A woman brought a folding chair. The old fella sat there looking dazed and disorientated.

The next morning it was clear the malfunctioning left pedal was close to death. Somehow it was now twisted downwards, which meant over time my foot slowly slid off it. The decision to get the pedal sorted had been made for me. I cycled into Xanthi, got myself lost and found a bike shop. A few days earlier I'd bought a new set of pedals but didn't have the tools to attach them myself. The guy in the shop in Xanthi kindly changed them over for free. What a difference that made! It was like riding a new bike again.

It didn't last long. Five miles the other side of Xanthi my left foot went wonky and the new pedal fell off. It couldn't be reattached because its thread had worn away. I turned the bike around and headed back to town. Pedalling with one foot didn't work and so I pushed the bike while scouring the roadside for a temporary pedal, a metal rod or something, that could go through the hole, but nothing was suitable. On the edge of town, after pushing those five miles in the sun, was a handily placed bike shop. It seemed pointless to go back to the one that had fixed the pedal in the first place. For one, he'd done it as a freebie and I'd no idea where it was. A small team worked on my bike, fixing the pedals and generally giving it a makeover. Cycling away was a dream, smooth and noiseless and for the rest of the day nothing fell off. But it would soon enough.

Chapter 14: Let me polish your trainers

**Capitals visited: 23
Total distance: 10,328 miles**

I was at the Turkish border brandishing my passport for the first time this year. Entering the country was a needlessly bureaucratic procedure, taking four officials to do the work of one. First, I had to queue to buy a visa from one desk and join another queue to get it stamped. I bypassed the queue for car insurance but then stood in line for the final check to ensure I had all the things I'd previously queued for. If one of these desks is temporarily unmanned the whole system comes to a standstill.

There appears to be a lot of reasons why cycling in Turkey isn't a good idea. Stories abound of awful road surfaces, big hills, mental drivers and packs of wild animals. Within ten minutes of crossing the border I'd seen my first dog. Ten minutes later I saw another. Luckily, they were both dead at the side of the road but they looked terrifying. If you want an image of what I saw simply go and watch *American Werewolf in London*. These two had been run over. Apparently, they can only be killed by silver cars.

I'd discover whether or not the other warnings were true soon enough. There was, however, something that compensated for the potential horrors of Turkey that was immediately obvious: the Turk's legendary friendliness. Halfway up my first hill, a farmer offered to load my bike on to his tractor to save me the effort. People were forever tooting and waving and cheering. They were probably thinking: "Hooray, there goes another tourist about to be eaten by a wild dog. It'll save our kids from getting carried off."

I spent the first night in Keşan, a small, bustling town not far from the border. I wandered around its cracked pavements trying to get the measure of Turkey. This was the most exotic place I'd been so far by a considerable margin. Food seemed cheap but, to counter this, alcohol didn't. In fact, it seemed pretty scarce. Muslims aren't supposed to get trollied but Turkey claims to be secular with only a nod to Islam. That wasn't the case here if the paucity of beer was anything to go by. Maybe it'd be different elsewhere.

I found a baker's selling interesting-looking shapes and figured I'd give them a go. Deep fried dough covered in a sweetly cloying syrup sounds like Scottish health food but welcome to *tulumba*, Turkey's inch-long, crinkled tubes of heart disease. You buy them by the boxload. After five of the sticky, little buggers I already felt queasy.

Now that I was in Turkey I had a strange uneasy feeling and I wasn't sure why. Perhaps it was because I knew the further east I went, the less likely I'd find spares for my 700C wheels. Or perhaps it was meeting Sean Conway and hearing his accident story. The usually wide verges of Turkey's main highways disappeared as the route south succumbed to roadworks and a contraflow system. The traffic was fast and close and my gears were acting up, slipping as I went from one to another and sometimes changing of their own accord. The unease continued.

I was three days into Turkey, already in Asia, before I discovered some smooth tarmac. In the 23 countries I'd visited previously, a lumpy bit of road would improve in a minute or two. In Turkey, at least so far, it was all lumpy bits. So when I discovered an amazingly bikeable bit of road I slowed down to appreciate it. It carried on and on for about fifteen miles. Just at the point when I started to take it for granted, it reverted to its former lumpiness and stayed like that for the rest of the day. That'll teach me.

The winds wouldn't go away and were getting stronger. Ten miles from Bandirma I stopped at a petrol station. Hussain was the station restaurant manager during summer and an economics student for the rest of the year. He looked like a young Robert de Niro and plied me with tea after tea while we sat and chatted. Other staff arsed around, joining us for a bit and then leaving, happy to act the fool with the blessing of their boss. There was a lovely spontaneity about the Turkish people I'd met so far.

I'd read somewhere that Bandirma is the ugliest town in Turkey but whoever wrote this could only have seen the factories on its outskirts. Waiting at traffic lights, a policeman asked me where I was going. I told him I needed a hotel and he got me to follow him until we passed one in the centre of town. After checking in I wandered down to the waterfront, to the sparkling Sea of Marmara. Bandirma is a clean, relaxed, cosmopolitan sort of place, young people walking hand in hand. A few waterside bars displayed signs for local beers although no one was visibly drinking. A boy of about ten approached me, told me he was called Sulli and asked me my name. Friendliness starts young here.

The next morning I loaded up as well as I could with a Turkish breakfast. Hotel breakfasts here rarely deviate from the standard. Everywhere it's hard-boiled eggs, cucumbers, tomatoes, occasionally faux boiled ham and as much strong tea as you can manage. In a country with endless roadside fruit stalls, hotel fruit juice is the oddest component. It's an instant, powdered variety tasting of sherbet. It fizzes in your mouth like Space Dust.

On my way into Bursa, Turkey's fourth largest town with nearly two million inhabitants, I had my first taste of city roads. Just when I needed them most, the wide shoulders of the intercity routes disappeared, one lane became two then three and cycling on the pedestrian-free pavement was the only sensible option.

Bursa felt like Manchester in that there were lots of shops and not that much to look at. Fast food joints were everywhere. I had to walk through a metal detector to get into a shopping centre but my little rucksack was passed around the side. It wouldn't take a criminal mastermind to work out a way to smuggle a bomb inside.

I ate in a *lokanta*, a ready-made food, canteen-style restaurant, ideal for my non-existent Turkish. I could point at what I wanted. I went for what looked like a chicken breast covered in cheese but when I dug into it the chicken had already been pulled apart and reassembled for reasons I didn't want to contemplate.

I hadn't been looking forward to Wednesday. It was a longer ride than normal, out of Bursa, back on to the busy roads at least until I was clear of the city, with several mountains to climb and, if the last few days had been any indication, a hurricane in my face. As it turned out, with a cool-aired, half-six-in-the-morning start, nothing but a gentle breeze and an overcast sky keeping the sun off during the uphill bits, the mountains melted away.

Halfway to my destination a well-dressed man with salt and pepper hair stood at the side of the road, holding out snacks. He was Erdinç, a fellow cyclist although today he was in his car. His little, individually wrapped cakes gave me a useful boost of energy. It was like having my own support team headed by Mr Kipling.

I was an hour ahead of schedule with only five miles to reach Bozüyük, my destination. Life was perfect. But then it suddenly wasn't. First, I got a puncture. Normally that's merely a pain in the arse. I got out one of my spare inner tubes – one I'd previously fixed – and test-inflated it before realising I'd put it back in my bag with the intention of fixing it and never actually got around to it, the lazy sod. Not to worry, I had a second, brand new inner tube. I took off the tyre, inserted the new tube, inflated it and set off. But there's one thing you should always do whenever you change a tube: check whatever caused the initial puncture isn't still inside the tyre. When my second inner tube exploded I had no spare. No problem, I'd patch one up. And I would have if only I could've found my repair kit. My tube problems though were the least of my worries. I noticed a crack in my back wheel rim, the wheel that takes most of the weight. A spoke was spontaneously removing itself and destroying my wheel with it. I'd need a new 700C rim in a country that used 26 inchers instead.

I still had to get us to town. Now of course the overhead clouds had evaporated. I pushed the hobbled chopper the five miles to Bozüyük in the mid-afternoon, blazing July sunshine and I burnt my stupid face off. On the edge of town I found an old bike repairman. He couldn't do much about the cracked rim but he trued up the wheel so the knackered spoke wasn't deforming it and I repaired the puncture. At least the bike was now rideable for the final quarter of a mile to the only hotel in town.

Twenty-five miles up the road was the city of Eskeşehir. I cycled there the next day carefully avoiding any potholes that could have worsened the rim and found a bike shop, a dark hole on a back street. By amazing luck its owner had a single 700C wheel rim, a bright red, plazzy-looking thing from a manufacturer I'd never heard of. It'd have to do. While the gruff-looking Ibrahim built me a wheel I sat outside his little shack. Ümit, a slender man with a mischievous grin and a demonic pointy beard, worked in the shop next door but was having a quiet day. He came out to talk to me for the next two hours, a conversation that kicked off with an immediate misunderstanding.

"So you're from Africa?" I said.

"No, from here," he replied, looking confused.

"I thought you said you are a Berber."

"I did."

"I thought Berbers are from Africa."

"Barbers are everywhere."

"Ah, you're a barber."

Ümit ordered the teas, delivered from an unknown source by a small boy with a silver tray, and taught me a few words of Turkish. We had an instant connection when I told him I was from Blackburn. Turkish footballer Tugay had played for the Rovers a few years earlier.

A man came past handing out leaflets advertising fasting times for Ramazan, the Turkish version of Ramadan, due to start in a couple of weeks. Ümit asked if I was Christian. I'd heard from other travellers to Islamic lands that to believe in a different god was acceptable but to be atheist was incomprehensible. Not wanting any conflict before I had a fully restored back wheel I told him I was born C of E. It's true but it was a cop out.

The next morning I cycled out of Eskeşehir. My gears were still slipping. Ibrahim should have checked them too but in the panic to get a back wheel I'd forgotten to mention it. At traffic lights near the edge of town a teenage lad pulled up on his bike beside me. He introduced himself as Emre. We communicated in sign language as we cycled together for the next 25 miles. I was glad of the distraction through the flat, unremarkable scenery. Emre turned off while I continued to today's destination.

Wow, I'd found it – Emirdağ – a place for which I couldn't think of a single point on which Blackburn was worse. The place was falling apart, the pavements cracked, people glared with hostile eyes as I walked down the street, the food was tasteless and the beer expensive and hard to find. In addition, even Blackburn's weather was better. Every summer here was sweltering while the winters froze. The area was also prone to earthquakes. Bizarrely this dump had been twinned with a pretty town like Belgium's Ghent. I wonder if anyone from Ghent's council had ever been here.

I found a hotel. The squalor of the town had seeped into the owner's bones if his facial expression was any indication. His chubby, twelve-year-old son on the other hand danced around like a chimp. The lad showed me to my room. As he opened the door he kissed his fingers in the same way a French chef might to indicate the quality of his wares. I peered inside expecting something special but the room was shabby. This cocky little git was destined to be a salesman. He already seemed too big for Emirdağ.

I'd now been in Turkey long enough to discover the black bag issue. Supermarkets almost never sold alcohol and neither did most corner shops but if the bright blue logo of Turkish beer brand Efes or the easier-to-miss gold of Tuborg was shown around a shop's name it was an off licence. The sales procedure went like this:

1. I enter. The shop owner looks unhappy, unusual for a Turk.

2. I walk to the beer fridge. The shop owner has already located and opened a black carrier bag.

3. If there happens to be anyone else in the shop, especially someone under 18, he's now sniggering, as though I'm buying a stack of Gusset Munchers porn mags or something worse like Model Train Enthusiast.

4. The beer quickly goes into the black plastic bag and the financial transaction is carried out with the utmost haste.

5. I leave the shop feeling guilty for reasons I can't fathom.

I'm not sure of the purpose of the black bag. If you pop

into the same off licence and buy a can of Coke you get an innocent white carrier bag instead, unless you can tell the man in time you don't actually need a carrier bag for a single can of Coke. So the black bag doesn't hide that you've bought some naughties. It actually highlights the fact. But maybe that's the point. Maybe it's the black bag of shame, the Judas sack.

I rumbled ever southward through Ilgen, past Konya with its superior mosques and Rumi's tomb and on to Karaman. I strolled around town and was pulled into a café by its owner and his brother, a keen cyclist. They'd seen me cycle past earlier. A red-faced, sun-bleached, blonde-haired European was unusual around here. Teas followed and a small group gathered around the table. The bloke next to me was the size of a bear. Every time he cracked a joke he thumped me on the back, loosening my teeth. He told me I looked Danish. Given the recent furore in Denmark over the Muhammed cartoons this might not be the ideal look in these parts.

There was a Turkish culinary treat I was seeking and the guys told me where to find it. Down a dark alleyway was a shop that sold *kokoreç*, a sheep's intestine sandwich. I went inside and ordered one, a diversion enough to draw a few of the fellas from the street into the shop with me. The guy behind the counter finely chopped the offal, added it to a grill pan and frazzed it before tipping the lot into a pitta. The result was better than you'd probably imagine, greasy but tasty, and without the toilet odours of my last intestine experience, that French poo sausage.

Although I was now on Turkey's high central plain that kept the temperatures just about bearable I still had to get over the Taurus Mountains. I climbed for twenty miles before reaching the summit at 1650 metres. Requiring calories on the other side I saw a sign advertising *borek*, which in Turkey can be just about anything made of pastry. This roadside place was basically a tent and also the home of another Emre and three generations of women in his life, his mother, wife and two daughters. The women sat on the floor on a worn, burgundy carpet around a griddle. Grandma rolled the pastry and stuffed it with cheese, mum griddled and the girls flipped. With tasty food in my belly I rolled for 45 minutes down to 300 metres, the air heating as I descended, and completed the descent the next day, hitting the port town of Taşucu on the south coast of Turkey.

Two hours after wheeling the bike on to the catamaran I arrived in Cyprus. I decided to give myself a little holiday, my first day off the bike since Athens, nearly a month and 1,500 sweaty miles ago. While in Cyprus I intended to do very little except ride to Nicosia, my most southerly city, a place oddly proud of the fact it's the world's only divided capital. Surely it shouldn't be a source of pride to highlight your embarrassing inability to get along with your neighbours.

Back in Turkey I had to regain the height I'd lost a few days earlier, from sea level to 1,650 metres in the Venusian heat, and retrace my steps as far as Konya. Ten days earlier the city had been a different place. Since then Ramazan had started. A kebab shop operated by a German-speaking Turk I'd visited last time was just about to close for a month. He said most food outlets would shut for the fast but he knew one that was open and he took me there. I had a bowl of lentil soup while an middle-aged woman and a small child sat around my table watching me eat. They looked forlorn.

I'd heard Ramazan induces tetchiness and it's hardly surprising. It's a bloody silly idea. From first light until dusk – in July that's from half five in the morning until eight in the evening – not even the tiniest morsel of food can pass your lips. Nor can water, and it was 40°C. You're only allowed an abstention if you're travelling, if you're old or sick, or if you're menstruating, that old religious hang-up. However, if you're menstruating you'd probably be locked in the shed at the bottom of the garden and not much food would come your way in any case. You're also banned from smoking. You can imagine the effect this has on the normally gregarious Turks. God is great.

From Konya I stopped at a garage to get a drink. The cashier gave me my change, a few coins worth around two quid. I sat on the forecourt drinking fruit juice, got on my bike and left. A few minutes down the road, two men in a car were waiting for me. One of them presented me with my change again. I'd left it on the ground at the garage. That's impressive.

I continued due north towards Ankara, halfway on my capital checklist. Acts of honesty aside, Turkey had turned into a joyless place. The smiles and chats had dried up. After all, tea was the lubricant for conversation. If they couldn't drink tea themselves they didn't want to talk either. It'd been the Turkish spirit that'd made the dusty, often repetitive landscapes bearable.

On the way to Cihanbeyli I had a puncture. I put on my spare and off I went. Since the incident in Bozüyük I'd located my puncture kit but unfortunately the glue in its squeezy tube had evaporated so I couldn't repair the damaged tube. I'd taken to visiting *CrazyGuyOnABike.com*, a treasure trove of cycling blogs, and typing into its search facility the names of towns I was passing. The fewer results I received was a sign of how far off the beaten track I was. Within its 9,000 digital diaries only one blogger had visited tomorrow's destination, Kulu. That's remote. Tonight's town, Cihanbeyli, scored a few more hits but these included worrying stories about the roads being full of tyre-piercing thorns. I'd scoured the town unsuccessfully for a bike shop. If I got thorned tomorrow without glue I'd no way to make a repair. Maybe this is why only one person had made it to Kulu.

I'd heard the call to prayer in every town I'd stayed. It always surprised me how crap their public address systems usually were, crackly and distorted. The quality of the muezzin's voice was more variable. Rarely they were decent singers but more often than not it sounded like he'd got the job because he knew someone. The call in Kulu was the most painful so far. In attempting to reach the higher notes he'd either invented a new tonal system or impaled himself on a nail.

The bike's gears were still misbehaving. On the outskirts of Ankara a big climb appeared just as the lanes doubled and verge disappeared. Luckily, the city had so much traffic it could barely move. I located a repair shop and my bike disappeared into its back room. While checking it out Arkan the mechanic noticed three broken back spokes. This struck me as odd. Normally this would mean a very wobbly back wheel. I was suspicious. Arkan dicked around, repeating "Yeah, Turkish delight" at the quality of his work, but seemed a bit slapdash and received a bollocking from his boss towards the end of my visit that soured his mood. The bike was repaired but I felt like I'd paid for things I hadn't needed to. At least now I had a puncture repair kit.

I had a day off in Ankara and the highlight was the mausoleum of Atatürk, the founder of modern Turkey. Its wide open spaces removed from the traffic were an antidote to the mayhem of the city, its white columns with clean lines and its massive scale made it feel like a Parthenon imagined by communists architects.

Three days later I was back in the city of Eskeşehir. With a population of over 600,000 it was against all odds that within a few minutes of arriving someone I knew would cycle up to me. Emre, the student who I'd cycled out of town with a few weeks earlier, had me follow him for a few miles, through a great fruit and vegetable market, with tomatoes, peppers and aubergines piled high and strange mini-okras and unidentifiable veggies, to a tiny bike shop to meet his friends. Two of them were biking superstars in Turkey. Gökay was the country's mountain biking number two. Even better, his sister Eda was the female number one. (Months later I'd see a clip of them on *Turkey's Got Talent* doing bicycle tricks.) The shop had some novelty furniture made out of old bikes. One chair had hacksawed wheel rims for legs, tyres for arms and fourteen criss-crossed inner tubes as cushioning. It was as comfy as an old sofa.

I went to a lokanta around the corner and pointed out the dishes I wanted to eat, chicken as well as the mini okras I'd seen at the market. I sat down at a table. The waitress came over to check whether I'd really ordered the okra because "foreigners don't eat things like that". How little she knew.

I left the city behind and spent a couple of days cycling through steep, forested hills to İznik, the modern name for Nicaea, famous for the Nicene Creed that was dreamt up here in the year 325. The hundreds of bishops who descended upon the place also came up with a list of new church laws, the first of which was to forbid self-castration, a sensible if largely unnecessary rule. Or maybe in 325 it was necessary. Perhaps you couldn't move in Nicaea without having someone hurl their severed genitals at you.

Despite its history, İznik didn't seem as religious as the rest of Turkey. The town was located on a large, turquoise lake surrounded by rugged mountains on all sides and it was possible for me to have my first outdoor beer in a month while drinking in the scenery at a lakeside bar. Turkey was relaxing the closer to Istanbul I got.

*

In Yalova, it was morning and I was sitting at the bow of a ferry that would carry me and my bike across the Sea of Marmara to Istanbul. It was due to leave in a couple of minutes. I began to wonder if my valuables would be safe. I had my bar bag with me containing the small stuff like my passport but my laptop was in my panniers on the car deck. My passport? Oh no! I checked the bar bag. It wasn't there. I'd handed it in to reception at last night's hotel and had forgotten to reclaim it this morning. The ferry's engines started up. I could write to the hotel and get them to send it to my rented apartment in Istanbul. I was planning to stay there for a week. No, that was stupid. They might not send it, or the postal system might lose it. I needed that passport for eleven of the twelve remaining border crossings this year. My hotel was only half a kilometre away. Perhaps I could get my passport and make it back to the ferry before it left. I grabbed my bar bag, raced down to the car deck, untied the bike and, bursting past baffled-looking crew, dashed off the boat.

"I'll be two minutes," I screamed to them.

I sped out of the port, weaved through traffic and crashed through the hotel doors. The man on reception held out a hand containing my passport. I pocketed it and pedalled as fast as I could back to the port. The ferry had already gone. Had I discovered my missing passport one minute later I'd have been separated from it, which would've been much worse than having to wait for the next ferry eight hours later. It meant I'd be cutting it fine for meeting Nina. Now I'd have to kick around Yalova all day and then once in Istanbul race through unfamiliar streets and its famously horrendous traffic to get there in time.

At six in the evening the ferry docked at Istanbul's Yenikapi port. The traffic in Istanbul was worse than anywhere I'd been but meant it was practically stationary. Cars and cities don't mix. I squeezed between the vehicles and what passed for a pavement, following the signs for Taksim Square, the focal point of Istanbul's European side. The route hugged the coast, taking me beneath Topkapi Palace, home of the sultans, and across Galata Bridge with its shoulder to shoulder fishermen turned golden by the evening sun. The route from here was steep, stupidly so for a city. I powered up the hill, sweat dripping off me in the heat, determined to get to the bus stop before Nina arrived in two minutes. And then the power disappeared and my pedals spun pointlessly. I looked back at the road behind me and the new chain I'd bought in Ankara lay there like a dirty road-kill snake, the first casualty of Arkan's shoddiness. I pushed the last mile to Taksim and got to the bus stop expecting to find Nina already there. She'd been slightly delayed and arrived ten minutes later.

It's immediately clear Istanbul isn't simply a larger version of other Turkish towns. It feels very European. There are bars everywhere and people enjoying a beer in the sun. After a month in provincial Turkey this felt very alien. Istanbul is much more relaxed about alcohol although in the district of Sultanahmet there's still a rule prohibiting its sale within 100 metres of a mosque, just in case the faithful are so desperate for a drink they're prepared to walk 95 metres but not 105.

This wasn't the only difference between Istanbul and the rest of Turkey. The honesty I'd experienced elsewhere was reversed here. One day, walking across Galata Bridge behind a shoe shine man, he dropped his polishing brush. I picked it up and called after him. He turned around, thanked me and walked off. As an afterthought he turned around and asked if he could polish my shoes as a reward. I was immediately suspicious because I was wearing trainers and, in my experience, they tend not to polish up too well. I politely turned him down. The next day we saw him again. He dropped his brush in front of a couple of women ahead of us and a similar exchange occurred. They turned him down too. After all, they were wearing flip-flops. By now we were behind him and he dropped his brush again. Either he's the clumsiest man in the world or his brush dropping was a scam. Tempted to pick it up and throw it into the Bosphorus we just kept walking. He turned around sheepishly and went to retrieve it. Later, we learned the scheme involved taking his time to polish your shoes, or your flip-flops, and then pouring out a tale of a dying wife, starving children and a desperate need for cash until your conscience is defeated and he's more effectively cleaned your wallet than your footwear.

There was still generosity on offer though. Hiding from a downpour in the ADA bookshop's café we noticed the staff's funky black t-shirts emblazoned with the store's motto: Eat, Drink, Learn, Enjoy. As this could be the motto for my ride I asked if I could buy a t-shirt. Instead they gave me one for free.

The rain eased and we crossed town for the sensual assault of the Spice Market. Our noses filled with unlocatable aromas, our eyes with rainbow piles of turmeric and coriander, paprika and sumac. Then we hit the Grand Bazaar with smells of a different kind. It's less of a market and more a covered city, divided into streets, each one specialising in lamps or clocks or jewellery or anything else. Outside the clouds burst. The market started to fill with people. Those without wanted cover and those within wouldn't leave. The rain kept coming and the drains burst. A thick treacle of turds and rain water sluiced down the slight incline of the indoor roads. Skirts were raised and shoppers did a splashy, poo-dodging dance. That was fun. You don't get that at Bluewater. I wonder how often it happens here at Brownwater.

There are many reasons to visit Istanbul but one of the best is to sit at a restaurant on the underside of Galata Bridge enjoying a fish sandwich and a cold beer in the warm evening air as the sun sinks and paints the mosques pink. Vessels of all sizes, from rowing boats to liners, happily bobbed along the Bosphorus. The lines from the fisherman on the road overhead didn't obscure our view but occasionally a little fish was hoisted upwards and we knew someone had his dinner for tonight. As the sky darkened, the lights twinkled, bands of bulbs stretched from minaret to minaret to celebrate Ramazan. No city on this trip had provided so much magic.

With a repaired chain and fresh legs I once again fought Istanbul's traffic, avoiding the roads to the west that famously terrify many a cyclist. Instead I went north, almost to the coast, and then westwards. I traded my map of Istanbul for one of Bulgaria with a young American cyclist coming in the opposite direction and got chased by a pack of dogs luckily on one of the few flat stretches of road.

I'd enjoyed Turkey. Or rather I'd enjoyed Istanbul and the rest of Turkey until Ramazan raised its mood-souring head. I was glad to be escaping the often bland pastries and repetitive cuisine and was overjoyed to be next venturing into a saner society where beer isn't seen as the work of the devil. Bulgaria, I need you!

Chapter 15: The man who lived under a table

Capitals visited: 25
Total distance: 12,123 miles

I was over the Bulgarian border and the ride was flat and dull with a painful headwind. Speeding through dour-looking villages sad-faced people in tatters stared blankly at me. It was summer but the fields lay empty. I eventually reached my destination, Harmanli, a drab town filled with ugly, concrete tower blocks. So far Bulgaria wasn't looking too great.

Then the fun started. The only accommodation in town was a four-star hotel, usually well above my price range. I thought I'd better go in to ask how much it would cost. As I locked up the bike outside a woman came down the hotel's long but shabby white stone staircase. She seemed very keen to get me inside and she only wanted twelve quid for a room. I unlocked the bike and started to carry it up the stairs. She was frantic, shooing me along and grabbing the bike to get me up more quickly but, by doing so, actually hindering my progress. What was the hurry? Another woman came out of the hotel and an argument broke out. The second woman said I could have a room for eight quid. Their voices raised a tone and the first woman threw out an arm to prevent the other getting too close to me. I didn't understand why they were competing on price to get me into the same hotel.

Once inside, it was clear the hotel wasn't a single entity. Reception had three desks, each with a different hotel name. One was empty and the two brawling women went behind their respective desks still yelling insults to each other. I wonder if they greeted all visitors like this. Imagine how competitive it would've been with someone on the third desk too.

There was little to do in Harmanli. I went out for a stroll and found a café where a pint of decent lager cost 60p. As great as it must be to live in a place where beer comes so cheaply this grey town was a position or two down from Blackburn in the desirability league. I was hoping the rest of Bulgaria wouldn't be this dire.

The next morning I looked at my computer showing the current weather for Harmanli, a great, big, beaming sun. I opened the curtains to reveal a leaden sky with grey clouds scudding thickly overhead. I set off and the rain came down immediately. I took shelter in a garage. The blokes working there as well as all of their customers looked like bouncers.

I trundled towards Plovdiv, Bulgaria's second largest city. The previous day's headwind had disappeared, the road surfaces were good and the riding was fun if damp. I passed a large road sign advertising a McDonald's 93 kilometres away. Surely no one can want a shit hamburger that badly. And then there was a metallic thunk. Round two of Arkan's Revenge had been unleashed. A spoke on the back had snapped. Luckily the wheel wasn't deformed and I carried on. The sun came out and I rolled into Plovdiv, a thoroughly modern city, a vast improvement on yesterday's dump.

After finding a hotel with only one reception desk I went to explore the city centre. This was the first chance I'd had to see real Bulgarians wandering about. The women were dressed impressively sluttishly.

A busy terrace full of happy diners enticed me in and only once sat at a table did I notice the place was styled on Hooters, with the visible staff consisting entirely of young women, slim but well-endowed, in tight, white shirts and red, vinyl micro skirts. Is this sexist, I thought? Should I be encouraging this type of thing by giving it my money? This was an issue I mentally debated as I sat there until it closed five hours later.

Thinking back, maybe they weren't dressed so flimsily. Maybe I'd been starved of the sight of female flesh in Islamically buttoned-up Turkey. It was the same with the food. Looking at the restaurant's international menu I'd been amazed by the choice – salads and burgers and things made of pork – options I would've taken for granted before visiting Turkey.

After fixing the spoke, I left behind the city and cycled the back roads. People were friendly if I had a direct transaction with them but blokes in the street eyed me with uncertainty.

Today's goal was Sofia, capital number 26. Before then, in the forests south of the city, I had a hill to climb. At its summit I met a party of Belgians, an older guy with three lads in their late teens, who were spending three months walking from Vienna to Istanbul through the mountains, or on roads in countries with the possibility of land mines. That seemed wise enough. The countries with land mines still lay ahead of me this year.

Rolling down the other side of the hill Arkan's voodoo snapped a second spoke. The next village was Samokov and luckily a bike shop sat right on its main junction. The bloke working there looked typically Bulgarian with his World's Strongest Man physique but had the freakiest, high-pitched voice. It was like Giant Haystacks channelling a BeeGee. He said he didn't have the necessary tool – which might have explained his vocal range – but knew a man who did. Off I popped to what was basically a yard on an housing estate with the remains of 300 bikes and four fellas smashing them up or fastening them back together. Coco was in charge and spoke decent English. He fixed the spoke and filled my water bottles and didn't even charge me. During the repair an old woman walked through the yard with a voice deeper than Barry White's. Some sort of voice-swapping sorcery was going down in Samokov.

But things were going to get weirder. I stopped at a tiny café near a lake thirty miles from Sofia. Two blokes were sitting outside, one of whom, a bearded man of about sixty called Mario, was enjoying a beer in the sun. He turned to me and asked me if I spoke English. That was odd. That's usually my question, especially in Bulgaria. When I told him I was English it was as though I'd given him a sudden shot of amphetamine. He stood up and danced around. He loved England, he gushed. By this point, about twenty seconds into our conversation, it was already clear the beer he was slurping wasn't his first of the day. It might not even have been his eighth.

Mario was a private English teacher and wanted to practise on me. So I sat down and he bought me a coffee. I asked if I could take a photo of him and he replied that he had better things for me to snap. We went for a walk, me with camera in hand and Mario with a gaping hole in the back of his shorts enabling a clear view of his royal blue, bikini-style underpants.

First we went to the hotel and bar around the corner from the café. He showed me a painting of his he'd presented as a gift to the hotel's owner. It was a boat on a sea but the cunning part was that the sun was a mirror. He particularly liked that bit. He danced around some more. He liked dancing around. He next showed me his collection of windsurfing boards. Windsurfing was his thing and the reason why he came to this lake although he probably came for the beer as well.

During the warmer months, he told me, he lived in Sofia for three days and then cycled the thirty miles to his house by the lake for the rest of the week and it was now time for me to see his house. On the way, walking along a country road, he told me he'd like to sing for me and that he was really quite good but, if I'm being honest, he wasn't. He launched into Rod Stewart's "We Are Sailing" taking his time to murder each note individually. He could have moved to Turkey and made a fortune as a muezzin. We took a turn from the road into dense woods, then down a steep banking along a narrow path towards the lake.

"All these houses are illegal," he said.

"What houses?" I asked. I was confused.

"Do you know what my nickname is?"

"No. What is it?"

"Kunti."

"Really?"

"And here's my house!" he screamed excitedly.

Guarding the entrance – although entrance is the wrong word – was a miniature pirate flag and a small, plastic brontosaurus. OK, I thought, that's completely normal. And then we entered what I guess might be called his living room. Except that we didn't really enter anything because his house had no doors or walls or a roof or any of the things that a house usually has. What it did have was a washing line pegged with various tattered garments, a collection of tables containing the stuff a charity shop wouldn't give shelf space and a big mat, all sitting on a bit of flattened earth about ten metres up from the lake shore. The assorted junk included a plastic telephone, a pretend musket and, obviously, a full-size supermarket till.

"There's no electricity or running water here," he said, as though this was some sort of explanation.

Mario listed the highlights of his abode like an estate agent hoping for a sale. He ordered me to take a photo as each feature was unveiled. I obliged, only too happy to document these events, if only to prove to myself they were really happening. Next to the aforementioned mat on the floor was a table.

"I sleep on the mat when the weather's nice. When it's bad I sleep here." He crawled under the table exposing even more of his arse and switched on a little radio to show the entertainment system contained within.

"Lovely," I said.

"Do you know what my nickname is?"

"Kunti?"

"Yes. How did you know?"

"You told me. It's an easy one to remember."

Music was clearly important to him. He told me how, when windsurfing, he towed behind him a small inflatable containing his radio so his toons wouldn't be submerged even if he was. I could imagine him breezing along in the summer gusts engulfed by the mellifluous tones of Patsy Cline's "Crazy".

Then he showed me his 'fridge'. Remember, there was no electricity. This was under another mat, under which was a lid, under which was a polystyrene box containing bottles of water, bits of fruit and vodka. He threw me an apple. It was pretty cold. His fridge was an environmentalist's dream even if it was Aggie MacKenzie's nightmare.

Next up was a small cupboard where he kept his valuables. It contained, he said, his ID. He opened it up. It also contained a soft porn calender. I'm assuming the calendar wasn't his ID otherwise he looked pretty hot with his shirt off.

Finally, he reached into the pocket of a suit jacket – for, yes, one such jacket hung from the washing line, obviously for when he was entertaining – and removed two novelty hats. One was a pirate's and the other a small plastic crown. He modelled them both for me. As I focussed my lens on an old man with a drunkenly crooked smile and a gold, plastic crown lopsided on his head I wondered how much the drugs would cost to replicate such an afternoon.

The demonstration was complete. Although Mario came across as a bit of a nut job I had to admire a man of advancing years who cycled sixty miles each week and spent his nights under the stars, or under a table – whether the table in his 'house' or the hotel bar – just so he could pursue his passion for windsurfing. As with others I'd met on this trip he was living his dream and clearly enjoying himself. On the surface Mario might have appeared utterly, glue-sniffingly bonkers but he wasn't bonkers at all. The real madman is the miserable sod sat in his office, staring out of the window, wishing he was somewhere on a lake rather than preparing this bloody spreadsheet.

I said goodbye to Kunti and made my way to Sofia through a magnificent gorge. The route got busier and then mutated into a road too big and fast for my fragile, little wheels. I hadn't normally had a city map as I'd approached my other capitals but I'd picked up a cheap one in Plovdiv and used it to inch my way to the centre via the quieter city streets, pushing at times when the cobbles became too annoying.

I got a cheap if old-fashioned room in the city centre and hit the town, the first stop being the Pri Kmeta brewery. A tasty starter of dried horse meat – a first for me – and three different pints was later followed by sushi. The monotony of Turkish food was a distant memory.

The next day I did my favourite sort of city tour, wandering aimlessly through Sofia's streets and its parks full of Communist monuments only occasionally checking the map for any places of interest nearby. I stumbled upon the St Alexander Nevski Cathedral with its plump, Orthodox, green and gold domes. I went inside to have a look. It was full of people, mainly women, repeatedly crossing themselves vigorously. A little later, while I sat on some steps, a man with a big gun came out of the building to which they were attached and told me I couldn't sit there. Apparently it was the National Assembly.

I liked it here. It was a city in which I'd love to live for a while, to discover its hidden treasures and secret corners. But that would have to wait. I had places to go before then. For the rest of the year the capitals would come thick and fast. Over the coming month I'd average one every four days.

Tran was my last stop on my six-day tour of Bulgaria. The hotel had disguised itself by not having a sign or any outside clue as to what sort of building it was. Surely that's bad for business. Maybe this explained why it was completely empty. I paid sixteen quid for a large, modern room. On my way out the door to look for food the receptionist pounced on me to apologise. She said there'd been a mix up with the price. Here we go, I thought.

"I charged you forty lev," she said. "That was the wrong amount."

"Was it?"

"Yes, it should have been 35 lev. Here's the difference," she said, handing me back a couple of pounds.

In the hotel restaurant that evening I dined in style on chicken noodle soup and super soft lamb served with a gorgeous rice dish with liver, heart and dill, finishing with pancakes stuffed with creamy chocolate. It cost almost nothing. I love Bulgaria. If UKIP is correct, all those Bulgarians coming to Britain are going to be so disappointed.

To get to my next capital, Kosovo's Pristina, I had first to nip across Serbia. I crossed the border without hassle and had a lovely ride over a mountain, circumnavigating the large Lake Vlasina sitting at over 1,200 metres before freewheeling for forty minutes into Surdulica. Here people, including children, had been killed by NATO air strikes.

I continued to Vranje, a larger, scruffier town, and found a hotel, an old, communist monolith. The room price was the strangely exact 3,145 dinars. They hadn't let go of their old communist bureaucratic tendencies. The next morning I had to collect a breakfast voucher from reception to hand to the dining area a few metres away. I waited for my eggs while the only other guest had a liquid breakfast of coffee, water and a shot of something strongly alcoholic.

Being in Serbia reminded me of one of my first vehicles. In the early 90s a small company I worked for near Blackburn promised to get me a company car. I knew their budget wasn't going to stretch to a BMW but I hadn't realised it would barely cover the cost of a BMX. The boss took me to a knackered car emporium and told me I could spend £300 which, in today's money, is just slightly more than £300. The only thing in my price range was a ten-year-old, grey-blue Zastava Yugo, from the same Serbian company that had once manufactured machine guns only marginally more dangerous than the car itself. I amused myself for a few weeks with its Noddy-style parp-parp horn but then I must have accidentally pressed the self-destruct button because it quickly fell to bits. The same model was still everywhere in Serbia.

I was a little nervous this morning. I was going to Kosovo, a country that still carried travel warnings from the UK's Foreign and Commonwealth Office. Land mines littered the place and spontaneous bouts of violence kicked off from time to time. I approached the border with the internet unable to tell me for sure if it was open or not. I had to climb a hill to get there. As I neared the top, there was a tailback of cars, and trucks parked at the side of the road as though they'd given up any hope of getting through.

I waited behind the cars but a driver in front gestured that I should just sneak to the head of the queue and so I did. At the border itself there was chaos. Thirty people huddled around three office windows. The officials inside weren't doing anything. No one was going through. There seemed to be no system and so I thought I would invent one. With no security barrier to block my way into Kosovo I figured I'd just cycle through and see if anyone stopped me. At least I'd get someone's attention. It was a young, blonde official who flagged me down. She passed me on to her male colleague. When he saw my passport was British he simply said, "Olympiad!" – the London Olympics had recently finished – and, with a big smile, waved me through. That was it. I can't offer this as a top travel tip – in other countries I may simply have been machine-gunned – but I'd still be there now if I hadn't cheated.

I was out of Serbia but not yet in Kosovo. I rolled down the other side of the hill and approached the desk of the border control of this tiny, breakaway republic. No one was there but two officials. I was through in seconds.

It was odd being in a place with such a recent bloody history. Only ten years earlier Serbs were cleansing villages of Albanians. It's one thing to think of the horrors perpetrated by, say, the Nazis or Vlad the Impaler but there's a sense that in Europe we've all grown up and don't act like that any longer but it's not true. A little bit of hatred, especially borne out of thick-headed nationalism, goes a long way. It left hundreds of thousands of people starving at a country's borders unable to escape, with their neighbours refusing them entry as their AK47-packing enemy bore down on them from behind. Sadly, when the tables were turned and Kosovo's Muslims eventually took control, they acted with equal cruelty towards the remaining Serbs.

The first thing I saw once inside Kosovo was a one-legged man hobbling along at the side of the road. Images of land mine explosions flashed through my head but there are people with one leg in every country. Maybe he simply had diabetes.

Expecting a long wait at the border I'd originally decided to bed down in the first large town over the border, the unpronounceable Gnjilane, but it was still only lunchtime. I had time to make it all the way to Pristina. On my way out of Gnjilane I was flagged down by a man in his forties speaking in German. This was Ramo, an Albanian Kosovar, who'd worked in Austria – hence the German – but who was now struggling to find employment and living back with his mum and dad. Ramo invited me into his garden for a chat, plying me with cake, cherry cordial and an energy drink called Pit Bull before saying that he wanted to buy me lunch at the restaurant next door. I said I'd pay but this wasn't allowed because he'd invited me. I went for the cheapest option, only a couple of quid, but a huge plateful of kebabs, chips, rice and salad. We talked about Kosovo.

"It was better before the war," he said. "Now all the politicians are corrupt."

"And how do you get on with the Serbs?" I asked.

"The Serbs are fine," he replied. "The problems are caused by the politicians."

For the second poorest country in Europe, Kosovo had a lot of expensive cars. A big, sleak, black one with tinted windows – sorry, I'm rubbish with cars – pulled up outside the restaurant. The two long-legged blondes sitting at the table next to ours stood up, strode across the car park in their heels and got in the car. Wealth was very polarised here.

"I like Austria," Ramo said. "It's very clean. Not like here. People just throw their shit on the floor."

We went back to Ramo's garden. His mum came out and

he introduced me to her. She plucked an apple from a tree and gave it to me. I ate it and looked around for somewhere to put the core. She took it from me and was about to throw it over her fence when Ramo chastised her. He was going to tidy up Kosovo one apple core at a time.

I set off again. On a country lane I heard the squeal of brakes ahead. Around the corner, with the scent of burning rubber in the air, I saw another expensive car at a strange angle in the road. It was hard to see what the driver had been trying to avoid. He saw me, looked sheepish, and zoomed off.

The afternoon passed amid bucolic beauty. I'd been reading a book called *The Road To Kosovo*. The author had described Kosovo's countryside as ugly. I don't know where he'd been in this little land but it definitely wasn't here. The only indication of past tension was that most town and village signs had their names written in Albanian and Serbian and often one or the other had been spray-painted over depending upon who lived there.

I arrived in Pristina and found an over-priced hotel down a rubbish-strewn, cobbled lane. From first impressions there didn't look to be much here. It didn't feel like a capital, more like a provincial town, which is what it'd been until recently. People openly gawped at me, a condition known as the Balkan Stare. They don't get too many cycle tourists around here.

Breakfast the next morning saw me back in the land of fake pork. It was joined by a bit of cheese and a bread roll. It wouldn't have been enough to sustain a day's heavy sightseeing. Luckily, the previous night I'd prepared a shortlist of city highlights and it was a very short list indeed.

It was the end of Ramadan and everything, even the kiosks, was closed. The streets were deserted. It was like the beginning of *28 Days Later*. I went to see the iconic, and now ironic, Monument to Brotherhood and Unity. There hasn't been much of either since Tito died. I took a walk down Mother Teresa Street. She was big here, having spent her childhood in Kosovo. Later, I climbed a steep road to Martyr's Hill to see a crumbling memorial and the graves of Kosovar fighters decorated with plenty of fresh flowers. The only thing left to see was Pristina's number one tourist attraction, the National Library building. It looks like a lair built by Daleks, all domes and webbed surfaces and that was all Pristina had to offer.

Something felt wrong about the prices here. The hotel had been way too much, and despite Kosovo's GDP per capita being half of Bulgaria's, beer was four times the price. Perhaps this was the fault of the Euro, which they'd started to use here since independence. Ramo had blamed the new currency for rising prices, as had people in other countries, but prices always rise.

Kosovo's countryside and its people had been wonderful but Pristina was, if I'm being honest, a bit of a hole and so there was no reluctance to leave. Besides, later today I had another country and its capital to discover. To Macedonia!

Chapter 16: Fires, tunnels and bulls

Capitals visited: 27
Total distance: 12,621 miles

Escaping Kosovo to cross into Macedonia didn't involve the silly games Serbia had employed on the way in but maybe there were different silly games. The route to Skopje, a lightly trafficked country road, was full of No Cycling signs. With no other road or cycle path I'd no option but to carry on.

Rolling into Skopje, the city was a definite step up from Pristina. My mood was also lifted by the Macedonian flag, which has to be the happiest in Europe, with its sunburst of yellows and reds. I checked into a hotel near the old railway station whose clock had stopped at 5:17 on July 26 1963 following a massive earthquake that flattened 80% of the city, killed over 1,000 people and left 200,000 homeless. The clock survived.

Skopje was a city on the move. Wandering around Macedonia Square, the city's focal point, there were statues and fountains galore but looking at a photo of the place from only five years earlier none of them had been here. Building work was in progress, with new statues on the go, additional bridges stretching the Vardar, including what looked like a modern version of Prague's statue-lined Charles Bridge, and marble columned structures sprouting along the riverbanks. It felt how ancient Rome must have done, with additional grandeur added on a daily basis.

I was hungry and so crossed the 15th century Stone Bridge linking Macedonia Square to the Old Bazaar to hunt for food. The swift transition from the modern Western feel of the square to the Oriental mysticism of the bazaar felt like stepping out of the TARDIS. A busy place with only one empty outside table emitted a steaming cloud of kebab essence from its kitchen and drew me in. A waiter came out to take my order. I pointed to the plateful of food some local lads were eating at the next table. He returned not long afterwards with a massive pile of grilled meat fingers, a Macedonian salad – tomato and cucumber covered in grated goat's cheese – a plate of grilled peppers and onions and a hunk of bread. The whole lot cost four quid and was one the tastiest things I'd eaten on the entire ride.

Back in Macedonia Square its huge fountain had mutated. During the day it produced an impressive water show, of spurts and water clouds dancing around the classical Macedonian soldiers and lions that line its base. On top of its central plinth is a golden Alexander the Great on his horse, Bucephalus. Now that evening was here, flashing underwater lights of reds and blues and greens were added into the mix unfortunately transforming it into something you'd see at Blackpool Illuminations.

The next day, aside from a repeat visit to the grilled meat place, I visited the Museum of the Macedonian Struggle. I paid my entrance fee at the desk in a grand but empty, wood panelled hall and was told to look at the paintings until the tour began. They were waiting for other people to turn up. No one did so mine was a private tour. The guide's grasp of English was slender to say the least. As I was the only person in his group, perhaps he thought I was wasting his time and so what he lacked in vocabulary he made up for in speed, speaking at sixty words per second. What saved the day was his tendency to clip the last syllable from each sentence and, given this was a national museum, he often finished his sentences with the word 'country'. He may have been telling me that in the whole world Macedonia was the greatest country but that's not what my ears heard.

The museum was a propaganda machine, detailing the

nation's history from the 19th century to the present day. Macedonian heroes and heroines were recreated as waxworks, their life histories described in minute detail as the guide poured forth fact after fact. His ten million words could have been distilled down to "we da good guys, everyone else da bads". About halfway around we were joined by an English couple. This meant I didn't have to nod quite so often and I'd someone to smirk at whenever he finished a sentence with 'country'.

Macedonia was light on road options. Unless I wanted to make a massive detour into the mountains on a day forecast to hit 40°C I'd have to go on the motorway. Strangely, even though the road signs had banished me from the small road on the way into Skopje, I was allowed on the motorway or at least there were no signs saying I shouldn't be there. After 25 fast miles on a wide hard shoulder the first test of my ride's legality came at a toll booth. The man inside first looked at me like I was from outer space and then waved me through without taking any money. Result!

I left the motorway and the hills started. Sweat poured as I climbed 700 metres in the sticky afternoon heat. Freewheeling down the other side I pulled into a garage to ask how far it was to Kičevo, the day's destination. The two lads working there thought I looked tired and asked me to sit down, giving me a big bottle of cold water. I wondered if I'd ever find a country where people were mean. One of the lads, Vuki, spoke very good English. Like a lot of people I'd spoken to around here, his opinion of his neighbours was very black and white. The people in Kičevo were good apparently, whereas the people in Tetova, a town I'd just passed, were bad. That seemed hard to believe. Work was hard to find, especially in rural Macedonia. Vuki had a law degree and a master's and yet the only job he could get around here was dealing out petrol. He didn't want to move away. It didn't sound like he was giving himself too many options.

After a wonderful night by the placid Lake Ohrid, one of Europe's deepest, on the first campsite I'd seen for two months, I woke up to a rose-coloured dawn. Even standing there and seeing the scene with my own eyes it looked Photoshopped.

Today I had a long ride into Albania and to its capital, Tirana. I cycled up the steepening hill that climbed high above the lake and was surrounded by clear, mountain air and dense, lush forest. Eventually, after a few swear words and a lot of sweat, I reached 1,000 metres above sea level and the border with Albania. No one else was about and I got through the officialdom in minutes. I was finally in Albania. Of all the countries on this trip Albania was possibly the one I most wanted to see because you never hear anything about it.

How many facts can you tell me about Albania? I bet it's not many. Before I started to research this trip all I could've told you is the capital is Tirana, Norman Wisdom was popular here and they once came last in the Eurovision Song Contest with a ditty called "Goats Aren't Just For Kissing", although I'm pretty certain I've made up at least one of those.

It's a mystery is Albania. The reason for this is that it was closed to the outside world from 1944 until 1991. During this time religious organisations were banned as was the private ownership of cars. Most homes didn't own a TV and those that did had the choice of a single, black and white channel. To make matters worse, their one TV channel seems to have featured endless reruns of Norman Wisdom movies. With the Communists in charge, Albania certainly put the 'grim' in Mr. Grimsdale.

Not long before the Communists, Albania had a beautifully alien-sounding monarch called King Zog. The Zogster was famed for smoking 150 cigarettes a day, which seems a tad excessive until you learn that he survived over 55 assassination attempts. It's not easy to take seriously your doctor's health advice about cutting down when someone's permanently trying to gun you down. In one famous attempt on his life he survived by shooting back at the wannabe assassins, the first modern Head of State to do so. I can't imagine the Queen whipping out an Uzi and letting rip. Prince Philip could probably manage it if the assailant was from an ethnic minority.

Albania has interesting geography too. Although not on my route, Albania is home to the Cursed Mountains. As tourist marketing disasters go, the name of these hills is up there with Galicia's unwelcoming Coast of Death. Right now though, I was in some other mountains. Normally when you cross a border you don't notice much of a change in your surroundings. Perhaps the houses become a little shabbier or grander, the people a little better or worse dressed, the prostitutes fitter or fatter. But crossing into Albania, suddenly the thick forest was replaced with parched, yellowing fields as though I'd jumped 1,000 metres higher and was now above the tree line. The air was bluer too, and not in a good way. It couldn't be the heat haze as it was still only eight in the morning. All the photos I took looked like an abandoned travel agent's window display.

Coming down the hill from the border I noticed a large dog in the road. Then I turned to my right and saw a pack of fifteen of them. Luckily they were distracted by something in the opposite direction, maybe the partially eaten remains of the last cyclist who'd come this way. I pedalled on and whizzed past before they noticed me.

Down and down I went. Eventually I came to people. The first person I passed was a twelve-year-old boy. At the top of his voice he sang out to me in English: "I love you sooooooo much!" He even did X-Factor wannabe arm gestures. I laughed. He laughed. But I kept cycling. Freak.

And then there were the hoses. If you know an Albanian and you're wondering what to get him or her for Christmas my advice would be to buy a hose. They bloody love them. In the first two minutes of encountering civilisation I counted twenty or thirty, erected nozzle up, pointlessly spraying water. They were never in fields, mind. No, they were just squirting on to a bit of tarmac, making a big, unnecessary puddle. Sometimes they even held the hoses and sprayed them randomly at things that didn't need water – like a kerb or something – just for the hell of it. Maybe there was nothing on telly today, or maybe it was another sodding Norman Wisdom film.

I'd heard Albanian road surfaces were awful but today they were at least as good as Greece or Bulgaria's. The problem was the roads weren't wide enough for the amount of traffic. The route from the city of Elbasan to Tirana – basically Albania's M1 – was no wider than a British country lane.

After descending back to nearly sea level it rose up again to nearly 1,000 metres. Getting around Albania was slow going. Well, it was for me although not for the drivers. They just gunned it, the mad bastards.

Once at the top of the hill I noticed a burning smell and then saw smoke and bits of ash in the air and little forest fires just metres from the side of the road. There were dozens of them but no one seemed to be doing anything about them. If only there'd been loads of people with hoses.

I descended into Tirana, passing a herd of freegan goats raiding some bins, and found a cheap hotel. All negotiations were carried out in the few words of Italian I'd learned – Mussolini invaded the place in 1939, which makes the language of Italy the most useful foreign language for travellers – during which I think I insisted that rather than take my bike to my room I wanted to take it to bed.

There's nothing much I can say about Tirana that might make you want to go there. I mean, it wasn't awful. Not really. Its river was only three metres wide and, from its colour and odour, was of a similar composition to the liquid that escaped from those drains in Istanbul's Grand Bazaar. I had the next day off to explore the city but that didn't take long. The old Enver Hoxha museum, like an alien spaceship, sat crumbling and graffitied but was worth a look. Hoxha was Albania's communist leader and the museum, designed by his daughter, was supposed to be a monument to his good work. But after his death and the collapse of his propaganda machine people learned how life in Albania wasn't comparing too well to its neighbours – except for Hoxha who'd lived like a royal – and enthusiasm for the building waned somewhat.

I popped into the city's art gallery. A lot of space was given over to the socialist realist movement, the communist guff that raised the worker to the status of superhero in order to make its viewers think there was something noble about hard work. It was interesting for a while but the manipulativeness of it all started to make me feel queasy so I visited the modern art room upstairs for a bit of light relief. It's usually good for a laugh. Two pieces of two-by-four lay on a block. The artist really hadn't made any effort, not even in its naming, calling it simply 'Composition'. That must have taken him ages.

The ride out of Tirana was interesting. The road had the width, speed and traffic of a motorway but without a central reservation or any actual road markings. It was a gloriously Albanian free-for-all. To add to the excitement someone had nicked all the manhole covers. One of these holes was so large and deep you could easily have lost a Mini inside it. And there were no warning signs. Unlike the UK, Albania wasn't a nanny state. If anything it was a dangerously-unstable-uncle-with-a-gun state.

Although I was searching for a particular campsite I must have zipped right past it because I ended up in the city of Shkodër, a large, flat place with a grid of roads that was designed specifically to get me lost. A man gave me directions to a hotel.

"It's the big, communist one," he said. They were always the most fun. Inside them nothing ever works but the communal areas have a great sense of space. The bedrooms are usually poky, little holes with bizarre wallpaper and broken furniture but they're cheap, and cheap is good. The Rozafa didn't let me down. It was one ugly mutha.

I didn't like the idea that my bike would have to live outside but the receptionist promised me they had 24 hour security. My back tyre was very worn and so, just outside the entrance, I swapped the front tyre for the back. The security man came out to watch half-heartedly for five minutes and then got bored and trudged back to where he'd come from. I didn't want him burning himself out with the excitement of witnessing my tyre swap. I needed him alert for later so my bike wouldn't get lifted by the local Mafia.

I wandered back into town, hungry from the day's exertion. I found a bar with tables and chairs outside. I plonked myself down.

"Can I have a large beer?" I asked the young lad who'd come out to take my order.

"No."

Fair enough. I didn't think any explanation was necessary. Then he wordlessly pointed across the road to a café and so I got up and went there instead. I'd spied a roast chicken shop and if the café had no food of its own I was going to ask if it would be alright for me to eat some of their chicken here. The waiter came out.

"Do you want some chicken?" he asked. Yes, I do, you psychic charmer. Five minutes later it was on my table, a whole chicken and a giant tray of baked spuds for a couple of quid. Add in decent beer for a pound a pint and that alone would be reason enough to visit Albania.

That night the moonlit mosque outside my hotel window provided the most beautiful call to prayer I'd ever heard. The muezzin's gentle, haunting voice caressed each note. He soared and swooped and ascended once again in an incantation that had me transfixed. Didn't he know he was doing it all wrong, the idiot?

The next day was New Country day. They were always exciting even if their frequency had increased recently. But maybe not today. I mean, Albania had promised weird shit and had delivered, especially with its roads. But what was Montenegro? It promised nothing. If I was light on facts about Albania before this trip I couldn't tell you anything at all about Montenegro. I didn't even know how you pronounced its capital, Podgorica. I'd assumed it was Pod-*gor*-ika. It wasn't until months later, watching England play Montenegro here on telly, that I learned it should be pronounced Podgor-*its*-a. So I actually knew less than nothing.

I came down for breakfast in the Rozafa, down its oddly dimensioned, concrete staircase with pink walls and a mustard, speckly floor, all crumbling or crumbled. How could you not love a place like this? Breakfast arrived, a basket of bread and a plate containing two fried eggs, a block of feta-like cheese, a dish of pickle and a large ice cream scoop of something disturbingly yellow. I tasted the blob suspiciously. It was butter. There was enough for a couple of loaves.

Today the roads were far from typically Albanian, quiet, wide and painted with lines and stuff. It couldn't last though. Five miles before the border there was a big pile of bricks blocking the road. I think that would've come as quite a surprise if you'd been bombing along at sixty miles an hour. To avoid this I took a diversion through some dour little towns, the roads dirt and gravel and potholes all the way to the border.

An ugly lump of a guard started to prod my panniers like he wanted to look inside. Ah, c'mon, I'd nothing to hide – although the pills might take some explaining – but a search would be a pain in the arse. Luckily, at that precise moment, two young lads on foot decided to cross the border without bothering to show their papers. The guards, including Mr Ugly, went ballistic, shouting and screaming and pointing guns. The kids were sent back into Albania. The prodder didn't come back and therefore never found the kilo of heroin and the dirty bomb I've been lugging around Europe all this time. I showed my passport and cycled into Montenegro. First impressions count. Just inside my new country a pretty, young girl in a tight, fluorescent pink dress was climbing out of a bush with a fat bloke.

The road was very quiet. With such beautifully smooth tarmac and so many unnecessary road signs the Montenegrins seemed to be deliberately taking the piss out of Albania. I cycled by a lake that turned into swamp and then the wind went bonkers, gusting nearly fifty miles an hour in my face. It was tough going. Thank God I'd eaten all that butter for breakfast. I fought my way into Podgorica, a small, easily forgettable sort of place.

Desperate for something interesting to look at I visited the symbol of the city, its clock tower, but, well, it was just a clock tower. Then I saw the white pipes of the Millennium Bridge, which, like London's, didn't open until well inside the new century. Finally I visited a little art gallery and I asked the dusty, old fella in charge if I was allowed to take photos.

"I know that some countries let you take photographs in galleries and others do not. I have worked here for many years and I say you *can* take photos," he replied, obviously foreseeing his role in this book and milking his part when the script simply called for a "Yes, mate."

Out the other side of the city the fires were getting worse. The tiny blazes I'd seen in Albania were nothing compared to those in the forests in Montenegro. A great wall of flame ate its way across the landscape, filling the air with choking smoke.

Fires weren't my only problem. Like most cyclists I'm not a big fan of tunnels. Even when well lit they still concentrate the noise of whatever is in there with you until it sounds like it's about to gobble you up. And there's nowhere to escape if something really is coming at you. That painful experience is multiplied a thousandfold if a tunnel has got no bloody lights.

Bicycle headlamps are primarily designed to let other road users know you exist. They don't normally have the power to do much illuminating. Generally at night, with street lamps and even the moon, you aren't going fast enough to need additional lighting. However, when you're inside a dark tunnel you definitely do need proper headlights and yet a dark tunnel is the last place you'll find a shop selling them. I didn't have proper headlights.

I arrived in Nikšić and headed to its communist monstrosity of a hotel, a huge concrete cube balanced on an infeasibly small base. I was glad the winds had died down. I walked into its foyer and had the sort of conversation with the receptionist that'd become standard in hotels throughout the former Eastern Bloc. They simply didn't care, a hangover from their redder days.

"Do you have a single room?" I asked.
"Yes. We have one for 20 euros and one for 36 euros."
"What's the difference?"
"Not much really." Go on, love, sell it.

Yesterday's forest fires and today's windless air meant blue smoke hung around the treeless plain at the side of the road. But then came the hills. I climbed and climbed and left the fug behind. And then I saw a bull on the road. I stopped and so did he. He looked me over. This wasn't good. I noticed the rocky roadsides had been covered in an industrial chicken wire to prevent stones falling on to the traffic below. With enough motivation – such as that generated by a charging bull – I could drop the bike and scramble up the wire. But that was Plan B. For now, Plan A was not to make eye contact, sing a happy song and hope he didn't gore me as I kept cycling. I pootled on past to safety. But then I remembered something. Just because a bovine has horns doesn't make it a bull. It might have been a cow. Perhaps I'd been scaring myself unnecessarily. Look for the udders or lack of them. Ten minutes later I saw another bull. This time I did the udder check. Ah, soft bloke. She was a cow, a big, fluffy, non-dangerous she-cow. The other one I passed must have been a cow too, you idiot. I mean, no one lets killer bulls just wander about the place, do they? Calm down.

Half an hour later I saw another cow. This one was darker and angrier. It snorted a couple of times. I did the check. Gulp! It was udderless. The bull stopped, stood solid and looked at me from across the road. There was no emergency chicken wire here for me to scramble up. He lowered his head, pointing his horns towards me. I took this to be a bad sign. I looked away, avoiding eye contact, not knowing whether this was wise or the most stupid possible thing to do now I couldn't see him properly. He started walking towards me. He kept snorting and he kept walking but most importantly he kept walking. Right past me. He lumbered drunkenly into a field to mess with the udder ones. Phew!

Eventually the twisting, ever climbing road emerged into

the Piva Gorge, the longest canyon in Europe, with sheer, white limestone cliffs and a deep, sulphate lake above its dam. The road had little traffic but before I could make it to the Bosnian border I had another challenge.

Unknown to me this route contains thirty or forty tunnels, some only fifty metres long but a handful close to half a mile. And every one of these tunnels was unlit. Sometimes I couldn't see the exit as I went in. In the bright sunshine each tunnel's mouth looked like a pit of despair, an inky soup for me to drown in. Once inside I couldn't see anything, especially the potholes, and so I had to push. I put on my head torch. This was normally only used for bedtime reading. It chose this moment of all moments to retire its batteries. I could see my hand in front of my face but only as a silhouette via the tunnel's distant exit, if I could see an exit at all. But I couldn't see the road or the tunnel walls or even my bike. I walked and pushed, hoping my rear light would show the occasional passing car I was in there with them. The tunnel builders had added a lovely additional feature, a ditch at the side of the road that I'd stumble into whenever I misjudged how far I was from the edge. This wasn't any fun at all. Each time I emerged I was back from the cold, dank blackness into blinding 30°C sunshine and the most beautiful surroundings of the trip so far. And that was quite a long way by now.

But today, the gorge's beauty was fragile. Smoke would occasionally wisp up from the trees on the other side of canyon. The forest was slowly smouldering giving the place an eerie feel.

Although the narrow road through the gorge was all descent, it was a day of ups and downs, the glorious scenery providing the highlights but then turning the next corner and seeing a string of tunnels clinging to the rocks ahead would make my heart sink. And then it was over and I came to the end of the gorge. Another country was done and I entered a land with the saddest recent history in Europe and it made me think that, for whinging about those tunnels, I probably deserved a slap. If those tunnels were black, Bosnia and Herzegovina had tales much darker.

Chapter 17: Tobogganing in war zones

Capitals visited: 30
Total distance: 13,064 miles

I was sitting in a town nestled in a tree-stuffed valley, the evergreens as verdant as they're supposed to be, the deciduous just on the turn to amber. Three weeks from now this forest would be a fire of yellows, oranges and reds but hopefully not an actual fire like in Montenegro.

Here in town, looking at these terracotta-roofed houses from a distance, I could've been in Austria, with the laid-back tinkle of a river merging with the laughter of the other folk on the terrace sipping their wine. But this definitely wasn't a bumbling Austrian village. I was in a place where evil happened and very recently. I'd survived the bull and the tunnels and the fires but then I'd reached Bosnia's Foča and a lot of people here hadn't survived. Despite its tranquil setting on the river Drina, thousands of local Muslims were butchered here by the Serbs in the early nineties. To add to the horror, Foča was famous for its rape camps, imprisoned women, some as young as fourteen, who were selected at whim and gang-raped and sometimes later sold on as sex slaves with the full knowledge and participation of the local authorities. The head of police, Dragan Gagović, was a frequent 'customer'. He was gunned down before he could be arrested for war crimes.

It was odd sitting here, amidst the peace and beauty, to believe this place could have been at the centre of such genocide and torture. With a short wander around town though you could see pockmarked houses and anti-Kosovar graffiti. Not everything had been glossed over.

The future still wasn't secure. Bosnia and Herzegovina was split into two autonomous regions, *The Federation of Bosnia and Herzegovina* and the Serbian *Republika Srpska*, with the latter insinuating they wanted out. It could all kick off again. This place was as much a tinderbox as the surrounding forest. With a slight shudder I left Foča behind and headed towards a city that had suffered more than anywhere else in this country.

I slipped into Sarajevo on the road known during its famous siege as Sniper Alley. It was the route from the airport to the centre of town, a nightmare of a ride that would've seen your vehicle peppered with bullets from gunmen hidden in the tall buildings on either side of the road. And me without a cycling helmet.

After fixing a cheap room in a crumbling banana yellow and lime green concrete precinct near the centre of the old town I went out to meet Julian, a British OU student, and Fedya, his Bosnian colleague. Julian had been a UN peacekeeper here during the siege and was now back to help train army officers in peace management, using lessons learned from the Bosnian conflict when things hadn't gone as well as they might have done. He admitted a lot of mistakes had been made. Fedya was a local who now worked with Julian and had lived through the siege from age twelve to fifteen. Your teens are difficult enough without the constant threat of death.

We met in Baščaršija Square, known to visitors as Pigeon Square because of the difficulties in pronouncing its real name. Together we walked to Sarajevo's brewery. It had been an important lifeline during the siege, with its own spring and therefore one of the few sources of safe water in town. The locals would queue to get their share in a city starved of all basic utilities. Julian told me, as the thirsty hauled away their plastic tubs of water, cocky snipers on the nearby hills would sometimes aim to pierce their containers.

On the way to the brewery Fedya pointed out local attractions. First we passed the corner where in 1914 Gavrilo Princip blew away Archduke Franz Ferdinand thereby launching World War I and, 90 years later, a successful UK guitar band. Then we saw the Turbeh, the tomb of seven wrongly convicted and beheaded brothers. It is said that if you visit the site and talk to the lads in the right order, the question to which you desperately seek an answer will be relayed by the mutterings of the first person you hear upon leaving. I thought it might be fun to hang around outside and shout out cryptic answers but these people have had enough trouble.

Once inside the brewery's moodily lit bar, Fedya gave me a month's course of Balkan history in about half an hour. There was a lot to take in. Even Julian who was knee deep in this topic said he'd learned something new. But this was just one man's opinion. Everyone in former Yugoslavia has a version and someone else to blame. But maybe Fedya's position was more impartial than most. After all, he had a Bosnian Muslim father, a Serbian mother and a Croat uncle.

Fedya had to leave and so Julian and I went for something to eat.

"You fancy pie?" he asked.

I'm from Blackburn – of course I fancy pie – but he was talking about *burek*, a stuffed flaky pastry I'd had in various forms since Greece. They'd been uniformly bland in Turkey but as I'd headed farther north into the Balkans they'd improved massively. Here in Sarajevo they reached their zenith with the best meat burek I'd ever tasted, a circular dish filled with a spiral of filo pastry, crunchy on the outside, soft and buttery further in, with a thick sausage of tasty meat throughout the centre.

The next morning I explored the city on my own fuelled by a breakfast of *krumpiraca* – a wonderfully fluffy potato burek – and Bosnian coffee. My tour included the yellow and brown Holiday Inn from which teams of journalists had monitored the war, dozens of graveyards that climbed high on the hills around the town, a mosque with a sign that prohibited entering with an AK-47 – the spoilsports! – the small, open air market that'd been shelled during the siege and, finally, a woman with shaved eyebrows and new ones drawn on to portray the facial expression 'aggressively inquisitive'.

Late afternoon, the second part of Julian's tour required his car. Up into the steep hills we went, where the Bosnian Serbs had been positioned, shelling and sniping at the poor sods in the town down below. This hill is also the site of the old 1984 Winter Olympics toboggan run, now derelict, graffitied and with the occasional hole blasted through to make it the ideal defensive cover.

Julian told me it was perfectly safe to walk down inside the remaining half mile or so of track while he drove the car to the bottom. It was eerie being alone inside the concrete tunnel amongst the darkening woods on this perfectly still evening, knowing a few years before these trees would have been crawling with hundreds of paramilitary and their mortars. I reached the bottom of the track and needed to jump from the top of a small wall. At its base was a patch of grass and a patch of concrete.

"Er, best to aim for the concrete," Julian said. I looked at him uneasily. "You can't be too safe."

Bosnia, especially these hills, is littered with mines and many of the ruined buildings are still booby trapped. Finishing the rest of this ride with a leg missing would have been difficult.

Sarajevo is a wonderfully atmospheric little city – one of

the ride's surprise highlights – but it must have been hell during the siege. There are few places in town not visible to the hills above it. Even a walk to your local shop – if it had anything to sell – could have ended with a sniper's bullet.

Julian himself seemed like a gentle, nature-loving man. It was hard to imagine him as a soldier.

"When I'm back home, I like to run barefoot on Dartmoor early in the mornings," he said.

"That sounds great."

"Yes, at that time of day you see unusual things. I once saw a sheep following a fox. Another time I saw a deer returning home as if after a party."

"Was it a stag party?" I offered. He was clearly unimpressed by that. It was time to leave.

Two days later, back in Serbia, I approached Belgrade. With no other option I cycled in on a busy road. As I got closer to town the traffic got more mental. A guy on a motorbike pulled up beside me.

"This bit is dangerous!" he shouted.

Ahead was an underpass. He slowed down and hung about behind me, preventing cars from squishing me. Once through he tooted and sped off. The road got even busier and so I turned into a side street and got thoroughly lost.

Belgrade isn't a great place to cycle. Unlike most cities with too much traffic, here it's also fast moving. It all got too hairy. I got off and pushed the bike along the broken footpath.

I holed up at the Hotel Royal, which sounds expensive but isn't. I handed over my bike, which they put in a staff room. After an evening's exploration of Kalemegdon, Belgrade's fortress that weirdly has tennis and basketball courts built within its old walls, I noticed a nearby restaurant with plenty of offal options. One of these – joy of joys! – was veal testicles. I couldn't pass over my first ever bowl of bollocks, especially after failing to find them in Spain. I had them with a Serbian salad, which is exactly the same as a Macedonian salad, which is itself nearly a Greek salad. The testicles were delicious, savoury and pleasantly greasy.

The next day, after a visit to the massive St Sava's Cathedral, the largest Orthodox church in the world, I went to see Tito's mausoleum. As well as his tomb it included the many gifts he'd received from foreign officials and the dozens of batons relayed across Yugoslavia each year to be handed to him as a birthday surprise despite having organised the whole thing himself. On the wall was a relief map of former Yugoslavia. Someone had scratched out Sarajevo, the symbolism of which, having just been there, felt a bit creepy.

Tito, dictator though he was, is considered the most benign of the Eastern Bloc's communist leaders. Using his mantra of Brotherhood and Unity he kept this fragile country at peace. It wasn't democracy but thousands weren't being butchered by their own neighbours. The philosopher Rousseau said, "Were there a people of gods, their government would be democratic. So perfect a government is not for men." Britain has a system that looks a bit like democracy but it isn't really. Maybe some countries need even less of it.

I cycled a few miles out of Belgrade but something felt wrong. Then I noticed it. My bike computer had disappeared. Maybe it'd fallen off but this seemed unlikely as one of my two front lights had vanished too. The remaining one was a bit flaky and sometimes gave the impression of not working, which is probably what had saved it. The cycle computer didn't matter much. Its ability to calculate how far I was travelling had ended the day before I'd set off eighteen months earlier. Since then it'd simply been my clock. But, that said, a big thumbs down to someone on the staff of Belgrade's Hotel Royal for being my first encounter with crime, albeit very petty, in 13,000 miles. It wasn't worth cycling back to confront anyone. The light had only cost a few quid and they'd have denied it anyway.

It felt like every time I googled a place name I intended to visit around here there was some hideous story attached. I rode into the grim town of Sremska Mitrovica, made all the more unpleasant by knowing it'd housed a prison in which Croatian inmates were tortured to death. Blackburn was beginning to feel like Disneyland after this place. This continued the next day too. After a tedious, flat crawl I crossed the border into Croatia and hit the town of Vukovar, a name more famously used in the phrases 'The Battle of Vukovar' and 'The Vukovar Hospital Massacre'. The sky was grey and the mood sombre. I was ready to finish the ride for this year. Former Yugoslavia's history was getting me down.

The road from Vukovar to Osijek was flat, straight and fairly narrow. My presence here didn't matter. If an oncoming car wanted to overtake it was irrelevant if I was in the way or not. They gunned it and I had to move, sometimes off the road entirely. I always had plenty of notice but they could have waited, the impatient sods. One was a little close for comfort. I was looking down at my chain to find the source of a new squeak. When I raised my head a car was heading straight for me. There was no way he could've stopped in time. I wonder if he would've even bothered to brake.

The repeated sound of shooting came from the woods beside the road and a man was out cold in a parked car miles from anywhere. Was he asleep or dead? These countries' recent history takes your imagination into darker places.

I eventually arrived in Osijek and immediately cheered up. The town reminded me of Graz, with its architecture and its fondness for bicycles. I went to a hotel in the main square. Compared to what I'd been paying recently it seemed a bit pricey.

"Can you make it any cheaper?" I asked.

"No, sorry, that's impossible," she replied.

"Alright then. Do you have anywhere safe for a bicycle?"

"You have a bicycle?"

"Yes."

"Ah, it's 15% discount with a bike."

This seemed odd until I learned Osijek was on the EuroVelo 6, the cycling route that had so bored me between Bratislava and Vienna. The hoteliers around here are keen to cater for the cycling community, by first inflating their prices and then giving you a small discount if you're on a bike.

Two days later I was on the road to Zagreb, the scenery very Norfolk, all flat and arable. I stopped for a slice of pizza. As I was eating, two gaudily dressed American cyclists rode past. I said hello. The man nodded but they didn't stop.

"You see all kinds of people here, don't you?" the woman said to her partner. I wasn't sure what that meant.

I continued into Zagreb and found a hotel. Capitals were beginning to lose their appeal. They were coming so thick and fast there was no time to process what I'd seen. I had Capital Fatigue. To make it worse I hadn't been particularly looking forward to Zagreb. About fifteen years earlier I'd been here for an afternoon and it'd left almost zero impression upon me. All I could remember was a dingy underground shopping centre. The plan was to stay the night and carry on in the morning. By early evening I was questioning whether I'd ever been here before. This place was lovely. I'd only had a quick stroll through its streets but either it'd done some serious remodelling or else I'd visited somewhere else.

A little later I was waiting for a clown in a popular street café called Bulldog. A fat, hard-looking, middle aged bloke walked past wearing a t-shirt that said, "Remember my name.

You'll be screaming it later". That sounded a little bit Fred West to me.

I'd never met a clown before. To be honest, I hate clowns but Fleur wasn't that kind of clown.

"I used to paint my entire face but it scared some of the children. Now I just put a red dot on the end of my nose," she said. It was hard to imagine this beaming, pretty French-Danish OU student scaring anyone, even if she'd been made up like Papa Lazarou. Fleur worked for a charity brightening up the lives of children and the elderly and frequently moved between Zagreb, France, Germany, London and two million other places with the languages to match. She was an international clown of mystery, probably driving a multi-coloured Aston Martin with a novelty hooter and doors that fell off.

She was sitting with Nadav, a man whose entire face was made of a smile, an Israeli clown-in-training who'd lived in Zagreb for three years. I'd decided to stay an extra day and so I asked Fleur and Nadav if Zagreb had anything strange for me to see and, without even thinking about it, Nadav confirmed that it did. There was The Museum of Broken Relationships, which sounded perfect.

As you'd hope with a pair of clowns we had a laugh.

"Do you think that Krusty is a bad role model for your community?" I asked Fleur.

"I don't really watch The Simpsons," she said with a smile, "but I don't really identify with him."

"Did you know that Krusty is Jewish?" asked Nadav. Maybe he'd found his inspiration. Watch out kids!

Fleur invited me to a party but the last few days in the saddle had been long ones and I'd accumulated a bodyful of knackeredness. Thinking about it, I hadn't had a proper rest day since Istanbul, over 2,000 miles ago. Sure, I'd had a day off the bike in most of the capitals but that always involved schlepping around on foot for miles and miles. I just wanted to sleep.

"S'OK," she said. "There might not be anybody there."

"Why's that?"

"Croatians always say they'll go to a party and then cancel at the last minute. A friend of mine once invited twelve Croatians and a Frenchman to her party. They all said they were going. Only the French guy turned up."

In reception the next morning I asked where I could buy a tram ticket.

"There's a place around the corner. But you might not need a ticket," said the receptionist.

"What do you mean?" I asked.

"I never buy a ticket," she replied.

A little later I found myself outside a building with a broken heart drawn in chalk on the pavement. The best museums send you away with a feeling, something to think about or an inspiration to read up on its subject. The Jewish Museum in Berlin did that well but it was dealing with the genocide of an entire people. It didn't have to work very hard to create an emotional response. The Museum of Broken Relationships was at the opposite end of the spectrum, offering stories in many cases so mundane they could've happened to any of us. But that was its magic. It dealt with something universal: love and loss.

In most museums you marvel at the exhibits and only read a caption if you're compelled to know more about something. In this place the exhibits are almost superfluous – a pair of boots or handcuffs, a bicycle, a dildo – but it's the attached story that matters. These tales came from everywhere in former Yugoslavia but also Germany, Turkey, the USA and Ireland. Some were funny, some tragic and some as bitter as Heather Mills steeped in denatonium benzoate.

One exhibit was an axe. A woman had finally made the

decision to let a girlfriend move in with her. Things had gone badly wrong and, painfully, her partner left. The woman used the axe to chop her ex-lover's furniture into matchwood. With each chair and table reduced to splinters she felt better. Much better. The axe was her therapy. When her ex came around to collect her belongings, the woman presented her with a neat bundle of sticks. It wasn't big and it wasn't clever but it was cheaper than a shrink.

Another exhibit was a white suspender belt. The accompanying label said, "I never wore it. Maybe we would have lasted longer if I had."

Other tales weren't so lightly treated. One woman complained that her man had said he loved her and yet she couldn't understand why he wouldn't sleep with her, wouldn't give her the intimacy she craved. She finally discovered why when he died of AIDS and she realised how much he really had loved her.

A tiny dog collar light had a painful story attached. A couple had been married for thirteen years. They were still good friends but the romance had gone. The bloke made the difficult decision to leave and they both went back to their home countries. He let her keep their little dog because he thought she'd need it more than him. Shortly afterwards he realised he'd been suffering from depression. His wife couldn't come to terms with the separation. She kept sending him gifts, symbols of her love for him, to cheer him up even though she was the one hurting the most. One gift was the little collar light. She'd bought it because their little dog kept wandering off in the dark and getting lost. One year after they parted, she committed suicide, alone in a hotel room far from home. He'd carried around the little light ever since, its red, flashing light reminding him of her heart beat. Too sad.

Reading some of the stories you could feel the longing, that gut-tearing ache for a special person who enters your life, hangs around for a while, and then disappears, leaving behind a hole that wasn't there before he or she showed up, a person capable of amputating a part of you forever. That's something anyone who ever loved and lost can identify with and that's why this was such a uniquely bittersweet place.

After a tram ride to the beautiful, tranquil Mirogoj cemetery, a bowl of goulash and a pint or two (OK then, three) at one of Medvedgrad's small chain of beer halls I went to The Museum of Contemporary Art. Like a lot of modern galleries it has its fair share of pretentious arsework but more than enough thought-provoking material to keep me occupied for a couple of hours. The most memorable, and sickening, exhibit was a dual video. One screen showed the events at Gay Pride marches in Zagreb and Belgrade in 2000 and 2001. The other showed a dance re-enactment of the violence they sparked. I couldn't pay much attention to the dancing. Real life was too powerful. A bunch of people whose only difference was that they were attracted to members of the same sex were first jeered and then attacked by crowds of onlookers in the same streets I'd been walking earlier that day. One young bloke was knocked to the ground and ten or so thugs kicked him repeatedly, some stomping on his head. The police eventually – and it took some time – moved in and cleared the mob away. The victim lay there still, a corpse. Later you saw he'd survived but had blood gushing from every hole in his face, including holes that hadn't been in his face that morning. All because he fancied men.

It had been an emotional day but at least Zagreb had left more of an impression this time around.

Having crossed my last non-Schengen border of the year, two days later I found myself in Slovenia's Ljubljana. The ride here had been beautiful. After the recent heat it had been refreshingly cool to cycle in the shadow of deep valleys filled with mist, repeatedly crossing rivers, down the tiniest of lanes entirely devoid of traffic.

I found a virgin room. I would be its first ever guest as the hostel had only just opened. My room was decorated with a rug, the skin and head of a wild boar shot by the owner. Using the timer function on my camera I repeatedly attempted to take a photo with it wrapped around my body to turn me into Pig Man but the results weren't too impressive.

Tonight was the last night of this year's trip but I still had someone to meet, a Slovenian ballet dancer, in a bar on top of a skyscraper. When Mojca had originally agreed to meet me she'd promised to get me tickets to whichever show she was performing in at the time. It would've been a great way to end the year. When she turned up it was clear why this plan hadn't gone ahead. She was pregnant.

From an early age Mojca had been destined to be a medal-winning gymnast. The communist system liked its sports stars. She'd started rhythmic gymnastics aged six, being pushed hard. But at eleven she developed leukaemia. By the time she'd recovered it was too late to catch her competitors and so she turned to ballet instead. At eighteen she landed a plum job at the famous Béjart Ballet company in Lausanne. This was a big deal for a young Slovenian and she was suddenly famous, people recognising her in the street. But she wasn't having fun.

"It broke me," she said. "Morals were turned on their heads. People went bananas. It wasn't what I wanted to do."

Mojca had recently completed a degree with the OU while working for the Slovenian state ballet company but had decided, aged 35, it was now or never time if she wanted children and so the ballet was on hold.

We talked about Blackburn. She thought I was treating it too harshly.

"You take a lot of things for granted, things you had in Britain that others didn't have. You had a passport. You had the ability to leave."

Mojca had a point. If I'd been brought up in a communist version of Blackburn – I'd seen a few contenders in Serbia and eastern Croatia – and not been allowed to escape, a prisoner of my own government, life would have been considerably worse. So I whinged about Britain and the West's excessive capitalism and commercialisation.

"What you see as a negative, others see as a positive. When you've had nothing for a long time, having too much doesn't seem like such a bad idea. Slovenia is much better than it was before. Under Tito, my parents used to go to the market – they'd run there – to change the dinars they'd just earned into deutschmarks as quickly as possible. Inflation was so high."

The conversation moved on to national traits. After the mauling the British had been given by Joris and Joëlle back in France eighteen months ago, I was interested to see if we'd score better here. We did.

"We like how the British are modest and gallant, their sense of humour and adventure. Like you on your ride. We admire that about you."

Well, that was better than being called a scruffy, plug ugly bastard.

After a straight eleven hours in the saddle, cycling 120 miles over very lumpy ground and losing another spoke in the process, I rolled up to the front door of a house in the Austrian village of Mureck. I'd said I'd arrive around six. I looked at my phone, just as the time flicked to one minute past. Damian, my co-cyclist out of Graz last year, was there with his girlfriend and a couple of pals over from the UK. We might have had a drink or two.

There was only one thing left to do this year and that was to eat the black Chinese egg. I looked at the sell-by date. I hadn't realised it'd been four months out of date when I'd bought it. And it'd been heated up to around 30°C on a near-daily basis ever since. With my penknife I sliced open the packaging. It smelled alright. Actually it didn't smell of anything. That was very suspicious. I chopped the egg into six pieces and offered them around but only Damian was brave enough to try one. He didn't seem too impressed. I ate the rest. It tasted a bit eggy and slightly gingery. I wasn't sick, even if I was a little bit sick of cycling and capitals by that point. But a rest over winter would change all that and prepare me for the final leg of my journey.

YEAR THREE

Chapter 18: Who let the dogs out?

Capitals visited: 34
Total distance: 13,998 miles

It was April and I was back in Austria although unfortunately my luggage wasn't. I had a few days skulking around Graz in the same clothes and then got a call to say the airline had found my bags. They were in Hanover, an entirely different country. Well done, Air Berlin.

Eventually I was reunited with my luggage and was ready to leave, looking forward to another 8,000 miles of Europe. Capital Fatigue was a distant memory. In fact, I'd missed cycling so much during my break I'd decided it would be wrong to neglect Britain's other capitals. Cardiff, Belfast and Edinburgh were tagged on to the list.

The old back wheel, with the cheap, replacement rim I'd bought in Eskeşehir, had been abandoned and replaced in the hope that spokes wouldn't ping off it at regular intervals this time around.

What would go wrong this year? This topic came up when chatting with my friend Nem.

"The first year it was the tent, last year it was the bike, I wonder what's going to fall apart this year," I said.

"Probably you," she replied. That's the spirit.

Similar encouragement came from Susanne.

"This year, all those places you're going to..." – she actually shuddered – "...they're horrible!"

"Have you been to any of them?" I asked.

"No," she replied. "Yes, actually. I once went to Moscow."

"How was it?"

"I had a nice time."

I'd often come across this attitude in Austria, and perhaps

it's true in other countries too, that anywhere east is a desperate hole that no sane person would want to visit. Most Austrians don't get out much. In Britain, when someone at work says they're off next week, your first question is usually "Where are you going?" In Austria, they'd always give me a perplexed look and say they were staying at home.

So far, over my 14,000 miles, I'd been spectacularly lucky with the weather. In my twelve months on the road I'd only had around fifteen days with rain – often little more than a shower or two – and six of those were in Britain right at the beginning. Temperatures ranged from pleasant to boiling, and even boiling is fine if you're moving. All that looked set to change. It'd been a long, cold winter for Europe. On the night before I set off, it was snowing an icy chowder of depression.

At least this year I wouldn't get too distracted by my studies. Last year's lower marks and lack of tutor comments meant studying maths with the OU while away from home was precarious. Any other subject would have been fine. I could simply have submitted my assignments and received my tutor's comments electronically but for reasons known only to the OU you aren't allowed to do this on maths courses. I'd rather have given myself a year off entirely but then I wouldn't qualify for the OU's special, pre-Clegg-lies course rates and so I opted to do a smaller course and finish the degree later.

On the morning of the 7th of April we – my mate Pete and I – trundled off into the freezing air made all the brisker by a fresh breeze. Today we were cycling to Hungary.

What interesting facts could I discover about Hungary? Well, Hungary was already quite famous for inventing things we couldn't live without, like the biro and the, er, Rubik's Cube, but did you know that in 1996 Ferenc Kovacs launched the world's first musical condom. It played a tune as you unrolled it. I don't know which tune. Maybe Johnny B. Goode.

The language of Hungary is a problem. It's not related to any of those around it and so knowing bits of other languages wasn't going to help. I'd prepared a crib sheet containing important Hungarian words, written phonetically based on the pronunciation of Google Translate. For some words though I wouldn't need the crib sheet. It was hard to forget that the Hungarian word for 'cheese' sounds exactly like 'shite'. Or that one version of their word for 'no' is 'minge'. Or that 'trees' sounds just like 'faaaak'. I could be wrong about all this. Perhaps Google Translate's virtual speaker had been hacked.

Ninety miles was ambitious for a first day. I'd hardly cycled over winter and thanks to a bread-making machine from Santa I was carrying a couple of stone more than last year's start. And keen cyclist though he is, Pete had never cycled so far in his entire life. By the time we hit the Hungarian border, with forty miles still to reach our destination, we were tired and starved.

We stumbled across a transport caff. The staff spoke a little German but we tried out the crib sheet. Something that sounded like 'kate scher' got us the two beers we desired. Scanning the menu, my eye was drawn to their 'shiteburger'. In the end we went for the 'extraburger' without knowing what the extra was. It turned out to be cabbage.

We struggled on to Szombathely, our destination, with a fierce headwind, saving energy by slipstreaming each other although Pete preferred to be in front because the fabric of my old cycling shorts was wearing a bit thin and when I bent over to cycle he could clearly see my arse. Eventually we arrived and collapsed into the only hotel we could find. And the only restaurant open on a Sunday evening offered me my first new taste experience of the year. Pigs' trotters are a bit gelatinous, aren't they?

Szombathely wasn't on the direct route to Budapest but I'd wanted to make the detour because in some ways the town was responsible for the entire trip. It'd been the reason I'd started comparing Blackburn to other places. Back in the mid-nineties, on a day trip from Graz, I'd visited Szombathely for an afternoon and thought how similar to Blackburn it was, with its surfeit of greyness, a drab shopping precinct and hardly anywhere to eat. But this town in Hungary had an excuse. It had been under communist misrule for forty years. What was Blackburn's excuse? I was interested to see whether Szombathely still reminded me of Blackburn. It didn't. It'd been tarted up, with a new and attractive cobbled main square. So now, even after those forty bleak years, it had caught up and overtaken its northern rival at least in terms of looks.

The next day Pete cycled with me as far as Sarvar before jumping on a train and returning to home and work, thankful he no longer had to stare at my arse.

After yesterday's cold it felt like we weren't going to bother with spring this year and instead jumped straight to summer. Cycling through frequent clouds of tiny, black flies my hi-vis jacket turned into something that sounded like a Geiger counter. I rode through empty village after empty village. No one was about. But when I stopped to eat a snack, people emerged to watch me, an old man in a brown suit and hat and a couple of potato-shaped women. They soon got bored and wandered off.

In Papa, a small town rebuilding everything, I found a cheap place and managed to complete almost the entire transaction with the aid of my crib sheet. The room came with a Bible and so I gave Revelation a read. It's an odd way to end the book, telling almost every Christian on the planet, bar a few thousand, male, virgin members of twelve Jewish tribes, that no matter what they do they aren't going to heaven. I bet that's a disappointment. I wonder if that Born Again New Zealander in Segovia knows.

Hungary was empty space. Being so flat the sky felt huge, the fields devoid of crops, no one anywhere except the occasional bus stop where I'd be gurned at by an expressionless gawper or that big, lurchy fella from *The Texas Chainsaw Massacre*. I never knew what I was going to get with each town I cycled through. Unlike Szombathely, tattered Tatabánya was the latest addition to my list of places worse than home.

There are a number of ways to approach Budapest and I chose the back door, the quietest but the lumpiest. A couple of miles from the edge of Buda, pumping my way up a hill, a woman waved and cheered me on, my first positive local reaction in four days. Once down from Buda and into its flat sister city Pest, I dumped the bike at a hotel and explored on foot.

Apart from Dublin and Edinburgh, Budapest was the only one of this year's capitals I'd visited before. After clean but anal Austria it'd seemed a shambling, mysterious place in the nineties. I remembered walking around its two-tiered indoor market and seeing half pig's heads hanging from hooks at a butcher's stall and imagining a great Hallowe'en mask by crudely stitching two of them together around my head, a pork-flavoured Frankenstein's monster. And evidence of recent painful history had hung about the place. Some walls had still been riddled with bullet holes. I'm sure I was wrong but back then it didn't feel as though there were many other tourists about.

Today though Budapest could have been an Austrian city, all spruced up, clearly benefiting from its EU membership. The market was still there but the pig's heads had gone. I walked to Hero's Square, a mostly empty plaza with the

Millennium Monument at one end. The statues were literally covered with tourists, young kids leaping from one to the other like monkeys. Presumably everyone had more money in their pockets but it was now a less interesting place to visit.

But perhaps my assumption about money wasn't true. I spoke to Robert, a Hungarian bloke in his mid-thirties working at my hotel although he'd been born and spent a lot of time in the Netherlands. He was a tall, solid man dressed entirely in black with a big smile.

"It's expensive here. The food is the same price as in the Netherlands but salaries are much less. Here 500 euros a month is a good salary," he said.

"How can you afford to live then?" I asked.

"My salary pays for the apartment, my girlfriend's for the food. We couldn't afford to live apart. Life was better under the communists."

I asked him how he knew this. I mean, he wasn't old enough to have experienced it himself.

"It's what I've heard. There was full employment. There were no homeless in the streets. Everyone had enough even if it wasn't much." This sounded like selective memory. Earlier he'd told me, "Bad things happened here in the fifties. People shooting each other in the streets."

But even though most people didn't seem happy to Robert in modern Budapest, at least he was satisfied.

"I don't need much. My friends know I speak Dutch and ask why I don't move there for more money but I'd be unhappier. My family and friends are here. And I love to take my guitar down to the Danube early in the morning and play. The boss of this hotel is famous in Budapest for his wealth and property. But I've only ever seen him smile once and that was when he told me how he'd won $150,000 in Las Vegas. He'll never be happy."

I was just about to leave when Robert gave me his last

story.

"I read a tale about a Spaniard. He's told that if he wants to find gold he must dig under the pyramids. So he does but he doesn't find anything. But along the way he meets a lot of people and realises their friendship and his adventure were the gold he was seeking. That's my parable for you."

Two days later, after some less than stimulating cycling across Hungary's plain, I arrived at my next border. There was no one on the Hungarian side and only a couple of Romanian officials, who checked my passport and waved me through with big grins.

After hardly raising a smile from anyone in Hungary I had two cheers and waves within the first five minutes here. Although the villages seemed a bit more knackered than Hungary's, with unmade roads, they were more colourful. Maybe spring had been here longer.

On the road I met a local lad in his twenties called Martin. We cycled the next twenty miles together towards Arad. Martin spoke a little English although the conversation couldn't flow too well with one of us cycling behind the other on a busy main road. Not far from Arad, before he turned off, we stopped and had a proper face to face chat. I was a little embarrassed that after preparing my Survival Hungarian crib sheet I'd done nothing for Romanian. Martin taught me the words for 'thank you', 'hello', 'one', 'two', 'three' and, most importantly, 'beer'. He gave me some biscuits and enigmatically told me there was a bulletin out about me. I've no idea what that means.

An hour or so later I rolled up to my destination, a campsite in the tiny village of Miniş. There I met Cornel, the owner, a Romanian with a Dutch wife who ran the site as a charity with profits going to the poorest Romanian families. I was the only camper today. Low on provisions I asked Cornel if there was a nearby shop. There was but it wasn't open. Never mind, Cornel told me, he and his daughter Andreea were going to a cheap restaurant a few miles away and I could come too. Perhaps he regretted it. While Andreea played with her phone I asked him questions, lots of questions.

"We've had it bad. Ceauşescu ruined the country. There was no money for infrastructure or anything. Then came the Iraq war. This was a disaster for us because Iraq was a major business partner. And then there was the war in Serbia, which was a big import and export market for us. One local farmer here had a million pigs. All their food came from Serbia. They had nothing to eat and so they ate each other. Now he has nothing."

"Maybe the EU can help," I suggested.

"Romania could benefit hugely from the EU but we misuse the money. The EU gives us grants, some of it gets used on unofficial side projects, the EU finds out and takes the rest of it back. One guy – he's also the owner of a Romanian budget airline – got a grant to build a new motorway. He used part of the money to buy two new planes. Now he's in prison."

In the end I'd finished my food and he was still only halfway through his. I stopped the interrogation for a bit before his dinner went cold. But Cornell wasn't done with his information yet. Back at the campsite, over a shot of his home-made *pálinka* – plum brandy, close to 60% alcohol – we perused the map and he pointed out places I might want to see, such as Dracula's real home town rather than the fake tourist one. He also pointed out a better, quieter route for the following day's ride. Having seen the state of some of the roads on my way into Romania – only the main roads had tarmac – I asked him if his suggested route would be asphalted.

"Oh yes," he replied confidently.

Back in my tent it took me a while to go asleep. Things barked and howled throughout the night. Cornel told me Romanians didn't like to use campsites. They preferred to wild camp.

"Doesn't Romania have bears and wolves?" I asked.

"Yes. Lots."

"Aren't they dangerous?"

He thought for a minute and then replied nonchalantly. "I suppose so."

"And are there any around here?"

"Yes, just up there. These are the foothills of the Carpathian Mountains."

Up until now I hadn't wild camped but with few campsites later on this year – I hadn't heard of any in Moldova, Ukraine or Belarus – and having no idea how easy it'd be to come by a hotel in the former Soviet Union, wild camping could be the only option. And in wolf and bear country.

The next day I headed off the scary, truck-filled main road on to the secret network of back roads Cornel had told me about and I'd otherwise have avoided. And yes, they were asphalted. For the first six miles. And then they weren't. For the next twelve miles they were dust and stones and potholes and, in their danker parts, mud. This would have been fine on a mountain bike but it was tough going on a heavily-loaded, thinner-wheeled road bike.

"Whenever I return from the Netherlands to Romania I'm always so angry about how terrible the roads are here," Cornel had lamented the night before. I knew how he felt.

I cycled through villages that transported me to a previous century. Houses were shacks. Chickens, ducks and geese wandered into the road. Although this was a Monday morning, children of all ages helped out in the fields. But unlike Hungary the streets were full of people and rather than staring suspiciously at me they waved and smiled. Eventually, via a boat across the River Mureş, I escaped the rough, muddy track and got back on to tarmac. Now I had to contend with fast, heavy traffic and a minimal shoulder full of little stones and assorted bits of glass and metal. This wasn't fun either. I gave up early in the afternoon just before Zam and checked into the ironically named Motel Paradis to calm my frazzled nerves.

Back on the road the next day nothing had changed. It was trucks and coaches and cars going at light speed all the way made worse by a strong, gusty headwind and, for the second day in a row, I quit when my nerves were knackered rather than my legs. I checked into another roadside motel. I thought a beer or a glass of wine, or in reality several of them, might calm me down and remove the heavy goods vehicles from my nightmares. But – obviously really – this motel sat right by that busy A-road. Each time a juggernaut went past, which was often, the walls of my room would wobble like the set of Crossroads. Every now and again a train would roar past my window too and then it felt like the whole room turned inside out.

Looking out on to the road through the window of the motel's bar something was happening. Two kids dressed in rags and holding buckets were striding cockily on and off the main road stopping the traffic. The trucks were backing up, hooting their horns. The smaller of the lads, who could only have been about ten, lurched about like a fifty-year-old troll. Then the older one went to talk to a truck driver. When the driver opened his door the boy threw something on fire into his truck. Just another day in Romania.

The morning after, the traffic had calmed down. I cycled past a shepherd tending his flock with his huge, vicious-looking dog. I said hello. The shepherd nodded. Then his dog noticed and legged it after me. He was fast. The shepherd shouted after him. The dog kept running. I pedalled like a nutter. Eventually, half a mile down the road, the dog gave up, just as I was about to come to a hill. A few seconds more and he would have had me.

Romania would present a new way to die every hour or so. Cycling through a small village I saw a child walking on the broken pavement. Suddenly, through the upstairs window of a nearby home, half a house brick arced through the air and landed on the road between the boy and me.

Without bite marks or a rock in my face I arrived at the village of Garbova. My map told me there was a track to Poiana, the direction I wanted to go. By now I'd worked something out. The red lines on my map were main roads and these always had tarmac and usually quite a few potholes. There existed a few yellow lines, which I assumed were B-roads, but I hadn't seen any of these in real life yet. Everything else was a white line, either a thin one or a really thin one. The thing I'd worked out was that the thicker ones were asphalted but the thinner ones weren't. This was useful knowledge and meant the track to Poiana was a tarmac one rather than loose gravel or sand. Unfortunately I couldn't find it. A thick-armed skinhead wearing a muscle shirt rode past on a quad bike. He saw me looking at my map and stopped. He introduced himself as Varsi and spoke some German. I asked him the way to Poiana.

"There's a track," he said, "but it'll be hard on a bike. There's a big hill."

Hills are fine. Besides, to go back the way I'd come would add several tens of miles to my day. He told me to follow him. He rode his quad bike around the next corner and then we went up and up and up. At the top of a very steep hill, he stopped.

"Here it is," he said, pointing to some mud in a field. It

was the sort of track you see in every farmer's field in Britain. In the UK it wouldn't have even appeared on a satnav. Here in Romania it was included on the 1:500,000 map of Romania and Moldova. And this was one of my map's thicker white lines. My asphalted road theory was in tatters.

Two days later I cycled out of Sibiu, one of the places Cornel had suggested I should visit. It'd been a pleasant ride into 2007's European City of Culture along mostly surfaced country roads on a vast, fertile plain between fields heaving with workers. The ride out of the town was on my first yellow B-road and made for near perfect cycling with light traffic and adequate surfaces. People waved from the fields, farmers still using horses and wooden ploughs. I passed a line of six Roma wooden caravans, brightly painted and overloaded with bags and kids, being moved along by the police.

I arrived in Sighisoara, the second of Cornel's recommendations. This had been the real home of Dracula, or Vlad the Impaler. A long and unlit, 17th century, covered wooden staircase, constructed from dark, ancient timbers, led up to his house on the hill overlooking the town. From below there seemed to be a spooky castle, the perfect haunt for Vlad, but once at the top I realised this was a church and that Dracula's house was a disappointingly modern looking mansion. Maybe that's why tourists are directed elsewhere.

Back in the countryside I passed a family walking with a twelve-year-old on a rickety bike. He decided to give chase. He overtook me and with his little legs pumping hard on his rusty pedals, bits started to drop off his bike, first a mudguard, then something off his handlebars. He carried on regardless as metal clattered to the ground, cheering as I regained the lead.

The route took me through Brasov, a vibrant town with brash, Hollywood-style lettering spelling out its name on its local mountain. I stayed in a room with a fridge containing a free packet of condoms. If I'd been in Hungary I'd have opened them up to see which tune they played.

I kept moving. In the Carpathian Mountains, in the heart of Transylvania, I reached the village of Bran with its creepy looking castle – Dracula's gaff as far as tourism's concerned – the sort of place Christopher Lee would rent for his holidays. At the entrance to the castle's grounds was a small market aimed squarely at the foreign tourist. They sold vampire mugs and vampire hats, vampire balls and vampire bats. For around a fiver – expensive for Romania – I could climb the stone staircase to enter the castle. Inside they told me about the history of the place, about the life of Bram Stoker, and the history of Vlad the Impaler. Nowhere did they mention Vlad had lived here. That's because he didn't. The only time Vlad saw this mountain fortress was when he tried to smash it up in the late 1400s and even that isn't certain. It was only billed as Dracula's castle because it looked scary. This place was a triumph of marketing over historical fact.

After being chased by several dogs, sometimes in pairs, I reached Bucharest. I've always associated being chased by animals as a countryside phenomenon. Rolling into the city I realised Romania didn't like to limit itself in this respect. At one point, down a busy road near the centre of town, I had four snarling canines after me at once.

Bucharest contains an amazing building. Although in the late eighties Ceaușescu – the man who put the first syllable in 'dictator' – was failing to balance the books he decided to build himself a little palace. This edifice turned out to be the largest civilian building in the world as well as the heaviest and the most expensive. Hey, we're all in it together. Given the squalor of a lot of Bucharest's apartments – judging by their crumbling exteriors at least – building such a monument to himself was hardly going to endear Ceaușescu to his people. The building itself – now called The Palace of the Parliament – is fuppin' huge. It has 1,100 rooms on twenty stories, eight of which are underground. A lap of the building's exterior is a two mile walk. The total floorspace is the size of fifty football pitches. And then there's the opulence of its building materials. They used a million cubic metres of marble and 3,500 tonnes of crystal. The building has nearly 500 chandeliers, for gawd's sake. And this wasn't a green field site. To build his one home, Ceaușescu demolished a vast area of Bucharest's historic district including nineteen Orthodox Christian churches, six Jewish synagogues, three Protestant churches and 30,000 homes. For being such a man of the people he was shot before it was finished.

The dangers of Romania aren't limited to the countryside. Bucharest's Arcul de Triumf, a half-sized version of its Parisian near-namesake, is, like its French cousin, surrounded by a busy roundabout. Traffic pings off it in all directions on to speedy dual carriageways. Where the roundabout joins the roads there are zebra crossings. There are lights to tell pedestrians when to walk but – this is the good bit – no corresponding lights for the cars to tell them to stop. It's as if the lights are saying "Go on. I dare you!"

I left Bucharest and moved towards Moldova. Passing through Galați I bought a pastry and, with the sun beaming down, started to eat it in the shade of an abandoned petrol station's forecourt canopy. Within seconds I was surrounded by a pack of mangy dogs all with protruding ribs. I decided to move on rather than get savaged for the sake of a Romanian Ginsters.

The road was a pleasant although badly potholed country lane through rolling countryside with almost no traffic. The lack of vehicles was at odds with the number of roadside memorials, each shrine with a photo and flowers. I saw one for a three-year-old girl. If only they'd slow down a bit.

Initially, Bârlad, in Romania's far east, seemed like a hole. On its outskirts were "No Photography" signs. Perhaps this was because it contained a military installation but more likely it was just telling me not to waste my time. Once inside, the town didn't seem too bad – lots of people milling about and a sweet, little park near the middle – and so I decided to stay. It wasn't until I reached the centre that I saw my first possibility of a bed, the Hotel Moldova. At reception they were charging a little more than I wanted to pay. I asked the receptionist if the town had any other hotels.

"No, not here," she replied.

I reluctantly paid, went to my room and opened the curtains. There, right outside my window, was another hotel, the lying toad. With damage to the daily budget already done I popped out to find a supermarket and ingredients for a self-assembly dinner. I was seeing more of the Romanian-style grocery store the further east I went. The women and all available produce are behind counters, on shelves or in fridges. Getting enough for a meal involved lots of pointing and miming. And having been in the country for a fortnight I could confidently say a Romanian fridge is merely a storage device and indicates nothing at all about the temperature of anything that comes out of it.

I was particularly looking forward to today. Moldova would be interesting if only for one reason – its poverty – because it had the sort of poverty that'll be coming our way in the not too distant future. Let me explain.

There's a measure of the Earth's resources called the global hectare. A hectare in this sense isn't a measure of land although there's a connection. Basically, if we add up all the world's usable stuff – its fertile land, its fish-giving seas, its fossil fuels – there are, at the time of writing, about twelve billion global hectares. With seven billion people on the planet this means we'd each be able to use around 1.8 global hectares if shared fairly. But there's an imbalance. While countries in Africa use hardly any of their allowance the West uses far more than its share. Denmark is Europe's biggest culprit using 8.26 global hectares per person on average but even this is comfortably beaten by the United Arab Emirates, Qatar and Bahrain, artificially turning their deserts into gardens at great environmental expense. Environmentally speaking, only one country in Europe lives within its means and that's Moldova, its poorest by a considerable margin. (The second poorest, Kosovo, has twice the GDP per capita of Moldova.) If you're poor you're forced to stretch what you have, make things last longer, grow your own greens or, in other words, be more environmentally friendly. As poor nations – India, China, Brazil – become richer and billions more people ache for a Western lifestyle our environmental budget will have to be shared more equally or face collapse. The way Moldovans live today is the standard of living we'll all have once everything is shared out equally.

I rolled up to the border. The officials of former Soviet nations don't have a great reputation when it comes to honesty. Ukraine's are famously bribe-extracting. I hadn't heard much about Moldova. It wasn't a country known for its tourism and so information was less forthcoming. The Romanian guards were as friendly on the way out as the way in.

"Got anything to declare? A gun? Drugs?" He looked at the state of me. "Ten thousand euros?" he smiled.

"No, twenty thousand," I said but then remembered the story of a lad who had joked with airport security in the UK about having a bomb and the next sound he'd heard was the thwack of a rubber glove. I shut up.

Next it was Moldova's turn. Despite there being four cars

in front of me the Moldovan official singled me out and beckoned me forward. He seemed genuinely surprised to see a cyclist. He stamped my passport and off I went.

The southern part of Moldova is like one big farm but it's a hilly, little sod, going repeatedly up and down 10% gradient slopes, usually one or two hundred metres at a time. It was hard work in temperatures close to 30°C. On the way down one hill, two large dogs emerged from a garden and went for me. I don't mind being chased downhill. I could always outrun them. I upped my speed a bit but the extra velocity made it all the more painful when a fat bumble bee decided to thump me in the eyeball. The most difficult aspect of the descent was dodging the potholes. Moldova's surfaces are considerably worse than Romania's.

After 75 lumpy, bumpy miles I reached Chişinău, the capital, home to over half a million people. Through its hectic streets I located my massive communist pile, the Hotel Cosmos, a shabby hole but cheap. Wandering around the city didn't turn up much gold. There's a scabby, little park where people played chess with four foot tall knights and bishops although quite a few pieces had been nicked. Someone in Moldova has a rook-shaped garden table. There's also an eternal flame memorial to commemorate some people with guns being killed by others with guns. And there's a statue of Pushkin, although he was exiled here by the Russian government and so, given he didn't want to be in Chişinău, perhaps it wasn't anything to celebrate. I doubt you'll add Chişinău to your bucket list.

At least I had a chance to try a couple of new drinks. I'd read beetroot juice is good for reducing blood pressure but this was the first time I'd seen it for sale. It's like over-sweetened tomato juice and is decidedly minging. Better was *kvass*, the barely alcoholic beer made by fermenting bread.

The country as a whole was desperately short on road

signs. Finding my way out of a strange, car-stuffed city like Chişinău without any help at junctions or roundabouts was taxing. Perhaps it was their way of keeping me trapped in the city and spending my money. Luckily, using my compass, I escaped the hell. The first road sign confirmation that I was on the right road out of town came fifteen miles from the centre. I was heading north on a busy dual carriageway with lots of traffic but no lines, Albania-style. I shared the space with old, dilapidated Soviet buses and the metallic shriek of lorries belching stinking smoke. Massive potholes were indicated with a single, easily moveable traffic cone.

I was discovering Moldova isn't particularly good at cities or large towns but it excels at countryside. It's a giant allotment of a country with, it seems, every household growing fruit or vegetables in its back garden, maybe out of necessity but it still looked pretty.

I was heading to a tiny village, Trebujeni, with a little, pink house I'd read about. Turning off the busy main road I hit some idyllic country tracks cycling through gloriously green scenery dotted with flowers of a thousand colours, through forests, past lakes and eventually rolled down a steep hill to the little town. By Western standards, Trebujeni was seriously poor. My target, the Vila Rosa, called itself an *agro-pensiune*, the hint at violence a little unfortunate.

The owner, Liuba, was in her garden. Before setting off I'd learned a few words of Russian, the default, if not always most popular, second choice language throughout the former USSR. With that vocabulary and the three or four words of Romanian I'd picked up, Liuba understood I wanted a room and I understood one was available. She grabbed her phone, stabbed in a number, said a word or two to the person on the other end and handed it to me. I was speaking to her daughter, Olga, from a location unknown. Her English was good, almost too good. We finished the transaction.

"Thank you for choosing our services," she said in an American accent, as though reading from a call centre script.

During negotiations I'd accepted the option that included dinner and breakfast for not very much. Before it was time to eat I went to explore the village. It had a dusty cultural centre that looked like no one had been inside for years. There was also a crumbling church at the end of sloping dirt track. Some kids came by and said hello. A man raced past a couple of times on his wooden cart pulled by a horse and foal. Some young women walked by in simple dresses but no one was smiling. Old people were bent double hoeing their fields. The country may have looked pretty but it wasn't a lifestyle to romanticize.

Back at the house I sat in the large vegetable garden for a couple of hours, reading in the evening sunshine, drinking a beer, feeling like I was on one of those relaxing sort of holidays that I never go on. Then the food arrived – a mountain of it – vine leaves stuffed with rice, a plate of pork and omelette covered in grated cheese, *mămăligă* – Moldova's take on polenta – and cheesy flatbreads. Oh, and a litre of wine.

Breakfast the next morning was similarly huge. There were two fried eggs, a schnitzel and cucumber plus a large pile of bread and biscuits. And twelve – count 'em! – twelve pancakes stuffed with fresh, sliced cherries and jam. Just like the evening meal I couldn't eat it all and so half of the pancakes and some of the flatbreads kept me going on the road later that day.

Halfway to Bălți, I met Alexi, a Russian lad with a harelip. He claimed to be walking to Russia although it'd take him a long time, not because he was on foot but because he was going in entirely the wrong direction. He shook my hand a lot and asked if I had any water. I gave him some and in return he grasped my head and gave me a big kiss on the cheek.

Like Chişinău, Bălţi had little going for it. The hotel I found had corridors that smelled of burning brake fluid. For safekeeping, the hotel's old odd job man stored my bike in what I thought was a spare room. The only available space was in front of a television. Then the bloke whose room it was appeared from the balcony. I was pretty sure he wouldn't like my bike blocking his telly. Perhaps it'd be over the balcony in the morning. As I left, I noticed it was room 101.

I was heading for the border with Ukraine. One of those crossings was in Soroca, a town known as the Roma capital of the world, not because of how many live there but because of the grandeur in which they live. Although the town's streets were the same old potholed and neglected roads I'd seen throughout Moldova, as I wheeled into town I noticed something odd. Some of the houses here were huge, but like the dresses worn by *Big Fat Gypsy Wedding* brides they were far from tasteful. Everything was over the top, with ornate columns and flouncy statues. Most were still in the process of being built. It was clear some sort of one-upmanship was going on, the newer houses a brick or two taller than the older ones but still in the same gaudy style. This was where rich Roma built their homes. There was a certain amount of speculation online about the source of this money. Some suggested it was drug dealing or kidnapping babies which they'd mutilate to aid begging. The Roma need a new PR man. The most lucrative form of begging in the world wouldn't fund mansions like these.

That night I read the border crossing near Soroca had been closed a few weeks earlier because the river Dniester was too high but I couldn't find any information to say it'd reopened. Because of the hot, dry weather recently I assumed it'd be possible to cross by now but checked with the young woman on my hotel's reception. She assured me it was.

I cycled the six miles towards the border, down a steep hill to the river. I couldn't find the crossing. I asked a couple of blokes. As one gave me directions the other did a swimming mime that threw me until I arrived at the border and found it entirely submerged. The guard told me the nearest crossing was forty miles away in Otaci. I knew there was no accommodation between here and there – Moldova is extremely light on hotels – and I'd no idea how far I'd have to go to find one once inside Ukraine. Maybe this would be the first wild camp of the trip.

I re-climbed the hill back to Soroca and then battled strong headwinds, awful road surfaces and several packs of dogs to reach the border at Otaci. According to what I'd read, the three European countries with the most fearsome border reputations were Russia, Belarus and Ukraine. If the Ukrainian officials found my collection of blood pressure pills then a bribe might be the least of my worries. My non-Cyrillic prescription was unlikely to offer any relief. Here we go!

Chapter 19: Stealing wine from church

Capitals visited: 37
Total distance: 15,590 miles

The border crossing into Ukraine was a long, wooden bridge across the Dneister with a set of officers at each end. On the Moldovan side a young lad with a stupidly large hat spent ages analysing my passport, looking at it from various angles, repeatedly flicking through it and tapping it on his desk. I don't know if he was looking for a financial incentive to hurry him up but he didn't get one. Eventually he let me through and I crossed the bridge.

I wheeled the bike into a dingy office containing an antiquated X-ray machine. There were three lesser guards but the room was dominated by their boss, an imposing lump of muscle in a daft uniform. While a younger guard took my passport, his leader asked me where I'd come from. I showed him my route map, which seemed to impress him. After a few minutes he gave me back my passport and wished me a good trip. No bribes necessary today.

Out of the office I was in the small town of Mohyliv-Podil's'kyj, a name generated when an official closed his eyes and bashed his keyboard for a bit. It didn't seem large enough to offer an hotel but on the road out I found some rooms. Sitting at a table in what you might call reception, although hallway would be more accurate, were two middle-aged women, one with a big smile and another with a big moustache. Luckily the latter could speak some English and German and, via a linguistic hotchpotch, I got my cheapest room of the entire tour.

The moustachioed woman was Maria, also a guest, a Pole here for Orthodox Easter. Despite my insistence that I didn't believe in God she invited me to the local church the next day to witness a liturgy. Not being into made-up stuff I'd no idea what a liturgy was but figuring my trip was all about new experiences I accepted, especially as Maria had said it'd all be over by ten. I could still get in a decent day's cycling.

The next morning, around eight, we arrived at the church. The interior was plain with no seating. A few dark, faded paintings hung on the walls. People milled about, crossing themselves, women outnumbering men by ten to one. Occasionally a priest would wander through and the punters would stop him for a kiss. The church started to empty as the congregation gathered on the lawn outside in the early morning sunshine. We formed two lines. At the head of the two groups were four priests, wrapped in expensive-looking carpets, who each took a turn at chanting while their colleagues yawned. The choir sang hallelujahs sweetly but unfortunately this exchange of chant and hallelujah went on for, approximately, ever.

In front of the priests' table was a collection of bottles and demijohns that belonged to the congregation. Each was nearly full of water with its cap removed. As the priest sang out, people would go up to him and slip him money and a piece of paper. An elderly priest with a ponytail, looking like David Seaman's grandddad, swung around an ornate incense burner to make the air smell more holy while the chief priest dipped a large metal cross into a bucket of water and dribbled liquid into the bottles and demijohns.

"What are the bits of paper for?" I asked.

"They're prayers," replied Maria.

"And why is he dribbling that water?"

"It's holy water. It makes the water already in the bottles holy too."

Ah, so that answered the question I'd had in the Vatican. Holy water makes non-holy water holy. But if that's the case, surely all the water on the planet must be holy by now. They're doing themselves out of a job.

"And what do they do with the water in those bottles?"

"They take small amounts of it to ward off evil spirits." Then she smiled.

What was the smile for? Perhaps she realised how ridiculous this all was. Or perhaps it was a smile of beatific joy. The water fun continued. The priest got a big brush, dipped it into his holy vat and began splashing the crowd. This didn't seem to be a normal part of the proceedings because it raised a few laughs but we were glad of it on this hot morning. However, maybe the chuckles came because of the gusto with which the priest swung his brush. One old dear got a right faceful. It knocked off her head scarf.

The chanting stopped and things seemed to be winding down.

"Is it over now?" I asked, summoning up as much enthusiasm as I could.

"No, now it's time for the liturgy. That was just for Saint George, our patron."

We all walked back into church to listen to some more chanting, the priests singing one line and the congregation replying, like oggy-oggy-oggies at a Max Boyce concert. Then the priests went into a back room in which they were barely visible. They took turns in putting on fancy hats and taking them off again. This part of the service lasted two eternities.

Ah, good, I thought, it was time for communion. My few visits to church told me this signalled the end of the party. There didn't seem much of a system with a huddle rather than a queue and people shoving themselves to the front to gobble down a piece of holy biscuit. After receiving their snacks they went outside. Maria was lost somewhere in the scrum but at least it'd be over soon. With only three or four people left to be fed the church started to fill up again. Oh no, what was going on? The chanting started up again. After another fifteen minute call and response it suddenly stopped.

"Is that it?" I asked with fake disappointment in my voice.

"No, I think there's something outside now."

"Goody."

In the garden Maria introduced me to Acsenti, a slim, fresh-faced, forty-something Ukrainian man with a fine top row of gold teeth. He spoke no English but did so at a million miles an hour. He got Maria to translate something for him.

"He says this is the one true church."

For some reason we now had to do a lap of the building. We dawdled at the back while Acsenti whirled passionately about the *pravosláviye* religion – Orthodox to you and me – and Maria beamed radiantly as though hearing all this for the first time. Back around the front of the church we gathered, this time for a twenty minute, non-chanty speech from one of the priests and then it was the turn of the guest acts. A group of kids got up to sing on badly set up microphones that squealed and screeched with feedback in a homage to *The Jesus and Mary Chain*.

"It's the blessing," said Maria. "This is the last bit."

Inside my head I punched the air with joy. We all formed a line with cupped hands and the priest walked down it infecting everyone with his piety. Apparently I'd cupped my hands the wrong way – either the left on top or the right on top, I don't remember – and got told off by the person next to me. I'm sure it made all the difference.

The service was done, and then came the buffet. Over the course of the morning a long series of trestle tables on the church's lawn had been slowly filling with food. There was more grub than the tables could realistically hold, with plates piled on top of wobbly plates containing strange bun-type things, meat patties, rice wrapped in cabbage leaves, cheesy pastries and bits of salami, chicken and pork. It wasn't like a British buffet, where we all form an orderly queue with our little, floppy plates and then after collecting our goodies stand around in the middle of the room with the plate in one hand and a drink in the other wondering how the hell we're going to eat that pasta salad. Not in Ukraine. Here you stand around the table with a spoon in your paw and you dig in.

My plan was just to have a mouthful as I hadn't contributed anything but the others around me had a different idea. Once they learned I was from Britain there was a quick survey to see if anyone around the table spoke English. An old woman five bodies away from me leant forward and spoke.

"I love you!"

The table roared with laughter. It was nice to know that my appeal stretched from twelve-year-old Albanian boys to eighty-year-old Ukrainian grannies. Actually, please forget I ever wrote that sentence.

Next to me was Julia, a soft spoken, German-Russian lady in her sixties with a lovely, open face – 'open' as in friendly, not an axe wound or anything – and we spoke in German. She repeatedly topped up my plate, made sure I had plenty of wine and water and sneaked chocolates into my rucksack.

"Go on, go on!" she kept saying. "It's healthy."

Acsenti nodded in agreement and indicated I needed the calories via a frenetic cycling mime with twisting hands and a lolling tongue. As the feast slowed down Julia got carrier bags and started to tip platefuls of food into them, stuffing them into my rucksack. She wandered off and came back with a bottle of wine she'd nabbed from another table. That too ended up in my bag. A younger, bubbly women called Leana, a local English teacher, joined in, collecting more things. My rucksack was full. That didn't stop them. They started to fill more carrier bags. It was time to leave but before I could go another woman approached me and thrust yet another bag into my hand, containing a bottle of lemonade and a load of cakes.

Maria's insistence we'd be finished by ten hadn't panned out – it was now midday – and so when I was invited to a nearby monastery I figured I'd write the day off. We climbed into the back of Sergei and missus's car – friends of Acsenti – and off we headed towards Lyadova, the eleventh century home of Saint Anthony on the deep green banks of the silver river Dniester.

I got to experience Ukrainian roads for the first time. They're awful. As a driver you have two options. You can scream along at top speed hoping momentum will crash you through the potholes rather than rip off your wheels or you can weave around the holes adding hours to your journey. Today Sergei chose the second option but most Ukrainians go for the first. In the back of the car Acsenti provided an endless monologue about the Orthodox religion. When he mentioned the names Melchior and Balthasar and was grasping for another to complete the trio I offered Caspar, which was a mistake because it made him believe I could understand Russian but, more worryingly, that I cared about this stuff other than for pub quiz reasons.

We arrived at the monastery and wandered about. I separated from the group for a second and a bloke approached me who looked very much like one of today's priests. He asked me where I was from and if I had any kids and then he leant forward. I think I was supposed to kiss his cheek. Instead we sort of nuzzled beards in a disturbing way. Back with the group we shuffled down a dark tunnel lit only by Sergei's lighter to a tiny chamber filled with piles of bones and skulls set in recesses in the wall. Scooby wouldn't have been happy.

Whenever I tried to take a snap of something, Maria muscled her way into the shot. She clearly liked to be photographed but she could have occasionally smiled. I have thirty photos of that day and each one contains a glum-looking, moustachioed Polish woman.

We all followed Acsenti to the gift shop. A 200-year-old woman with a beard and dressed as Terry Jones from *The Life of Brian* sat behind the counter. The shop was heaving with Christian tat, a wall full of what appeared to be religious Top Trumps, gaudy, laminated cards containing various theological imagery. In an attempt at a conversion Acsenti bought me two cards. The first, guaranteeing good health, depicted Jesus's first icon and the other gave me high religious power. It's a Dungeon and Dragons thing. No one could mess with me now.

We walked back to the car. Acsenti continued his sermon. He decided to demonstrate to me the difference between Catholic and Orthodox belief with a visual parable. Maria translated. He ripped a large branch from a tree and stuck it in the ground to make a smaller tree.

"These," he said, pointing at his new tree's shoots, "these are the branches. Catholicism is a branch. But this" – indicating the trunk – "this is Orthodox. Without the Orthodox church there'd be no Catholic church."

Sergie's wife piped up. "Protestant is lies. Is that right?" Did she mean her English or the sentiment?

Acsenti's was a great analogy. His Orthodox tree had no roots, no foundation, and without this – evidence for the existence of God – the tree falls over. I didn't mention this. They'd all been far too nice to me.

Someone called out to us. For no reason but friendliness a family of Moldovans invited us all to join their picnic. We drank their wine and ate their jars of meatballs, their ham and cheese and their spring onions. Maria had a huge slurp of tomato juice and turned her moustache red. There we were, sat around their little table, Ukrainians, Moldovans, a Pole and a Brit. When he learnt of the nature of my trip, the Moldovan family's dad spoke.

"Your ride is a mission of peace," he said.

I'd never thought of it like that. Maybe the religiosity of the day had got to me or, more likely, the wonderful and entirely unnecessary friendship that'd been shown to me by absolutely everyone I'd met today but he was right. It was about peace and it was about new friends, but some of it was also about old ladies sneaking bottles of wine into my rucksack.

Acsenti and Maria invited me back to church for the evening ceremony but I was all Godded out. Back at my room I surveyed my haul. I had wine, water, sweets, pop. They were all bottled or wrapped and would keep. I also had cake that'd need eating pretty rapidly. But there was also a bag of chicken, potato and stuffed cabbage leaves that had been in Sergei's car boot for two hours at over 30°C and had already started to ferment. It was probably best not to risk delving into that one.

At close to ten Maria and Acsenti returned from church and knocked on my door. Acsenti presented me with a tiny pendant of Saint Alexi. That was very kind of him. He really wanted me on his team but – sorry, fella – I need proof rather than nice stories.

The next day I got to ride on those terrible Ukrainian roads, the worst so far in Europe by a considerable margin. As well as the potholes I'd experienced in Sergei's car, plenty of roads could only be described as small-stones-thrown-on-to-wet-tarmac, making for a bumpy ride. There was always a good-sized shoulder but unfortunately it was filled with sand and grit and only rideable on mountain bike tyres. Ukrainian drivers also came a bit close.

Twenty miles out of Vinnytsia I was nearly killed. Riding on a long, straight road, the weather was lovely, a bright, sunny day with a gentle breeze and very light traffic. Road surfaces aside it was perfect cycling. Suddenly, from behind, I heard the squeal of brakes. Skidding off the road to my right at sixty miles an hour on to the gravel shoulder was a Dacia Duster. It regained its ability to steer and slid around me back on to the tarmac and parked up a hundred metres farther up the road. A dark-haired man in his thirties got out.

"Are you OK?" he asked, in good English. It must have been a close call because another car pulled up to see if we were both alright.

"Yes. What happened?" I said.

"You were too far out."

"No, I wasn't. I was at the side of the road. Didn't you see me?"

"No." Which sort of undermined his you-were-too-far-out argument.

"You didn't see my fluorescent jacket, my bright yellow, fluorescent jacket?"

"No, it's not as good as a Ukrainian one. Ukrainian ones have more reflectors."

"Mine has reflectors. Anyway, reflectors are only for night time."

He tried another excuse. "It's been a bad winter. The roads are not in a good condition." That was true enough but they'd been neglected for decades. One cold season couldn't have turned a decent road into something resembling Baghdad's airport runway during the Gulf War. On a quiet road, he'd been texting, or playing Angry Birds or something, the daft sod, then he'd looked up and I'd been in his way. We chatted a bit longer. He was called Oleksandr and seemed like a genuinely nice bloke, if an awfully shit driver. He drove away and it occurred to me that at no point during our chat had he apologised for nearly splatting me.

I continued cycling, more nervous than before. As I approached Bila Tserkva, a one metre wide, gravel-free shoulder appeared that calmed me down a little. Coming in the opposite direction were a few groups of lycra-clad racing cyclists each followed by a support car to prevent Oleksandrs from wiping out their entire team.

Today had been the longest day's ride of the entire three years. Although I'd done 130 miles it hadn't felt too difficult in such a flat country. Still, I needed food and a hotel and therefore I needed to get some money. Once in town I found a cash machine. I asked for 1,000 hryvnia – about 75 quid – and the money was delivered. I waited for my card. It didn't come. The machine reverted back to its default welcome page. The attached bank was already closed. Oleksandr had said it was a holiday weekend. The bank wouldn't be open again until Monday – in five day's time – and I'd only have 75 quid to last all that time. It wouldn't even cover the hotel costs. What was I going to do? I'd have to wild camp. And then a full two minutes after giving me my cash, the ATM spat out my card. If I'd walked away it would've ended up in someone else's wallet.

The busy main road into Kiev had a large, clear shoulder. It was the first time I'd felt entirely safe since meeting Oleksandr. It'd been a challenge to get this far. None of today's junctions had any signposts. Fortunately there was usually someone hanging around for me to ask directions with my dodgy few words of Russian. The road into Kiev offered a tasteful collection of roadside hoardings. Bra-less, dungareed girls advertising DIY equipment competed with posters for Miss Blonde Ukraine. Along this same stretch large, plastic castles – the sort of crap you'd expect in America

– housed restaurants, outside of which costumed maidens lured in passing drivers. The tackiness continued once in the city. Those with money felt a need to flaunt it. A bright, red Ferrari roared down the city street with such a throbbingly angry engine it set off the alarm of a parked Lada.

I'd been lucky. Despite lacking a map I'd found a hotel within ten minutes. They wanted an amount well over the odds for poor Ukraine but what I'd been expecting in ostentatious Kiev but when the receptionist demanded another three quid to house my bike – I hadn't had to pay anywhere else – I walked away. If I'd found a hotel so easily, surely I'd find another soon.

I didn't. The next three hotels I approached were all full, the fourth hotel's only remaining single room was 'premier', whatever that means, for which they wanted 140 pounds, and such was the quality of my local language skills, the fifth one was, ahem, a dog hotel. Swallowing my pride and returning to the first place I'd tried wasn't an option because without a map I'd no idea where it was. It's always a good idea to head towards the railway station if looking for cheap rooms in a strange town and I found somewhere just before I was about to admit defeat and give the dog hotel a tenner for a cage.

I wondered if all this city-seeing was making me jaded. Kiev had some lovely churches – the glittering, onion-domed towers of Orthodox architecture – but it also had a lot of the crap that comes with tourism, people dressed up in costumes to winkle the cost of a photo out of a passing punter. You could choose from a rabbit, a pharaoh, Scrat from *Ice Age* and a manky-looking, home-made Bart Simpson with a nose that would have been more more suited to Worzel Gummidge – all national icons of Ukraine, as you well know. There were also plenty of those turnips who dress up as statues and then stand about. I think if you've looked at the balance of your talents and decided your only chance of income is from standing still for hours on end it's probably time to get that CV moving with an OU course. Still, Kiev had its highlights. I saw a woman whose jeans were so ripped it looked like she'd been mauled by a fashion tiger.

The next two days saw me cycle towards Belarus. The closer I got, the more the locals' inability to hold their alcohol provided the laughs. In Korosten a paralytic old man argued with his wife. He tried to throw a punch at her but was so legless he missed her and hit himself in the head. Further on, still mid-morning, a farmer stumbled drunkenly down the side of the road. Seeing a lamp post with which to steady himself he reached to grab it, missed entirely and fell over backwards. In a third case I couldn't be sure if alcohol was involved but other explanations seemed unlikely. Three men wearing nothing but Speedos were standing in a field. There was no water anywhere nearby.

After the non-event at the Ukrainian border I'd decided not to worry about Belarus's. On the Ukraine side I was given a piece of paper with a stamp on it and was handed over to the baggage guy, a dark haired, clumsy-looking bloke. He rummaged through my bar bag like a monkey looking for a banana, moving things from side to side and being a bit shouty.

"'Pistol?" he demanded, making a gun with his fingers.

I laughed. Yes, I've often been involved in many a cycle-by shooting. He wanted to search my panniers. I unfastened each one but didn't open them up. If he wanted to search them he'd have to do the work himself. He did a pathetic fumble and decided he couldn't be arsed. Instead he leant forward and said something in a whisper. I looked blank and he repeated it. I said I didn't understand. He was probably after a present but eventually gave up.

I got into the queue to see the passport woman. It'd rained

the previous night and this area is covered in swamp. It was also only a few miles outside the exclusion zone surrounding Chernobyl, still an area with lethal radioactivity. I felt something tickling my uncovered legs. I looked down to see hundreds of mosquitoes plugged into me. Maybe they'd only just arrived and hadn't started to suck yet. I swiped them away leaving a huge, bloody smear. It suddenly dawned on me. I'd just been bitten by hundreds of radioactive mosquitoes. In the footsteps of Peter Parker, I now knew that from this moment onwards I would forever be Mosquito Man. Perhaps my superpower, like mosquitoes themselves, would be to annoy people but speaking to friends since, apparently I already possessed this power.

Eventually, it was my turn. Still being eaten by supermossies the passport official said she was impressed simply that I'd managed to cross Ukraine. Maybe she knew about Oleksandr. She stamped my piece of paper and sent me on my way with an English "Good luck!" I cycled to the exit and was approached by a soldier. He took my piece of paper from me and kept it. What a great system.

For the next ten miles I was in no man's land, neither Ukraine nor Belarus. What would happen if you murdered someone here. Which side would care, if anyone? I suppose your decomposing body would slowly be eaten by mosquitoes.

I finally reached the Belarus border. Apart from the pretend Turkish visa that you buy when you arrive, this was the first time I'd needed a real visa, one that required application forms sent to consulates and special letters. I'd been given a contact without whom I'd have struggled to get a visa at all. A recent change in the Belarusian visa system meant you're supposed to pre-book, and pre-pay, accommodation for every night of your visa. Although I'd only be here for little over a week, my visa was for three weeks to cover any delays. This would've meant paying over a thousand pounds for overpriced, government-approved hotels that I couldn't use because none of them was on my route. My contact was so good we managed to bypass this formality altogether and you'll meet him soon enough.

The entry process included more mosquitoes but also numerous tests on my passport with a magnifying eyepiece and a UV light machine. The guard asked for something in Russian which the man in the queue behind me translated as 'medical insurance'. I showed the official my insurance documentation. Not speaking a word of English he obviously couldn't read it – it could've been a letter to Santa for all he knew – but he nodded his approval and I was off.

I was now somewhere special, a place not visited very often at all. It was, after all, Europe's last dictatorship. It was also the last country in Europe to hang on to communism, which suggested poverty, shifty secret police and endless queues for basics like bread. Is this what I'd find? I'd so many questions about Belarus but the internet couldn't answer them.

As I've mentioned before, the website *CrazyGuyOnABike.com* with its 9,000 cycle tour blogs is a good place to get the measure of the popularity of a town or country. Of all those thousands of blogs, only two had visited Belarus, and one of those was a quick two-night stay in the far north-west corner of the place. No one cycles here. There must be a reason for that, over and above the visa difficulties, especially since visas weren't always as difficult to obtain as they were now.

The roads for the first two miles were just as useless as Ukraine's but soon they improved and for the rest of my time in Belarus they were the best roads of the entire former Eastern Bloc. The tarmac is smooth, the roads are wide and, outside of the towns, the traffic is nearly non-existent.

I was approaching Mazyr which I knew to have a hotel and saw a cash machine, a relief as I'd not known whether I could use my debit card here. I already knew the exchange rate but it still seemed like a dangerous extravagance to request a million Belarusian roubles. In reality it was only 75 quid. Belarus doesn't have any coins. Even its lowest denomination – the fifty rouble – is a ratty-looking note worth only half a pence.

After the excellent condition of the roads, the next big surprise was how clean the country was. In Romania and Ukraine I'd seen plenty of litter strewn at the roadside. Here there was none. It was on a par with Austria or Switzerland.

The hotel was pleasant enough. The young woman on reception spoke decent German. I'd been given a small form at the border on which I was to collect a stamp from each hotel I visited. There was only enough room for three stamps. I asked the receptionist what happened when the form was full. She looked at me like it was the first time she'd heard this question and admitted she'd no idea. Despite being close to a border they don't get many foreign visitors here.

I went out to find food. I couldn't locate an obvious centre to the town. There were lots of tower blocks, concrete, ugly but not crumbling like those in Romania. A favourite pastime here seemed to be leaning out of the window in your vest and smoking. People stared at me as I walked down the street. I quickly realised there was nothing to see and walked back to the hotel via a place that might have been a supermarket. There was no obvious outside sign but I waited around and people came out with the odd grocery.

Inside it felt like the place was illuminated by twenty watt bulbs but there was enough light to see that at least the shelves weren't empty. I decided the best way not to get constantly stared at was to act like all the other customers. I adopted a blank expression and made no eye contact. Only drab thoughts were allowed. I bought some green cheese studded with caraway seeds that tasted of nothing.

Back at the hotel a dark haired man in a suit was sitting in reception. He looked up when I came in and watched me. Belarus still has the KGB. I pitied the poor sod if he had to follow me in his car tomorrow.

The next day's ride was tedious in the extreme. The road was flat, the landscape occasionally fields but usually dense forest but the worse part was the constant headwind. Although today's hundred miles required seven hours in the saddle it felt more like a week. The road only encountered civilisation when it entered a big town and the only towns today were Mazyr – the one I'd left behind – and Babruysk, my destination. Everywhere else was somewhere down a very long lane, rarely visible from the main road.

As in previous years I'd been fortunate with the weather. A freak period of spring sunshine had followed me since Hungary but on the outskirts of Babruysk the sky started leaking. Thunder rumbled and forks of lightning cracked down around me. I dodged the rain, hiding in a bus shelter. It was full of people on their way home from work. In pretty much any other country someone would have cracked a joke or asked me what I was doing. Here, everyone remained schtum, their eyes looking forward. I was invisible.

The rain eased a little and I cycled into the centre of Babruysk. The road took me through a shanty town of dark brown, wooden hovels. I was in Middle Earth. The rain had been heavy but short-lived although it'd been enough to flood the town. Cycling through puddles is dangerous when you don't know what's underneath. The town had more potholes than the main road and I slammed my front wheel a couple of times in holes obscured by muddy water.

I found a hotel, basically a building site, and went shopping. Over the last 24 hours I'd come to realise that working with this currency was a nightmare. There were too many notes and too many noughts. Cashiers expected exact change every time and weren't happy if you handed them a huge note worth, say, two quid. In order to slim down my stash of worthless cash I decided to bin the lower denominations to make it easier. I managed to reduce my pile of notes by half even though I'd only discarded about forty pence. But it still felt wrong chucking away paper money.

The next day I was heading to the rendezvous point with my Belarusian contact in a town called Marina Gorka. Once again it was flat with the same landscape but, without a headwind, it didn't seem so boring. Close to Marina the traffic increased – it's not so far from Minsk – but still not enough to make it seem remotely busy. Occasionally I'd see a fish tripod at the side of the road, three bamboo canes strapped together at the top to form a frame on to which dried and salted fish were attached for sale.

Once installed in town I walked around. As in the other places people didn't seem happy. Maybe they had good reason though. After all, it felt like a cursed land. It had suffered Stalin, then Hitler and then Stalin again. Despite the nuclear plant being located in Ukraine, the worst of Chernobyl's radiation landed here. Its south-east corner has been abandoned. And now they had Lukashenko, a dictator who rubbed out those who got in his way. The country is a vast swamp, teeming with mosquitoes. Maybe you could excuse their lack of smiles.

On the Saturday morning of my 43rd birthday I met my contact, the one who'd eased my visa application. He was Bruce Bucknell, the British ambassador to Belarus. Along with four others – Chris, the number two from the American embassy, Martin, the husband of one of Bruce's team, and Denis and Pavel, two young Belarusians – we were going to cycle into Minsk. For one day only I handed over responsibility for route planning and simply rode without knowing or caring where I was going.

Befriending Bruce had been via a slightly tortuous path. Nem, my weird chocolate-providing friend in Austria, has a sister married to a British diplomat in Russia – I planned to meet them in Moscow – and because he knew Bruce liked to cycle he put us in touch.

Martin presented me with a collection of gifts: a bright red Belarus t-shirt, Belarus socks and the official water bottle of the British cycling team when they'd visited Minsk recently. He'd no idea it was my birthday.

Bruce clearly loved a challenge. Of all the European ambassadorial roles this one had to be the trickiest. He had to make connections within Belarus but he couldn't get close to the regime. He had to be positive about the country but remain critical about it too.

"So what's Belarus like?" I asked him.

"It's clean, it's safe, everyone has a job," he replied.

It sounded like there was more to follow. "But?"

"It's clean, it's safe, everyone has a job," he repeated.

I heard him repeat this mantra on a couple of other occasions during my time in Minsk, his way of appearing positive about the situation. In the gaps between these three phrases were where his real feelings about Belarus lay.

Diplomats are only allowed to remain in a position for three years before moving on and Bruce had only been here since the end of the previous summer. Martin had been here longer. He told me Bruce's approach to bridging the gap between the British and Belarusian mentalities was by fostering better business and educational links between the two countries. The previous ambassador's approach had been more confrontational and pulled up Belarus on its human rights abuses. She didn't get very far with that but was openly followed and videoed by the KGB for her trouble.

The American embassy had even greater problems. They used to have a staff of 25 but when the US imposed sanctions on the country in 2008, Belarus wouldn't allow them to have more than five diplomats here. If another American diplomat needs to visit Minsk, one of the resident five has to leave temporarily, such is the maturity of international politics.

Still, having a dictatorship rather than a free market could sometimes work in your favour.

"Last year, all the meat disappeared from the supermarkets," Martin told me. "The farmers had started to sell it to Russia for a higher price."

"What happened?" I asked.

"Luckashenko simply ordered the farmers to sell it locally again. Within two weeks we had meat again."

We took the back roads towards Minsk on tracks not shown on my own map. The roads were quiet, occasionally unsurfaced and sandy but never impossible to cycle. At one point down an obscure lane we saw two hundred cows staring at four women of various ages stood in their underwear. Ten miles outside Minsk, passing through a village, we met a dishevelled bloke on his second bottle of vodka.

"He's a policeman," joked Denis. "He wants to see your papers."

Someone tried to ask him whether we should turn left or right up ahead but the drunk launched into a sales pitch.

"What did he say?" I asked.

"He said if you want anyone killed, he can arrange it." This time he wasn't joking.

We eventually hit Minsk and found a cycle path. Clean, functional but austere tower blocks loomed over us as we penetrated the city's outer edge.

"So, Bruce, tell me something interesting about Minsk," I asked.

He struggled with that for a minute before giving up. In the past he'd had diplomatic roles in Milan and Madrid. Although he was now top dog for the first time in his career I got the impression this wasn't his ideal location.

Just like my first impressions of Mazyr, Minsk was also very neat and tidy.

"Is it clean because people don't throw stuff on the floor or because there are lots of people to pick up the litter?" I asked.

"The second one," Denis said. "Belarusians are pretty bad about littering. They know someone else will pick it up."

The cycle path joined up with a better surfaced one running beside the Svislach river. There were many other cyclists but even more weekend parties of sunbathers, some clearly hammered, stretched out by the water's edge. As he cycled, Bruce waved flamboyantly and greeted everyone he passed in Belarusian. He later told me he only knew a few words of the local language. Instead he was having Russian lessons.

"The English taxpayer doesn't want to pay me to learn Belarusian. It can't be used anywhere outside this country."

After stopping in Victory Square, the home of another eternal flame, we said goodbye to Chris, Denis and Pavel and made our way to the embassy. To get inside we had to walk through a metal detector and through three security doors each requiring codewords. A large, plushly carpeted staircase led to Bruce's apartment on the top floor. A framed photo of the queen greeted us at the door. The apartment was huge, the function room big enough for a game of five-a-side, richly decorated with a piano and a dining table that cried out to have maps opened and perused upon it.

After a cup of Earl Grey and a slice of home-made cake, Henrietta, Bruce's wife, showed me to my room. The curtains and bedding were emblazoned with the Prince of Wales's crest. I went to plug in my laptop and saw they had three-pin plug sockets. This was a little piece of Britain abroad.

Over dinner we chatted about the country. I mentioned that no one seem to want to start a conversation with me.

"If I ask directions they'll answer but that's all," I said.

"It's difficult to get an opinion out of people. They're suspicious that it may be used against them later."

Through a cultural exchange between Belarus and the US, that night Project Trio, a Brooklyn-based flute, double bass and cello combo, were performing modern jazz in one of Minsk's larger concert halls. Bruce had tickets for the three of us. The US Embassy's Chief of Mission – there was no longer an ambassador – introduced the show in Belarusian, drawing a round of applause with each sentence. I think this made Bruce a bit jealous or at least spurred him on to learn more of the local language.

Out of the concert hall, Minsk was heaving. A large, white stretch limo rolled past full of drunk teenagers leaning out of open windows. This was all new to Bruce and Henrietta. Soon after they'd arrived the long, cold Belarusian winter had descended – that year's had been particularly harsh – and now in mid-May temperatures had only just started to warm up. On the way back to the embassy we decided to get a drink. One bar was ruled out as it was in what Bruce called "regime square".

"Now that the weather's warming up, do you ever have a drink on your roof terrace?" I asked.

"I've never been up there," replied Henrietta.

"And I don't think the taxpayer would like it either," said Bruce. It wasn't clear how the taxpayer would know whether he drank his wine in his living room or on his roof.

"Are you not allowed to be seen to have any fun?" I asked.

"No," he smiled. "No fun."

Outside the embassy I looked at its plaque by the door and it suddenly hit me that this ride had taken me to some unusual places.

"This feels a bit surreal to me," I said.

"It still feels surreal to us too," said Henrietta.

The next morning Bruce had arranged an interview for me with a Belarusian newspaper and a photo session with a freelance photographer. The photographer was a bit naughty. He knew it was illegal to take pictures of the Presidential Palace but he snapped a photo of me with it as a backdrop. A soldier guarding the building came over and made him delete the images. Instead he took another picture of me in front of the building across the road. Its huge reflective windows meant the Presidential Palace was clearly in the shot with me.

Bruce had arranged lunch at an unusual restaurant, Expedicia. On the way there in the car I figured it was time to bring up the two questions I'd been aching to ask since he agreed to meet me.

"So, how often do you serve Ferrero Rocher?" I said.

Bruce smiled and rolled his eyes skyward.

"I always keep a box in the house for a joke," replied Henrietta, "but I don't pile them into pyramids."

My second question wasn't quite so frivolous.

"In *Lethal Weapon 2* the South African ambassador to the US went around killing people and then claimed diplomatic immunity. How much could you get away with in reality?"

"Diplomatic immunity covers everything. But in reality as soon as you're caught doing something illegal – no matter how small – you'd be whisked away to another assignment. You've been compromised." He gave me some examples that I probably shouldn't repeat.

We arrived at Expedicia, a Siberian restaurant, liberally sprinkled with animal furs. A video on a permanent loop showed Putin and Medvedev eating here. If I'd struggled to hunt out new food experiences in other countries, here they came like a landslide. We started with frozen slices of sturgeon served on a block of ice and a plateful of assorted pickled mushrooms. This was followed by a thick reindeer soup with cranberries served with reindeer liver pâté on rye toasts. Main course was a tasty steak of pan-fried elk on cabbage stuffed croquettes and we finished with a Siberian tea made with eighteen different plants and sweetened with a runny raspberry jam.

It was all absolutely delicious but it should have been. It was only after we'd ordered I realised how eye-wateringly expensive it was, though I could've been out by a factor of ten in either direction what with the daft Belarusian currency and all its zeroes.

On the drive back I thanked Bruce for my Belarusian experience, the one that had included an American jazz band and a Siberian restaurant.

"Yes, it wasn't very Belarusian, was it?" he smiled.

The next morning Bruce cycled with me to the city limits, heading south-west, and wished me luck. I told him what a great time I'd had and how I'd enjoyed Minsk.

"You know," he said, "if you like it here, it's probably because you've only seen it skin deep. And so have I really. But there's something darker underneath."

The next three days were spent aiming my bike towards Warsaw, cycling on entirely flat, well-surfaced roads fringed with dense forest in beautiful sunshine but with the wind annoyingly in my face. The towns on this side of Belarus seemed less dependent on concrete than Mazyr had done. Even so, I never saw anyone smile although I still saw people being a bit free and easy with the booze. At a hotel in Baranavichy one morning, the three blokes on the table next to mine polished off a bottle of vodka with their breakfast.

On my final morning in Belarus I noticed something had happened to my bike. As I put on the panniers outside my cheap and fairly nasty hotel I realised my chain had somehow become entangled with my derailleur. I worked it free but the derailleur was now loose. The tiny piece of metal by which the bracket was fastened to the bike had snapped off. As I cycled, the derailleur would flip up, rubbing the chain and making a horrible, metallic grinding sound. I could no longer change gear.

I limped over the border into Poland hoping to find a bike shop. I'd seen none in Belarus. The derailleur got worse and would flip up any time I wasn't actually pedalling. I found a small stone and jammed it into the mechanism, holding it in place. I now had to stay on the largest chain ring until I could get it fixed but as Poland was another flat country it wouldn't be much of a problem.

Cycling-wise Poland felt a lot like the UK. The roads were too narrow and contained pointless traffic islands that forced the cars into the kerb and that's where I was. There was also a lot more traffic than Belarus. The weather had taken a British turn too, overcast and threatening rain.

On my second day in Poland I'd intended to reach Warsaw. I'd set off that day on the E30 but after only a few miles it was clear from the signs my presence wasn't wanted. With the speed of the traffic it wasn't a road I wanted to be on either. Before setting off I'd bought a map of Russia – the only one I could find – and it was 1:2,000,000 scale. It included Ukraine and Belarus and even the eastern side of Poland. But for a country as densely populated as Poland the map was useless and only the busiest main roads were included. I needed a new one.

I popped into a garage in Siedlice but the cupboard was bare. Another customer who'd heard my request took me to one side and started to draw a detailed map that used two sides of A4 to instruct me how to get on to the road I wanted. I thanked him and, as I was about to leave, he kindly handed me an old but very usable map of Poland. I followed his elaborate, hand-drawn map. As I left town I saw the aftermath of an accident. A train had hit a car. The resulting carnage had drawn such a crowd that someone had set up a tent selling drinks and snacks. Poland had come a long way since the days of communism and now embraced the spirit of merciless capitalism.

The grey sky looked ominous. About thirty miles from Warsaw it started to rain. And then it became heavy and steadily got worse and worse. The busy road was flooding, the puddles full and of unknown depth. There were no hiding places on this stretch. I had to keep moving. The density of the traffic increased and, as everyone rushed home, it seemed to speed up despite the reducing visibility. I put up with miserable conditions for 45 minutes, desperately hoping every upcoming sign was for a hotel. The traffic got thicker. The rain came down harder. A lorry screamed past, hit a puddle and nearly drowned me. This was horrible.

And then I saw it. A hotel. But one that looked painfully expensive, like a stately home. Accommodation this year had averaged around eighteen quid a night. This one was going to scupper the budget but the roads were too wet and dangerous to carry on. I crunched up its gravel drive and, leaving my bike outside, plopped through the large glass door and dripped my way to the reception desk. I asked how much it was, ready to cringe at the response. It was 45 quid – a lot by my standards – but it's rare to get a Premier Inn for that. At least this aspect of Poland didn't feel British. It was more like a suite than a mere room. As well as a large bedroom I had a living room with a sofa that faced an enormous flat screen telly and a large bathroom including a real bath – only the second I'd seen this year. This felt like real luxury. Most of the hotels I'd stayed in recently hadn't even had hot water.

With my filthy, soaking cycling clothes I felt like I didn't belong here. Looking out of the window, however, the rain was getting worse if anything and so I'd have to fake it. I dressed for dinner as best I could – my black lightweight trousers and a black t-shirt – and went to the hotel's restaurant. My trainers still squelched as I crossed the marbled lobby. I sat down and ordered a feast.

It was still raining hard the next morning but the weather forecast had said it would stop soon and with only twenty miles to Warsaw I hung around until it did. The ride into the city was uneventful although the busy roads meant it was sometimes safer to get off and push.

Exploring the city I visited the imposing Palace of Culture and Science, Stalin's gift that dominates the city. It's the tallest building in Poland and looks like the tower block in *Ghostbusters*. Many consider it hideous and claim the best views of the city come from its viewing platform on the thirtieth floor, mostly because from there you can't see the Palace itself.

The next day the greyness had disappeared and had been replaced by glorious blue skies. Even though I was now forty capitals into my list I'd had at least a day's great weather for all of them except Douglas and Saint Helier. That was some luck. On that sunny afternoon I stumbled upon exactly what you'd expect to see in Warsaw, a stage containing the Three Amigos singing Mexican classics while a sombrero-wearing hombre made a huge paella.

I had three more days in Poland, cycling in pleasant sunshine on flat roads – I still hadn't got my derailleur sorted, lazy sod – but the north-easterly wind that had plagued me as I cycled south-westerly out of Belarus was now south-westerly as I cycled north-easterly towards Lithuania.

The routes were often through forest but the dense trees

didn't seem as oppressive as Belarus's, with more variety to them here. The days passed enjoyably and *pierogi*-filled but without incident. That wasn't entirely true. In the not at all humorously named town of Pisz I saw a man in a wheelchair being huskied along by two Alsatians. It'd like to try that.

But I was now heading back into the former USSR. Poland had seemed a little tame, a bit too western, after Ukraine and Belarus. I hoped Lithuania, Latvia and Estonia would be just as quirky as their erstwhile soviet chums.

Chapter 20: Warnings about Russians

Capitals visited: 40
Total distance: 17,072 miles

Not far inside Lithuania I rolled into the small town of Lazdijai hoping to find a hotel. I hadn't seen any on the way in and so headed to the tourist information office on the main square. Inside I thought I'd arrived in Gatlin from *Children of the Corn*. The office had a staff of four, the oldest no more than seventeen and the youngest about twelve.

"Is there a hotel in town?" I asked.

They looked blankly at each other. Then one of them went to a cupboard and got out a map. For the next five minutes all four of them hunched over, inspecting it carefully. Eventually, the eldest raised her head.

"We don't know," she replied. Perhaps they'd only recently murdered the adult staff and were still getting up to speed.

I left the office and was about to remount the bike when I noticed the back wheel. Its rim had split in several places and two of the spokes were loose. It had only survived 3,000 miles. I wobbled my way the thirty miles to Alytus, the first town large enough to have a bike repair shop. I could finally get my broken derailleur sorted at the same time. I knew I'd get through plenty of tyres on this trip. I just hadn't expected to eat my way through quite so many back wheels. I was already on my fourth.

Not far from the centre of Vilnius a snazzy car was parked in a layby. Three men in dark suits milled around it, the largest of whom flagged me down. He spoke in German although his wasn't a German accent. He came from somewhere farther east.

"I need your help", he said as he thrust a business card for an import-export business into my hand. "We've run out of petrol."

I looked down at my non-motorised push bike. "Er, I haven't got any."

"No, we need some money." This seemed like an odd request from three businessmen in such an expensive car.

"I don't have any money," I lied. "I've just got a card."

"That'll do. We'll come with you to the machine. I'll get the money back to you. You can have this gold bracelet as a deposit."

So three men had set off that morning and not one of them had thought it a good idea to bring a couple of quid or a credit card. And in return for my investment I was going to get a bracelet that may or may not have been gold. I wasn't buying it.

"I'm sorry," I said and cycled off. I felt bad afterwards thinking about all the kindness I'd received from others, and here were strangers claiming to be in need but something seemed bogus and not just the bracelet.

Once in town I found a cheap hotel. The middle-aged woman on reception asked where I'd come from and I gave her the story. She pulled a sad face.

"Is it OK travelling alone?" she asked in a soppy voice.

"Yes, it's fine," I said, as upbeat as possible. "Besides, I'm not really alone. My Facebook friends are following what I do."

Her face went even sadder. I felt I needed to raise the mood.

"My girlfriend sometimes comes out to see me."

She looked like she was going to cry. But the truth was

Nina hadn't been able to visit me this year and it didn't look like she'd be able to for some time. Now I felt sad.

Vilnius is a city within a city. In 1997, the bohemian residents of Užupis, a once-neglected district of Lithuania's capital, declared independence. They have an anthem, a flag and an army of eleven. To understand the tongue-in-cheekedness of their claim, April Fool's is their national day. But what's the point of this elaborate joke? It was simply because they could. In previous centuries, dominated by the Soviet Empire, even a jokey insurrection would have been quashed. Now Lithuania was free. Satire was possible. And like all good satire the humour is allowed to be daft but the message serious.

The city was enjoying its annual Vilnius Challenge – an event that included cycling, orienteering, climbing, paddling and rollerblading – with 1,000 competitors from fifteen different countries. The participants amassed by the Neris river, separating old Vilnius from the modern skyscrapers and office blocks of the new. A siren sounded and they legged it into the distance filmed by a swooping remote control model helicopter overhead. I was meeting Frank there. He ran one of the companies involved in renting bikes to the athletes. He'd been a champion of local cycling initiatives and coming from Germany, a land with plenty of cycle lanes, he was exasperated with the Lithuanian approach.

"For lots of reasons we need to get people cycling. The mayor acknowledged this. He started a scheme where the city provided 300 city bikes but they were all stolen within a couple of weeks," he said.

"Ah, that's not good."

"And then the town introduced measures that make cycling unpopular. Government workers are promised free parking in Vilnius – which costs a fortune – and prevents people from changing to bikes."

"But at least you've got some cycle lanes."

"They're not cycle lanes."

"They're better than nothing."

"No. They're worse that nothing. Just lines painted on pavements."

"Pedestrians seem to like them," I said. Except in the most cycle friendly countries – Netherlands, Belgium and Germany – cycle lanes are like magnets for oblivious pedestrians.

"Yes, the lines are very good for drunks. It helps them walk in a straight line. There's only one real cycle path in town and that runs outside the mayor's office. It starts nowhere and goes nowhere but he can step out of his building and claim to be doing something for cyclists."

The mayor, Artūras Zuokas, is one for grand gestures. Two years earlier, as a publicity stunt, he'd crushed an illegally parked Mercedes by personally rolling over it in a tank.

"Vilnius is very flat. It's perfect for cycling. I'm surprised there aren't more people on two wheels," I said.

"There's no cycling culture. A lot of people in town never had bikes as children and so they never learned to cycle. And then when Lithuania left the USSR and people became wealthier they wanted stuff. Cars have prestige. Bikes don't."

I was interviewed by a guy from the local television station and Lithuania's largest newspaper group. In a conversation that felt strangely like a job interview ("and what have you learned from this experience?") he asked me what I planned to do with the rest of my time in Vilnius.

"See the KGB museum, visit the contemporary art gallery and eat a zeppelin," I'd replied enthusiastically. I'd be disappointed on all three fronts. The KGB museum was closed because it was, er, Father's Day, the Contemporary Art Centre was rearranging its displays and not open to the public and the restaurant had sold out of zeppelins. Instead I wandered through town watching an eccentric sports display.

A busy main road had been closed off so that people could indulge in judo, karate, tennis, giant chess, dancing and a strange type of sword play.

As I'd discover, the Baltic States are very keen on the concept of 'beer snacks'. I had my first in Vilnius. The packaging's English translation explained the contents were dried yellowstripe scad, which sounds like an STD. It's like eating a salty piece of fishy plastic. With enough grinding I could break it down but every so often a shard of dried fish would pierce my gum.

I escaped Vilnius on a combination of badly connected bike lanes and foot-wide, dried mud tracks – that's not twelve inches wide but the width of my foot – and then made my way on quiet country roads. That night I checked to see what interest there was in my news story on Facebook and was delighted to see it'd been shared by someone called Milda Minge.

I love silly names. Long ago I did a short cycling tour of Orkney, where I picked up the regional rag. Inside there was a photo of a local lady's recent birthday gathering. Just as Tony Blackburn's surname originates from my home town, other places become surnames too. Unfortunately, in Orkney there's a village called Twatt. You can see where I'm going with this. Being saddled with such a surname is unlucky enough but you wouldn't thank your parents if they then christened you Violet.

Jump forward a few years and I took my silly name research international. In 1996, on my first evening in Graz, in a company apartment with no telly or radio, while waiting for my gear to arrive from the UK, I got bored. This was the sort of crippling ennui that causes you to get creative with alternative sources of amusement. All I had to read in my spartan flat was a local telephone directory. I did what any Englishman might do in such a situation and decided to see how many Hitlers lived in my area. I'm not exactly sure what I was going to do with this information. It's not like I was planning a putsch or anything. There were no Hitlers but I noticed an outstanding number of silly names.

When I arrived at work for the first time the next day it was obvious that silly names weren't confined to telephone listings. The company email system was full of them. There was good old Harold Fuchs and the painfully honest Roland Wanker. My own department contained two great ones. Despite his tragic name Peter Piswanger really was a lovely fella. And when you appreciate that a 'd' at the end of a German word sounds like a 't' you'll understand the childish joy I felt whenever Marina Kuntzfeld's name was mentioned. Even the Brits in Austria had dodgy names. I knew a bloke called Richard Cheese. He rarely contracted his first name.

I never met the man behind the phone book's most beautiful name. To me he was the superhero of daft monikers and he was called – wait for it! – Andreas Wankhammer. Isn't that just gorgeous? I saw him as a Thor-like creature battling evil with his giant penis. He probably wasn't. He was probably an accountant or something, calculating profit and loss accounts. With his giant penis.

The city of Siauliai, in the north of the country, sits on a plain. Despite the flatlands that surround it, a hill has appeared. Although I'm not religious I'm still impressed by some of the things humans manage to do that, on the face of it, seem religious but are really more about being human.

In 1795, Lithuania became a part of the Russian Empire, a curse it wouldn't truly shake off until just over twenty years ago. Uprisings against the Russians would periodically happen and Lithuanians would die with their bodies lost in forests, never to be returned to their families. People took to remembering their unrecoverable loved ones with a cross on this hill. During Soviet reign, religion was banned but still the crosses came. The KGB stationed men around the hill to prevent the addition of new memorials. They twice bulldozed the site and even schemed a reservoir plan to put it under water. By the 1980s the hill contained a couple of thousand crosses.

Then, on the 11th March 1990, liberation came and the people of this little country, with a population of just over three million, had the freedom to add crosses to the hill legally. And they did. And then people abroad heard about the hill and they started coming to Lithuania to add their own crosses too. One of those people was Pope John Paul II. He came here in 1993, added a cross, and celebrated mass for around a hundred thousand people. The hill is now the most surreal religious location I've ever seen, bunches of smaller crosses hanging from larger crosses in an almost infinite regression – several hundred thousand of them – each one a symbol of a loved ones who died or prayers for those still managing to cling on. There's more beauty and humanity on this tiny hill than in the grandest cathedral. This place was built with love, not money. It isn't the release of godliness here that's to be celebrated but the release of something a nation had desperately craved for decades that was suppressed by the Russian Empire and then the USSR. They wanted to express love for someone and they were denied that.

That night, not far from the hill, I found a campsite. At first it seemed idyllic, with four small houses, each in a different local architectural style, and in the fenceless field between them two tiny lambs were munching away on the grass. Ahh, I thought, how lovely, until I realised the lambs were chained into position.

In the campsite's restaurant I got a chance to try out some new Lithuanian food. I ordered another beer snack. This time it was a boiled pig's ear. It tasted alright but crunching the cartilage took some getting used to. And I finally got a chance to try a zeppelin – a Lithuanian speciality – a potato-heavy dough around a boiled stick of unspecified meat covered in a creamy sauce containing other lumps of meat. It's reminiscent of school dinners but very filling and a lot easier to eat than the ear.

I'd noticed a clicking coming from down below. It only happened on every third or fourth revolution of the pedals and so I figured it was a problem with the chain. I did what I do with all mechanical problems and left it to get better all by itself. But it didn't. After a twenty mile stretch of forest it snapped, right outside the village of Kuršėnai.

I pushed the bike into town. Outside the first shop I came to, a middle-aged man was smoking. I asked him if he spoke English. He didn't but he said he spoke German so I asked him where there was a bike shop. Unfortunately this was too much for him and he scurried inside the shop to find his wife, a local English teacher. Nijole came out and introduced herself, a dark-haired woman in her fifties with the clearest, pale blue eyes. They hopped into their car and had me follow them. Outside the bike shop Nijole told me that when I was done I should come to their house. She wanted to make me lunch.

When I arrived the table was laid out with cakes, salami, cheese, cucumbers, grapes, tea and coffee. We talked. She'd been an English teacher for thirty-five years. I told her how much I was enjoying Lithuania and how amazing the Hill of Crosses had been.

"Yes, it's a very special place," she said. "I don't think there's anywhere like it in the whole world. I'm very proud to be Lithuanian." She noticed I hadn't countered with my own national pride. "Aren't you proud of where you come from?"

I told her I didn't understand national pride. Being British is an accident of birth. It's like being proud of having two legs or blue eyes. It's not an achievement of mine. And I knew Britain wasn't the best place in the world. There probably isn't a best place in the world.

"I love Britain," Nijole said. "It provides jobs for our young people."

"Yep, some people in Britain have a problem with immigration."

"For us the problem is emigration." I'd heard this from others here. "Too many young people are leaving. They go to Britain and pay their taxes there. We have too few paying into our pension scheme."

I'd had a lovely lunch but I still had a great distance to my destination that evening. I got up to leave.

"Isn't it sad to cycle alone?" she asked with a pained expression. C'mon, don't you start too.

"No, I meet loads of friendly people. Like you."

"Haven't you met any bad people?"

"No, not yet." Well, apart from the guy who tried to bottle me.

"You'll probably meet those in Russia," she said.

Near the coast I crossed the border into Latvia, headed off the main road and disappeared down some rough gravel tracks using directions I'd been given. I was hunting for a tiny village called Jurmalciens.

Paul was a recent OU graduate, not long into his sixties, who was more or less self-sufficient. His garden, where he grew onions and leeks, carrots and beets, all types of fruit and even his own tobacco, morphed into sand dunes and then into beach. The beach was deserted and stretched out a pale gold north and south on the chilly Baltic Sea. In the distance stood a defunct Russian watchtower, no longer searching for spies sneaking into the USSR via the water.

His house, part of which he'd built himself, was like the lair of a mad scientist. A lot of his fruit was turned into country wines fermenting or stored here in large demijohns, liquids of various colour. I sampled a couple of them, a light bilberry one and a richer chokeberry. They were both much tastier than home-made wine has any right to be.

Paul seemed a bit of a loner. His partner was Latvian but they conversed in German because Paul didn't speak much of the local language.

"I'm a bit embarrassed about it actually," he said. "I know just enough to get by at the market."

"Do Latvians speak much English?" I asked.

"Not here."

"So what do you do for conversation?"

"I don't. That's why I'm monopolising you right now."

"It must be difficult though."

"I get the occasional opportunity. I was introduced to someone from England a while back but he wasn't the sort of person I felt like I wanted to talk to again."

Paul seemed happy with his own company. He also liked to do things his own way, which didn't always work in his favour. He'd been doing an environmental science degree with the OU and had disagreed with some of the content. He knew if he wrote the essay his tutor wanted to read he could've got a first. Instead he wrote what he believed to be true and ended up with a second.

"I don't know if I regret that now. I could have swallowed my tongue and done a lot better. But I believe what I believe."

Paul is sceptical about certain aspects of climate change. I reckon there's a simple answer to this topic. Either there's climate change or there isn't. Either we do something about it – develop greener technologies, reduce carbon emissions, etc. – or we don't. There are four possible combinations. If we decide to do something about climate change, in one case we avert disaster and in the other we unnecessarily improve our technology, although it's technology we'll need anyway once fossil fuels run out. If we don't do anything about climate change, in the best case we don't have the technology required when fossil fuels run out and the worst case is environmental disaster. So whether there's climate change or not we should develop the technology anyway and stop quibbling over whether or not the scientists have got it right.

After a night cap of his home-made blackcurrant port I returned to my tent. Paul had found me a sheltered spot in a hollow between a circle of dunes. That night I drifted off to the sound of lapping waves.

My bike was slowly dying. My right hand gear cable – the one that changed the gears on the cassette – snapped just as I pulled up to my hotel in Saldus at the end of a long, ninety mile day. There was a bike shop around the corner but unfortunately it was Saturday afternoon and it'd already closed for the weekend. I had a maths exam in Latvia's capital, Riga, on the Tuesday. I couldn't risk staying in Saldus until after the weekend to get it fixed. There were still ninety miles to Riga. Any mishap along the way on Monday would mean I'd miss the exam. I'd have to manage with the remaining gears.

As I was storing away the bike at the hotel I was approached by a middle-aged man with a pan-European accent who'd been listening when I'd told the hotelier why I was there.

"I'd like to buy you a drink," he said in a way that didn't sound remotely like a chat-up line although it does now I've written it down.

"You are a fascinating man, Mr Bond," he said. OK, he didn't add "Mr Bond" but his slightly sinister European drawl would have stood him in good stead as a Bond villain. "You've cycled all over Europe. It would be difficult to drive the route you have taken. And you are in Latvia alone. You are some kind of hero."

"No, I'm not." I was just a dick on a bike.

"I should introduce myself. I am Heinz Schassman."

He told me he'd worked for the European Commission but was now retired. We talked about Europe and I said how I'd like to live in a borderless world.

"That's what I was working towards my entire career," he said and then shook my hand.

Once I realised he didn't have a swimming pool full of piranhas in which to throw me we got on well. As always, it seemed, the conversation swung around to differences between our home nations. He was from Austria.

"I've been amazed by how friendly everyone has been. The only place I experienced any unkindness was in the UK," I said.

"Yes, but that's because you're from the UK. The only people who are rude to me are Austrians. But when I'm in the UK everyone is kind."

But then I thought back to a conversation I'd had with a young Pole who'd worked in Kingston upon Thames. I'd asked him if the locals had been friendly to him. He'd replied that most had but quite a few hadn't. Maybe you only get treated kindly if you're the right sort of foreigner.

The conversation continued amiably until, after overhearing the noise of a wake downstairs, I mooted the idea of recycling coffins instead of burning them during cremations. He found this idea appalling and stopped talking to me.

The road to Riga was mostly flat and I could luckily do the whole lot in one gear. The city was heaving with tourists, a lot of them on stag dos or hen nights. A group of lads went past in matching red t-shirts, each emblazoned with their individual nicknames, or perhaps they'd been randomly allocated. You had to feel sorry for guy with 'paedo' on his chest. Or maybe not. The humans-as-statues reached a new low here. A man sprayed from head to toe in gold paint couldn't even be arsed to stand up. He just sat there scowling at passers-by.

The next day was Monday, the day before my exam, and I locked myself in my room for a final lengthy, tedious revision session. I was in there for so long two women from the hotel came to check if I was alright.

The next morning I found the exam centre, sat the paper all alone except for the invigilator and devoted the rest of the day to seeing Riga. This included the harrowing Occupation Museum. It was almost impossible to comprehend just how recently these grim stories had unfolded.

I made my way slowly up the coast towards Estonia. The mosquitoes were a pain. The tent had a fly sheet to keep them out although it reduced how much breeze could get inside and made for stickier conditions. They did not seem to respect that, as Mosquito Man, I was their leader.

At one campsite I was confused by the signs for the toilets. One door had the symbol of an upward-pointing triangle and the other door had a downward-pointing one. I tried to reason it out. Was the downward-pointing triangle indicating the normally broader shoulders of a man or a female triangle of fluff? I noticed the young woman serving here didn't smile much. Maybe because she knew I kept using her toilet.

I edged nearer to Estonia. Close to the border I saw a man covering a full-size tree in bright orange paint. I've no idea why.

At my first campsite in Estonia I received another warning

about Russians from its owner.

"It's the alcohol. What will you do when they challenge you to drink a 200 millilitre glass of vodka in one go?" he asked. I'd give it a go.

"Some of them get loving," he said. "But a lot of them are aggressive." It sounded like Blackburn. "One other thing," he said. "Don't smile during a transaction or else they think they're winning."

"I've heard the driving is bad," I said.

"It is. They all know they can bribe a policeman if they get stopped for drink driving. So there's a lot of drink driving."

From watching the videos on YouTube I knew a lot of Russian drivers had video cameras installed on their dashboards so they could prove the accident wasn't their fault, unless of course it was. But the accidents posted on the internet were horrific. I wondered what it would be like in reality.

I stopped in Pärnu. After a lunch of smoked pig's tongue, pickles and horseradish in a local bar I returned to my tiny campsite that sat beside a small man-made lake. Outside the wooden hut that served as reception were a table and chairs. I sat there with a couple of cold beers reading my Kindle in the evening sunshine. A taxi pulled up. Out of the car climbed a family led by an unshaven man in his forties visibly swaying and clutching a half-empty bottle of vodka. The young lad running the site came out of his wooden office and said something to me in English. On hearing this, Mr Vodka fixed me with a wobbly-headed, drunken glare and staggered towards me with a clenched fist. The young lad ran forward and shooed the man away, diverting him to a nearby field.

"Fucking Russians," he said on his return.

The drunk stayed in the field for the rest of the evening, stripped to the waist, wrestling and slapping the other, younger male in his party. At first it seemed to be a bit of fun, a drunken picnic rumble, but occasionally he got out of hand and had to be held back for his own good. His wife and two teenage children screamed at him to calm down. Then there was a loud slap and the younger man hit the deck. Eventually the taxi returned and they all climbed back inside. I bet he's an absolute joy to live with.

Estonia is flat and green and full of mosquitoes and trees. Endless bloody trees. Eventually the trees thinned and I approached the almost Disneyesque prettiness of Estonia's capital, Tallinn. Although Tallinn was a Hanseatic port it felt more like a theme park recreation of a Hanseatic port. In parts it could be overpoweringly twee with lots of restaurant staff dressed in period costumes and done up like serving wenches. Poking around the edges it was less twee. The wonderful old alleyway that is Laboratooriumi Street retained the cobbles but added several homeless men sleeping snugly in the recesses of the city's wall.

As an antidote to Disney Tallinn I walked a mile from the centre and found a darkly special place that'd been recommended to me. A minuscule entry fee got me a ticket into Patarei Prison and a torch. I'd need it. The place was a health and safety nightmare with dodgy, crumbling stone staircases, rotten floorboards and debris scattered around the dark cells. Outside the temperature was well into the thirties but in these dank corridors it was icily cold. Imagining what it must've been like to be one of the two thousand prisoners locked up here made my spine go all wobbly. Although originally a sea fortress built in the 1800s, the prison had only closed in 2002.

Some of prison's cells had views of the Baltic. Would seeing the freedom of the ocean improve your stay here or rub sea salt into your wounds? In any case, the proximity of the water would be at best a mixed blessing. During stormy weather sea spray gets blown through the bars.

The prison was drenched in menace. One murky cell, with peeling plaster, had a hole in the floor and a hook in the ceiling. This was the hanging room, where prisoners were executed.

With no signs to guide me, I poked around, getting deeper inside the massive complex. There was no one else in there with me. I didn't want to get lost. I found rooms that felt like I really shouldn't be there. And maybe I shouldn't have been. I came down one flight of steps heading for the central courtyard and stumbled upon a member of staff who told me the building I'd just been looking at was only permitted with a guide. With no signs of any kind I didn't know how I was supposed to know that. It didn't matter. I'd seen all I wanted to see. I needed some sunshine to remove the chill.

I went for a walk in Kadrioru Park and had a surprisingly good bread-flavoured ice cream before arriving at the Kumu gallery. Four foot high metal letters spelling the Estonian word for 'art' – KUNST – were clumsily arranged outside. From certain angles it spelled a different word entirely.

I was camping fifty miles east of Tallinn in the tiny village of Jäneda. It was early evening. I was in my tent, avoiding the mosquitoes. I could hear a football being kicked outside by a group of lads. Their ball hit my tent. A head appeared at the entrance to my tent to apologise but they didn't move any farther away. The ball hit the tent again. I figured I'd get out, join in and then hoof their ball as far away as possible.

I emerged from my tent. A lad in his twenties asked me what I was doing there. I told him and was then descended upon by the entire group of six blokes and five girls. They thrust a paper plate of kebab meat and salad into one hand and a beer into the other. It was a special day, the longest of the year – this far north it wouldn't actually get properly dark – and they planned to party all through the night and I was now their guest.

I got talking to Alice. She looked how Jordan would if the model didn't wear the make-up of a drag queen. I asked her how she coped with the mosquitoes – at least Blackburn didn't have mosquitoes – and she popped to her car to fetch something.

"A present!" she said, and sprayed me from head to toe in repellent.

We all sat around slowly getting very drunk. They were a group of Estonian Russians. Despite being born in Estonia, between themselves they spoke Russian. One of the guys, who'd studied at Oxford, said his English was better than his Estonian. They asked me where I was going next.

"Oh, be careful. Russians are dangerous," one of the blokes said.

"You're all Russian," I replied. "You're not dangerous."

"But in Russia, the Russians are more Russian than us," said one of the girls.

"How often do you go to Russia?" I asked.

"I've never been."

"Neither have I," replied another.

The night wore on and some people had clearly had more than they could take. Two blokes had fallen asleep and then the woman to my right put her arm around the girl sobbing next to her. The crying woman got up and left the circle.

"What's the matter?" I asked my neighbour.

"It's your fault," she said.

"Eh? What have I done? I haven't even spoken to her."

"It's your bike ride. She said that instead of cycling you should be leaving your mark on the world."

"How?"

"By having children."

"I don't want children."

"It's OK," she said. "She's crazy."

At four in the morning the party broke up and I toddled back to my tent and tried to go asleep in the brightening daylight.

After a brief snooze and a round of handshakes I cycled off while they got stuck into the beer again. I kept to the edge of Estonia, cycling through more trees on flat roads with shops few and far between. I stayed at a campsite in Mustvee on the shore of Lake Peipus. I thought it'd be great to go for a dip – and it was – but I should have known it'd be Mosquito Central. They nearly drank me dry on my way back to the tent. Inspired by Alice's gift I looked for mosquito repellent but nowhere seemed to sell it. Maybe that was just as well. Too much of it might have been like kryptonite for a superhero like me.

The rain came down. Despite there being few signs of human life the roads all had bus shelters every mile or two. They were usually covered and became my hiding place until the worst of the weather passed by.

On the bridge that crosses the Emajõgi river in Tartu I heard the familiar thunk of a spoke removing itself from useful service. This new wheel had only managed 1,400 miles before it'd been compromised. When I checked the wheel properly it turned out that another spoke had already died. I found a bike shop and they fixed the wheel but, if past experience was anything to go by, once a wheel loses its first spoke the others start pinging soon after.

The receptionist at the hotel in Tartu dished out some more ex-commie customer service.

"Do you have a single room?" I asked.

"No."

"OK, do you have a double room?"

There was no answer but the stern-looking, peroxide woman started to fill in a guest card.

"Er, how much is it?"

"It's 26 euros." That was alright. "Would you like breakfast? It's six euros."

"Is it a good breakfast?" I asked.

"It's not worth it," she replied.

A little later I was back at reception while she checked in another couple.

"Would you like breakfast?" she asked them.

"What sort of breakfast is it?" the man asked.

"It's so so," she replied. I hope she's not on commission.

My hair was long and straggly. It was time for a cut. I went to the barber's in Tartu, sat on a long bench waiting my turn. Busily working away were seven women, one in her early twenties and the others all in their sixties. Nobody spoke, not the client to his hairdresser, nor the hairdressers to each other. They took an age to cut one head. There's was only one guy in front of me but I still had to wait twenty minutes. Fortunately the one who became free was the youngest, non-dour-looking one and she could speak English.

I told her I liked Estonia but wasn't too keen on the mosquitoes.

"Ah yes," she said. "The mosquitoes are a problem. But they'll be gone soon."

"Really? That's good."

"Not really. That's when the big black flies come. They bite and they hurt." Brilliant.

After the haircut – I'd gone from bedraggled hippy to bank teller interview candidate – I went to visit Tartu's tiny KGB museum. It was basically a little dungeon in a house off a main road. In order to make visitors feel as comfortable as possible they had sound effects, like gunshots and people screaming in agony. It only took a few minutes to see it all but the overpowering memory was of the solitary confinement cell. At a smidge over three quarters of a square metre of floorspace there wasn't even enough room to lie down. All a prisoner would get to eat was half a litre of water on days one and two and then half a litre of soup and a hunk of bread on the third day. The KGB kept people in this tiny hole for up to ten days.

On the way back to the hotel I passed a drunk man in the street covered in blood and fresh Frankenstein facial stitches. He was screaming while throwing stones at a window. I was inching closer to Russia.

Back on the road, the hairdresser's prediction came true. Every time I stopped a black fly or seven would land and bury their faces into my skin, the little sods.

In Võru I met a fellow cycle tourist, a Czech called Jan. He looked a little like Hannibal Lecter. He seemed to be eyeing up my liver. Jan and I were apparently having a competition even though I didn't know this yet. I asked him where he was going and he puffed out his chest and proudly announced that he was going to Murmansk, a trip of 6,000 miles or so. After asking where I'd been he looked a little downhearted. So he wanted to compare other things. How many punctures had I had? How many gears did I have? How many this and how many that? I didn't know who was winning. Or care. Then he looked at my handlebars and saw my compass. He smiled a smug smile.

"I don't need a compass," he said. "I use the sun for navigation."

We both looked up at the overcast sky. The sun could've been anywhere up there.

"Which way is east?" I asked. He shrugged his shoulders. Whatever the score was, surely that was an own goal.

We parted but not before Jan told me that Russian roads were dangerous. He'd cycled there before. They really were awful. But he'd survived. How dangerous could they be? I was about to find out.

Chapter 21: From Russia with fear

Capitals visited: 43
Total distance: 18,644 miles

The first myth about Russia is that border formalities take ages. I'd been told the process would take up to three hours and include a full bag search, not something I wanted with my dodgily labelled blood pressure pill bottles. I arrived at the border and showed my passport to two or three different people. The visa woman looked at it quizzically and then it was the turn of the baggage bloke. He simply waved me on. The whole process took ten minutes tops.

I'd also been warned about the quality of the roads here, but the main highway from the border to Pskov was quiet with a decent surface, although it had the Ukrainian-style sand pit as a shoulder. Secondary roads, wandering off to unseen villages, looked less attractive, merely gravel tracks that would have suited a mountain bike but not mine.

The forty miles to Pskov passed only a single settlement. The rest of the time I was staring either at trees or forests of giant hogweed, that human-sized, white-headed monster that gives you a nasty burn if touched.

Once near the city the traffic got a little more aggressive and so I took to cycling first in the grit – it was shallow and doable – and then, in town, on the pavement but they were badly broken. In the end I got off and pushed. Another broken spoke was the last thing I needed.

I found a hotel located on a street called something like Risky Prospect. As with many of the places in Belarus I was warned there was no hot water. The hotel had an old woman who guarded the keys on each floor. This was once standard commie practice. During a tour of the KGB-observed Hotel

Viru in Estonia the guide had said how old women were chosen for the job because they were less likely to be picked up by foreign visitors and defect. The old women would also let themselves into each room and line up the visitor's goods that she was prepared to buy. Selling on Western stuff in Soviet Russia was a money spinner.

I went for a walk but, aside from the gold-domed cathedral, the place seemed down on its luck. I don't know if it was my imagination, especially given the bad press Russians had been given of late, but the town had a threatening air, hard-faced blokes, many stripped to the waist as Russians seem to like once the temperature gets above zero, and some clutching bottles and stumbling drunkenly along the pavement.

Cycling out of town the next day was made trickier than necessary due to the lack of sign posts. I guessed the right way and put myself on the long road to Moscow. It was immediately clear that yesterday's nice road from the border had been unusual for Russia. The roads had the potholes and cavalier approach to road maintenance of Ukraine but with a lot more traffic. Unavoidably banging up and down the bumps it wasn't much of a surprise when another spoke committed suicide. This time the damage was more serious because the wheel was buckled enough to rub on the mudguard every time it went around.

Although my original plan was to reach Opochka sixty miles away I decided to duck into the only other settlement of any size, the town a few miles up the road called Ostrov. With twenty thousand inhabitants, around these parts Ostrov is massive. I figured it'd have a bike shop. In the past, most bike malfunctions have resulted in some serendipitous interaction with the locals. Given the warnings I'd had about Russia I doubted it'd happen this time. Ostrov was a shabby, scabby-looking town, appearing grimmer than anywhere I'd seen in former USSR. Russia hadn't made the leap forward that many of its former soviet pals had.

I saw a man with a bike. He had his head down. In my mind I managed to string together a real Russian sentence by adding 'bike shop' to the word 'where' – you don't need 'is' in Russian – and so I let it out into the world. He looked up, pissed as a pint glass full of newts, with food and vomit all around his mouth and slurred me a "Da!". OK, maybe he'd misunderstood and so I tried again. But no, I got another "Da!" And then another. I wasn't getting anywhere.

The next cyclist I asked, Alex, a man in his late fifties, spoke about ten words of English. He told me he'd once been in hospital in Greenwich or, in his pronunciation, Green Witch. He took me to the bike shop, which was really just a hardware store, and waited outside with me until it reopened after lunch. Once inside he purloined a fresh spoke and a spoke key – I didn't see any money changing hands – and took me to his garden. There, he introduced me to Valya, his wife who, like Nijole in Lithuania, had been an English teacher. Like the British, Russians are famous for not speaking foreign languages. I'd got lucky again.

In Alex's garden was a workshop, which gave me the impression that, unlike me, he might know what he was doing. I'd watched enough spoke repairs by now to be able to do it myself but unfortunately the broken one was on the side of the wheel that required removal of the cassette and I'd no means of doing that. Alex made the decision that before we attempted any repair we should have a drink in his garden. From somewhere a can of beer and two glasses appeared. Alex poured half the can into each and gave me one. We chinked cups and necked it. Then Alex asked me to follow him. We went around a corner and down a little lane where Alex stopped for a piss and indicated I could do the same. I didn't need to and so I just stood around while he finished, feeling like a bit of a perv.

Now was the time to fix the bike and it turned out that Alex had less of an idea about how to fix it than I did. He had no tool with which to remove the gearing. Instead he tried to poke the spoke through the minute gaps in the cassette and that was never going to work.

Valya had told me of a hotel in town and if I wanted to stay, which I did by now, she'd accompany me and help with the check-in. I'd never had a problem getting into a hotel anywhere else but then she admitted it wasn't actually a hotel, rather a barracks for visiting officers to the local air base.

I left my bike in Alex's garden and we walked to the hotel. If this was where the officers got to stay then I wouldn't want to see where the cannon fodder lived. The place had the feel of Tallinn's Patarei Prison with murky corridors, cell-like rooms, crumbling concrete stairs, peeling plaster and ancient, rusty beds. Once again there was no hot water.

The bathrooms were shared, with two toilet bowls next to each other with no dividing wall in between so you could conveniently shit and chat at the same time. Any thought of avoiding this situation by locking the bathroom door had to be abandoned because someone had thoughtfully nailed bits of plastic to the door's edge to prevent it from shutting let alone locking.

Valya negotiated my entrance with a large, dour woman in a lengthy process that involved lots of forms and bizarre questions but I eventually got my key. My room stank of stale fags and the bed's wire mesh base was so slack it was more like sleeping in a hammock but, on the plus side, it only cost a tenner.

Alex and Valya decided it was time for lunch. In order to make some space the bike went back into the tool shed, puncturing the back wheel in the process, one more thing to fix. We ate in their garden – meat patties on bread with cucumbers – and Valya gave me a book from 1976 about a town on my route the next day that'd been the home of Pushkin. They recommended I visited it.

Their garden wasn't big but in it they were growing tomatoes, cabbages and herbs. There were also two bee hives.

"How much honey do the bees produce?" I asked.

"None yet. Last year all the bees died. These are new ones." Ostrov felt like a town with a lot of bad luck.

After lunch I tried to fix the puncture but the pump adapter I'd got on my way out of Berlin had disappeared. Alex's own pump was knackered and so it looked like before I could solve the problem of the broken spoke I'd have to solve the problem of having a non-functioning pump.

We walked back towards the hotel. I didn't want to load the bike without the back tyre inflated and so Alex carried some of my bags on the handlebars of his own bike. On the way, Valya told me about her children. It was a few years since she'd retired and her English was, like Alex's bike, a bit rusty.

"We have two children," she said. "Our 33-year-old daughter is a calculator. And our 25-year-old son is electric."

The route took us past the grim housing blocks in which Alex and Valya lived. Their garden was basically an allotment.

"I have lived here all of my life," said Valya.

"You must have seen a lot of changes," I said.

"Oh yes," she said, and smiled.

"Better or worse?"

"Worse. A lot worse."

I said goodbye to the couple and thanked them for their hospitality and help. So it seemed that another myth was exploded. Russians, at least some of them, are lovely.

Back in my hotel's cell I did a thorough search of my

panniers and found my pump adapter. I managed to inflate the inner tube and so now I'd only one problem left to solve.

Tomorrow's destination, Opochka, was only half the size of Ostrov and so the chance of its having a bike repair shop was slim. There was nowhere bigger for miles around. I'd have to hope I could limp on to Velikiye Luki, a town of a 100,000 people, but being 140 miles away this made me nervous. If another spoke popped and the back wheel buckled any more I'd be thumbing a lift or pushing, possibly for days on end.

There was one final myth to explode. I was told that roads in Russia are bad. They aren't bad. They're absolutely bloody atrocious. They'd make the transport minister of a banana republic blush with shame. And today I'd discover just how bad.

Since Pskov, the hard shoulder had become another sand and gravel pit, alluringly rideable at times, when the intimacy of a speeding juggernaut three inches from my left-hand cheek got too much, which was every few minutes. Either I was invisible to truck drivers or they were driving so close just to terrify me. It was bad enough when cars missed me by inches but when it's a truck the suction effect of its huge wheels dragged me even closer.

The edges of the tarmac were broken and potholed meaning at times I had to swerve into traffic to avoid too deep a hole. As the trucks got closer, the sandpit became even more tempting but, like all sandpits, I couldn't tell how deep it was. I had to try it. The next truck could be my last one.

For a few minutes I was safe, far enough from the traffic to feel just about comfortable, although the cycling was tougher on the softer surface. And then it happened. My front wheel hit a patch of deeper sand and sunk into it. The handlebars flipped to the left. I was thrown from the bike, into the middle of the road, skinning both knees and an elbow on the tarmac. I quickly spun around to see how close the next vehicle was, expecting to be slammed at any second on this busy road. There was a curiously clear stretch, the next car a couple of hundred metres away. Had I fallen at any other time today I would have been splattered.

Not wanting the shock of a forced dismount to unnerve me I continued immediately, back on the tarmac, with a racing heart and stiffening, bloody knees. It was a couple of miles before I stopped and took stock of what had happened. Then I carried on, chose the sand pit again and the same thing very nearly happened again, this time with a juicy truck hovering just close enough behind to squash my head like a melon. Luckily this time I caught the bike before it threw me from it.

Roads in Russia are scarce. There was no alternative to the route I'd been taking. It took the rest of the day to come to a big decision. The roads were deadly and so were the sandy shoulders. This was stupid.

For the rest of the way to Opochka I stuck to the rough tarmac of the road, hoping my luck would hold with the trucks. Once in town I got a hotel. Luckily it was the first one in Russia with a working internet connection. I used Google Street View to see the condition of the road between here and Moscow, and then from Moscow to St Petersburg. It was the same in all the places for which there was information, except the traffic would be much denser the closer I got to either of those massive cities.

My nerves wouldn't take sixty miles a day of this sort of crap, five hours dodging trucks or falling into the road. And doing that daily distance it'd take me three weeks to escape Russia, 21 days of waking up not knowing whether today would be my last. And what would I get in return? I'd see two great cities but the rest of the route was endless forest, teams of horseflies, hotels without hot water – tonight's hadn't even got cold water – and a skanky, small town every fifty miles or so on a bike that was falling to bits in a country without any bike shops. But boredom or the state of the bike weren't good reasons to stop. My death, or its prevention, was the reason.

To compound the feeling of despair I realised I'd left my phone back at the hotel prison in Ostrov. So if I were knocked from my bike into a ditch, broken but conscious, I wouldn't be able to contact anyone for help.

I skyped Nina to run my decision past her. She said I looked haunted. Today was my last chance of an easy escape from Russia. My route so far had been due south from Pskov. It was only forty miles to the border with Latvia and then another forty to a large town in a land that didn't want to kill me. Nina told me to get a stiff drink. That'd always been my plan.

So my challenge to reach every capital had failed. But I was still going to see more capitals than the fifty I'd originally intended to visit. Even missing Moscow, by deciding to include Cardiff, Belfast and Edinburgh, I'd still have done 52 capitals and that wasn't to be sniffed at. If at first you don't succeed, redefine your original goal so that your miserable failure seems like unadulterated success. I wasn't visiting every *capital* in Europe. No, I was visiting every *country* in Europe and I was still on target for that.

The escape road the next day was gravel from start to finish but, with an even depth, it was never dangerous. The wobbly back wheel made for slow progress. Being a back road it had almost no traffic, a massive relief after the day before. Giant hogweeds lined the track like Triffids ready to attack.

I reached the border. It took a little longer to leave Russia than it'd taken to enter but not much. At one point I was ordered into a room by a dumpy guard in a massive hat. I had to walk through a metal detector although the bike remained against the wall outside. I couldn't help thinking if I was going to smuggle firearms I wouldn't have put them in my lycra shorts. Not unless I was trying to impress someone.

I was right outside the front door of the bike shop in Latvia's Rēzekne when a second spoke decided it'd had enough. The timing was perfect. It rendered the bike unrideable. The wheel was patched up and fixed for less than a fiver but, sixty miles later, I had another spoke go. I struggled on forty miles to Smiltene and got that one mended too but seven miles outside Tallinn, another spoke went. Having spokes snap on me on a near daily basis was a pain but at least in the Baltic states it wasn't expensive to get them repaired. Over the sea in rip-off Scandinavia this would be a different matter entirely.

Chapter 22: The cost of being bored

Capitals visited: 43
Total distance: 19,222 miles

The bright blue morning skies of Tallinn had become thick, grey cloud hanging two feet above my head by the time my ferry reached Helsinki. The weather matched my mood. I'd researched costs for my next few lands and it wasn't looking good. Finland would be painfully expensive, Sweden would be significantly worse and Norway might require me to sell an organ or two if I hoped to stay anywhere near my daily budget. I was imposing my own Ramazan. Alcohol would have to be off limits until I reached Denmark.

For mid-morning in the middle of what was supposed to be the height of the summer tourist season, Helsinki had the atmosphere of a library. Plenty of people milled about, looking cautiously skyward, but no one talked. I suspected nobody wanted to overuse their jaw muscles and waste unnecessary calories knowing how costly they'd be to replace.

I was hungry. I examined a few menus but it was clear that restaurants would also have to be excised from my spending plans. I looked for street snacks and found a makeshift fish market but the cheapest takeaways cost around a tenner for very little. Perhaps I'd have to forgo food entirely. I found myself thinking fondly of Blackburn and a time when I could afford to eat.

I wheeled around Helsinki, bumping on the regular drainage gutters that cross every pavement-turned-cycle-path. I saw all the recommended sights but, with each capital I visited, it was taking more and more to impress me. Knowing rain was imminent and the only campsite in my direction was sixteen miles away I zipped out of town, stopping at a little supermarket on the edge of the city to get a drink. A can of Coke cost three quid. I came out empty-handed. It didn't matter. Soon it'd start to rain. I'd drink that instead.

By the time I arrived at the campsite near Lake Bodom I was soaked. I'd popped into the small town of Espoo looking for food but this wasn't particularly successful. The supermarket had provided a miserable stash of disappointing fare. Thinking they might be custard tarts I'd bought a packet of *rukiinen riisipiirakka* – clearly you want a rackful of 'i's when playing Finnish Scrabble – but they turned out to be tasteless, soggy rye pastries. I'd also got a tin of meat to cook with my camp stove noodles but, once eaten, I couldn't tell for sure I hadn't bought a can of dog food.

Peering through my tent door flap at the rain lashing down into the misty lake I reflected upon the last few hours. Despite a thoroughly depressing first day in Nordicland I resolved to buck myself up or at least try to find a more imaginative way to whinge about absolutely everything.

I was on my way to Turku, the port from which I'd leave Finland the next day. The roads were surprisingly shoddy for a country that charged three quid for a Pot Noodle. That said, proper, dedicated cycle paths made a frequent appearance. They weren't designed by a cyclist though. Every so often a tunnel beneath the road allowed you to get to the other side but the ramps from the tunnel back to the cycle path were so steep that the only way a non-Tour de France type was going to manage it without pushing was by charging full speed on the down ramp and hoping no one popped a head out of the tunnel.

I'd only been on the road for fifteen miles when my first spoke went and it was joined by a second casualty fifteen miles later, making the Tallinn wheel rebuild the worst yet. I found a bike shop in Salo and the wheel was repaired. And – bargain! – it only cost 23 times more than a similar repair in Latvia.

For the first time in Finnish history something fun happened and I was there to witness it. Screaming down a steep cycle track on a wheeled zimmer frame was an octogenarian in her pink and purple onesie. She must have been doing forty miles an hour. It was like a scene from *Last of the Summer Wine*. It cheered me up for a good four minutes.

The campsite was six miles out of Turku and so the next morning I needed to retrace my steps to catch the ferry. It was going to be a lazy day. I'd amble back to town, have a look around the city and, now the weather was heating up again, have a little sunbathe. And before catching the early evening boat I'd even find time to watch people eating food. But after two miles on the road back into town another spoke thunked and, like every spoke so far, it was on the side of the wheel I wasn't able to repair myself. I couldn't afford for this to keep happening. I wobbled back into town and I bought my fifth back wheel of the ride.

The ferry arrived in the remote portlet of Långnäs on the eastern shore of the Åland Islands. Unfortunately it was ten past one in the morning. There were no campsites nearby and it was too dark to go hunting for them in any case. The ferry terminal's tiny portacabin lights were on, burning gold on to the dark blue forest surrounding it. I went inside. A handful of people were waiting for a later ferry back to Helsinki. I decided to sleep there, a plan that was only scuppered when a ferry arrived about three o'clock, everyone left and the terminal closed down.

I waited outside for the sun to rise and enough morning light to cycle. This far north, overnight temperatures in the middle of July were low enough to require constant dancing. At half four there was sufficient light and I set off, teeth chattering, into the cold morning. I quickly warmed up as the sun boiled off the morning dew turning each meadow into a field of ghosts. It was only twenty miles of lush country road to Mariehamn, my 45th capital, a low rise town of 11,000, sitting on a large bay with a pretty harbour.

As the morning warmed up I spread myself out on some grass near the sea and caught up on the hours I'd missed that night. It's alright to sleep rough in public during the day. It's only at night time it upsets people.

As expected, in such a small town, there was no need to spend more than a few hours here and I caught the mid-afternoon ferry to Stockholm. On board I got talking to Julian, from Leicester, and his Swedish partner Carolin, who both lived and worked in Stockholm. When I asked about odd things to see in Stockholm he mentioned the site of the bank that gave the world the expression 'Stockholm Syndrome', when hostages show such empathy for their captors they sometimes end up defending them.

The approach to Stockholm was stunning, passing hundreds of tiny islands, some inhabited and others bleached white, with foliage stripped by the effect of the cormorants and their napalm-like poo.

Once disembarked I cycled around the centre of Stockholm, over its bridges. It's like an upmarket, well-maintained version of Venice. Knowing that tomorrow I'd have a full day to explore the city I left behind its grand buildings and raced off to the campsite ten miles away.

The girl on reception looked at my passport and started to write down my details, mouthing the words as she wrote them.

"Steven," she said. Then, reading my middle name, "Peter. Ha, ha! What's your last name?"

"It's there," I pointed.

"Smith? Oh my god, you have, like, the most British name in the world."

"I'd never thought of it like that before."

"Steven Peter Smith," she repeated, doing an accurate impression of Henry Higgins.

"Are you from Stockholm?" I asked.

"Yes, I've lived here all my life."

"From what I've seen it looks like a very beautiful city."

She pulled a face. "I hate it."

"Why?"

"I just do."

The next morning I stood waiting at the nearby metro station for a ride back into Stockholm. A young fella aged about twenty came up to me and said something in Swedish. I asked him if he could speak English or German. He then asked me for a cigarette in German and where I was from. I told him in the language he'd chosen.

"Then why are we talking in German?" he said.

"I thought you couldn't speak English."

"Hey, c'mon, I'm Swedish."

He asked me what I was doing in Sweden and we got chatting. The train arrived, we got on and stood together. He wanted to know which had been my favourite cities. I reeled a few off, including Istanbul.

"Wow! I'm going there on Wednesday," he said.

"For a holiday?"

"No, I don't work," he replied. "I can't work. I get paralysed, my whole body, for a few days at a time. I used to work but not any more."

"Could it happen now? I mean, could you just become paralysed here?"

"Oh, no. It's sometimes I just wake up and I think, y'know,

I don't want to get up."

"Isn't that depression?" I asked awkwardly.

"No, that's what the doctors said. You're depressed, they said. But I'm not. I'm really happy. I've been signed off work for a year now."

"But could you get up if you wanted to?"

"Oh yes," he replied, "but I don't want to."

I seemed to remember suffering from that complaint as a teenager. And I'd be really happy too if I'd been signed off work for a year because I didn't want to get up, especially in a country offering the benefits of Sweden.

"I'd like to do what you're doing," he said.

"What? Cycling around Europe?"

"Yes. But wouldn't it be easier to fly?"

"Probably, but that's not the point."

"Mmm." he finished. If he could be arsed to sit up in bed long enough to look at a map, he could attach a motor and drive it around Europe instead.

I had a pleasant day getting lost in Stockholm, seeing the nineteenth century Biological Museum with its animals stuffed in poses believed to be natural at the time – a mother bear had one baby in her arms and was leading another by the hand, just like real bears don't – and seeing the modern art museum with its cartoon Lichtensteins and Duchamp's found objects, his urinal he'd called Fountain.

Stockholm really was a lovely place. Why did the girl on the campsite reception despise it so much? But, then again, what was my problem with Blackburn? Maybe the towns themselves weren't the problem. Maybe it was just that we were stuck there and wanted to escape. Perhaps we wouldn't have liked to stay wherever we'd been brought up because we knew there was more to life and it was happening elsewhere. In the city that gave us Stockholm Syndrome, I'd discovered a second case of the recently discovered psychological condition known as Blackburn Syndrome, the crippling desire to leave somewhere you know too well.

I was on the outskirts of Stockholm. The campsite owner had told me to find the E18 motorway to Oslo. There was, he said, a cycle path running the whole way along it, although he'd never actually cycled it himself. There was a reason for that. On the edge of the city the cycle path disappeared. I tried to piece my way on other cycle paths that didn't seem to be going in the direction I wanted and then stumbled across a smiley Chilean on foot. He pointed to a road we could see.

"Follow that. It goes all the way to Oslo," he said.
"Have you been to Oslo on that road?"
"No."

It was no surprise when that road came to a roundabout whose only options were the motorway, a dead end country lane – I didn't discover it was a dead end until I'd cycled six miles down it – and a road that turned north, hardly the direction I wanted. The only thing that went the whole way to Oslo around here was the motorway itself.

After a tiring day with a strong headwind I entered Västerås, a city I knew to have a campsite. It was six o'clock by the time I found it, several miles the other side. I asked how much it cost and was told it was the same price as the most expensive site on this trip – twenty quid for one person to sleep in a field – and this one wasn't even near Euro Disney.

"Do you have a camping card?" the woman on reception asked.
"No."
"Oh, you need one."
"OK, give me one then."
"It's 120 krona [£11]."
"And what do I get for that?"

"What do you mean?"

"What is the benefit for me if I pay 120 krona for this card? Do I get discounts later on or something?"

"No."

"So why should I buy it?"

"Because you need it to camp here."

"In a country where wild camping is legal and free I need to pay for permission to pay to sleep in your field?"

"Yes."

"Fair enough," I said and left. There were no other campsites around and so tonight would be my first ever wild camp. I'd been putting this off for as long as possible. I headed away from the motorway hoping I could find somewhere nicely isolated. Suddenly all the forest I was cycling through was fenced off with twelve feet tall mesh. I rode about fifteen miles before I found a way to get into the forest via an unguarded track. I wheeled my bike into the woods. I was still close to the main road but the tent was well hidden and I figured the noise of passing traffic would ward off any dinosaurs or whatever lurked amongst these dark trees. With a springy moss base beneath the tent it was more comfortable than any campsite and I slept like a miser who'd just saved himself thirty quid. I might even be able to afford to buy some food tomorrow.

The next seven days were identical. Sweden was tediously beautiful. As I topped each little hill I'd see the same lake surrounded by the same trees. Yes, it was gorgeous but it never, ever changed. Each night I'd roll up to a campsite and each night the receptionist would try to charge me thirty quid. So each night I'd find a quiet hole in the woods nearby and bed down. I went days without anything approaching a conversation.

Only on one night was this tedium broken when I heard a

series of snuffling grunts outside my tent. Was it a wild boar or a wild bear? I was ill-equipped to deal with either and so I ignored it and it went away. I fell asleep to the sound of falling branches from distant and sometimes not-so-distant parts of the woods. If a branch landed on my tent at least I'd have something to batter Yogi with.

With no mirror I hadn't seen my own face for days. And with no showering facilities in the woods it could be filthy, especially as, in baking temperatures, I'd been doing long days of at least a hundred miles but sometimes considerably more. Or perhaps my face could be covered in something more suspicious. The tarmacked roads in Sweden were sparkly and so I spent the first few days desperately trying to avoid what I thought was glass in the road and the next few days fixing punctures because I'd run over glass in the road. One day while flipping the bike over to make a repair I smashed myself in the forehead with a pedal. It had bled but I didn't know how much. I probably looked like I'd escaped from somewhere. The only clue as to what I looked like was my shadow and that merely told me that my Estonian haircut had grown upwards rather than outwards and that I now resembled Vanilla Ice.

My alcohol ban was still in effect and that was probably just as well because the only beer available in the supermarket was that 3.5% rubbish your mum buys a crate of at Christmas thinking it's a bargain and only gets drunk once everything else has gone. If you want anything stronger you have to go to a different shop but these close at six in the evening. I'm not sure how Swedes working normal office hours ever get a chance to have a bottle of wine with dinner.

During this time I managed to pop over the border into Norway and head towards Oslo. The tunnels and No Cycling signs were proving to be a challenge and I tried to find my way on badly signposted cycle routes. Eventually I asked for directions from a mountain biking computer programmer called Rune. At quarter to ten in the morning he was already late for work. He told me to follow him. Although he blasted through town we chatted. He told me about his girlfriend. They'd been friends for years but had only recently got together.

"She's even started to like my favourite music," he said.

"And what sort is that?" I asked.

"Progressive rock."

"Wow, she must really like you."

"I took her to a Rammstein concert."

"And you're still together? Impressive."

I cycled around the capital for a few hours but I suspect I wasn't seeing it at its best. It was all being dug up, even the Royal Palace. The roadworks continued out of town too. On a cycle path leaving the city I had another brush with death. A juggernaut on the main road beside my cycle path turned right directly in front of me. He hadn't seen me or hadn't cared. Had I been one metre further forward I would've been a sticky mess under his wheels. Scandinavia, at least the parts I'd seen, hadn't been worth dying for.

From Oslo the route went back into Sweden and down its western edge, avoiding the busy coast roads. Not far from Vänersborg I flashed by a curious sight. At a bus stop a middle-aged woman in a purple top had her trousers pulled right down and was bending over showing her arse to an old man. Something was dangling from it and was clearly causing her some distress. Does Sweden have snakes?

On what I planned to be my last night in Sweden I found a packed campsite that waived the need for the rip-off camping card. It was still bloody expensive but I desperately needed a shower. My pitch was handily close to the toilets, bins and loads of screaming kids riding up and down the tarmac all night, an annoyance after the peace of the woods. I blew most of my remaining krona on a tasty chicken, peanut and curry sauce pizza but still baulked at the takeaway's drinks price list. They wanted six quid for a can of beer, eight for a shot and twenty for the cheapest bottle of wine.

As I rode the final few tens of miles the boredom with Sweden's endless rolling hills gave way to flatter lands and fields of wheat and barley and beaches full of happy bathers. I got talking to a Danish cycle tourist who told me that beer was cheaper in Denmark and I dreamed of sipping my first cold one in ages that evening. My Ramazan was coming to an end. Nothing could stop me now although a slow puncture in my back tyre was trying its best. I figured I'd keep topping it up until I got to the ferry terminal and repair it properly once I had my ticket. Having revived the inner tube for the fourth time I got back on the bike and heard a small explosion. The inner tube had blown, taking the tyre with it. There was no option of a patch up job.

I slowly pushed the fully loaded bike the seven miles to a bike shop in Halmstad, a town that'd been my planned lunch stop but now, with the delay, became another overnight stay. There'd be no cold beer tonight. Tomorrow I'd get to Denmark if I had to walk the whole way.

The next morning my bike had a brand new malady, a grating, metallic grinding whenever I twisted the handlebars. I'd spent a million pounds on this bike already. I just hoped it would last long enough to get me home.

After a short ferry ride on a dead calm sea I rolled down the gangplank on to Danish soil into Helsingor, Hamlet's gaff. What followed was a wonderful beach-side tumble down the flat coast into Copenhagen. I got slightly lost in its back streets looking for a city campsite. The town was a far more culturally diverse place than I'd been expecting. I was on a street corner looking at my map when a young black lad approached me.

"You appear to be lost," he said.

"Yes, I am." I explained where I wanted to go.

He gave me detailed instructions and then said, "I hope to have been of some service to you." Now that's polite.

Even ignoring the camping card, the site was half the price of those in Sweden. In a nearby supermarket I bought food but, more importantly, cold beer. Back at the tent I drank it in the early evening sunshine and feel merrily asleep.

The next morning, via the internet I'd been starved of in Sweden, I realised I had to change my plans. Scandinavia still had one more financial fist to swing. I'd originally hoped to get the ferry from Esbjerg on Denmark's west coast to Harwich. I now learned an overnight ferry including the most basic non-optional cabin would cost a painful £350. I could have had a decent weekend in the Paris Hilton for that. And she'd probably have videoed it. No, instead I'd scream down through Germany and the Netherlands again and catch a boat for a sixth of the price from the Hook of Holland.

This made me feel a little low though. Denmark was the last of the countries unknown to me. In two days' time I'd be back cycling in a land I'd already visited. This year had had its fair share of quirky nations and, despite being as dull as afternoon telly, a cost-cutting bloody-mindedness had got me through decidedly non-quirky Sweden and Norway. But it was all coming to an end. It'd once felt this silly idea would last forever but in less than a month it'd all be over.

I still had Copenhagen to explore and unlike dull Helsinki and Oslo it was clearly a rival to Stockholm. Copenhagen had so many statues they'd taken to displaying at least one of them – the Merman – under water at the bottom of a canal. Blackburn displays some of its supermarket trolleys like that.

The city's more famous amphibious ornament was so small she didn't stand up well to the hundreds of tourists gathered around her. Once or twice amongst the flowers and canal-side apartments I had to remind myself where I was. Parts of town could have been Amsterdam, particularly the area of Christiania, a self-proclaimed free town. But capital fatigue was setting in again.

My first, and last, full day of cycling in Denmark gave me the impression very little happened here. I trundled out of Copenhagen early in the morning and dodged the drizzly rain in deserted bus shelters. The cycle lanes were wide – second only to the Netherlands – but the scenery flat and not even tediously beautiful.

Knowing Guldborg possessed a campsite I stopped for an ice cream before setting up. The man in front went for one with seven different blobs of ice-cream, two kinds of sauce and biscuits on top. I hoped it tasted as nice on the way back up.

The next morning I caught the 45 minute ferry back to Deutschland. The boat had a deal. You could buy one duty-free pack of cigarettes as long as you smoked them all on board. The problem was you couldn't start on them until sixteen minutes into the journey. To puff your way through twenty cigarettes in 29 minutes seemed like a big ask but plenty of punters were up for the challenge. King Zog would have loved it.

Chapter 23: A fight in a holy land

Capitals visited: 48
Total distance: 20,400 miles

I cycled through Germany struggling to find a map. Shopkeepers told me nobody bought them any more. Everyone has a satnav. That's a shame. I love maps. In any case, maps and satnav aren't equal. A satnav won't allow you to peruse a wide area, letting you choose the most interesting route, whatever that means to you. A map won't let you down when it's run out of batteries. You can't roll up a satnav and batter a wasp to death.

I'd had to resort to the low cost route-finding technique of Mad Andrew, the Guinness-hatted bloke I'd met in France, and write down the names of the towns I needed to visit and the order in which I'd visit them. As expected it didn't work well. After the first diversion I was hopelessly lost and had no idea where I was. It was the countryside. No one was around. It was only luck that after twenty miles of aimless cycling I stumbled upon a name I'd written farther down the list. Andrew's probably in Kazakhstan by now.

Eventually I bought the last map in the world and crossed Germany. While en route I'd had some good news. I'd passed the maths course I'd taken in Latvia with a decent mark. Happy with this year's minimal studying I entered the Netherlands and made my way to Shane's living room on the night before returning to the UK.

Shane's own cycle tours make mine look a bit soft. He recently cycled 9,000 miles across Africa, from Cape Town to the west coast of Namibia and then across the continent, finishing in Nairobi. Soon he'd be off to Canada to cycle the remote Trans-Labrador Highway. In mid-winter.

I asked him if he fancied attempting a cycling record, like Sean Conway, who I'd met in Greece. He reckoned those types of rides are just "willy waving", something he wasn't interested in. But I suppose cycling across Canada in mid-winter could be classed as the same thing although in those temperatures no one will be able to see him waving it.

After kipping at Shane's and a tasty breakfast that included nettle cheese I fought my way against fierce headwinds down the Dutch coast to the Hook of Holland and jumped on a ferry. Strange thoughts filled my mind. Would I see Britain differently? Would it be a more enjoyable place to cycle now I'd seen what the rest of Europe had to offer? Would I rediscover the crap weather I'd left behind in Milton Keynes two years earlier and never really found again?

The ferry arrived at Harwich around eight in the evening. The campsite wasn't far from here but I wanted to get there before it got dark. It was almost inevitable there'd be a delay. This would be my 22nd and final border control of the last three years and it was the first with a faulty passport scanning machine. We all waited in line while the security guard made various unsuccessful attempts to fix it before giving up and switching it off and on again. I made it to the campsite at dusk and had an evening in the friendly pub attached to it. It felt odd to be back in the land of English once again. All the regulars were talking chimney sweep, doing bad Del Boy impressions with lots of cushties, luverly jubblies and bish bash boshes.

The next morning I was reacquainted with Britain's awful roads. Despite being Sunday morning the A120 was busy but without an alternative in the direction I needed to go. The cars came too close again. To calm my nerves I stopped at a burger van installed in a lay-by and bought myself something typically British.

"You wanna be careful, mate," said the stall holder. "This

road is faakin' dangerous."

I took a bite out of my really quite magnificent bacon sarnie.

"I was nearly killed a few years ago on this stretch on me bike," he continued.

"What happened?"

"Car was comin' out of a slip road. 'E saw me an' slowed dahn. Car behind overtook 'im and 'e faakin' smacked me one. Injuries still gimme gip."

We all need to slow faakin' down. The butty man and I chatted about my ride. He said I should write a book and put him in it. So I have done.

I cycled through Colchester and Bishop's Stortford and arrived in Ardeley, a tiny village on the outskirts of Stevenage. The village had a farm with a basic campsite. As I wheeled my bike into its field, I noticed another cyclist. Matt was on his way around Britain, cycling 2,000 miles to the areas of the UK where homelessness was greatest. His own mum and sisters had recently been evicted from his childhood home and, inspired by their difficulties, he was raising money for the homeless charity Shelter.

The campsite at Ardeley was unusual. It was part of a new farm bought by Tim, a local trying to breathe life into his dying village. In most of the smaller places I'd passed through in England it was sad to see the lack of facilities – no shop, no pub, no post office – but Ardeley was different. Tim's farm was designed to attract visitors, particularly children, who could help with various activities. There was also a team of international volunteers, and a shop and café selling their own produce. Recently Tim had bought the pub across the road. He was in massive debt but believed it was worth it to keep his village alive.

I cycled across England. The towns all looked alike, the

same shops in each one. Globalisation and ever expanding chains had created a land lacking any individuality. From east to west I cycled through the centre of a dozen sizeable towns but I can't now differentiate one from the other. They all merge into one congealed mass of Costa Coffees, Oranges and Greggs.

This part of England was an unpleasant place to cycle. Too many people live in too small an area. Roads in and around towns were heaving and fast, almost always lacking a hard shoulder. Country lanes weren't much quieter but were also too narrow so I'd constantly have to stop to let cars overtake. If you've ever entertained the notion of cycle touring in Europe but wondered how dangerous it would be, nowhere but Russia and the busiest roads of Romania should worry you if you've survived England.

If the roads were bad, at least the people I met were lovely. Each day would end with beer or a meal or a spare room or all three with fellow OU students. I met some fantastically wonderful people.

And then, after nearly being hit by a car in Cheltenham, I was in Wales. I sneaked into Cardiff via relatively quiet roads but Newport had been hellish. And I wasn't the only one who discovered that. A cyclist was killed there on the day I travelled through.

Riding north of Cardiff was easy enough apart from a junction in Tongwynlais that was designed to kill anyone on two wheels, having to cross four lanes of speedy traffic, from slow lane to fast lane, to take the only non-motorway exit. But what followed was three days of blissful cycling through the prettiest scenery of the year, landscapes that kept improving the farther north I went, over the Brecon Beacons, through the Cambrian Mountains and into Snowdonia. At last I had some real hills to test the legs. Falls of crystal water tumbled down the naked mountain sides and pooled in perfect lakes. The traffic even thinned out too.

I was feeling tired. I'd only had four proper rest days – those not involving a schlep around a city – in the last four months and the last one was two months ago. I needed to stop cycling but I still had over 600 miles to go.

The previous night I'd stayed at a campsite in Dolgellau. The nearest tent to mine housed a party of three American lads. Although my tent wasn't particularly close to theirs I had no trouble hearing them. They were discussing Bath, their next destination.

"Are there baths there?" asked one of them.

"We should definitely have one," said another. "Spend, like, twenty pounds for a bath."

"Awesome, dude!"

If they wanted to experience something genuinely awesome they should have cycled with me the next day. I'd arranged to meet Elton, a former OU student and keen cycle racer, in Bethesda. The A5 skirts the edge of Snowdonia, the remnants of ancient volcanoes sculpted by glaciers. There's something about the desolation of these mountains, the wild slopes stripped bare, that adds to their grandeur. Austria and Montenegro may be effortlessly beautiful but for the most part their mountains are hidden by trees. Snowdonia feels raw.

This place was Elton's playground – he's a keen walker and landscape photographer – but it's also his workplace. He'd fallen for his wife, Tabitha, working for the mountain rescue service. I met them both for the first time, along with their bouncy dog who licked the sweat off my legs as I sat drinking a cup of tea. Within minutes of meeting him I felt like I'd known Elton for years.

He cycled with me to Holyhead. The road through Anglesey was flat and not particularly busy but closer to the port the traffic thickened up. There was a cycle path but it was typically useless. Elton was in front. A car came too close, something I'd gotten used to by now. The passenger, a red-faced man in his fifties, leaned out of the window and screamed at Elton.

"Why don't you use the cycle path, you bloody idiot?"

We cycled a little farther and then Elton slowed down.

"I'm not having this," he said. He'd spotted the car containing Mr Angry pulling into a car park. Elton cycled across the road as the man and his younger driver were getting out. I thought Elton was simply going to deliver an insult and then come back again but from a distance I could see him and the older bloke yelling at each other. Luckily there was a small fence around the car park that prevented physical contact but if things escalated it could've easily been breached. I thought I'd go over and try to settle things down.

I arrived just as the man had finished screaming something.

"I bet you're a Daily Mail reader, aren't you?" replied Elton. The man looked like he'd been punched in the stomach.

"There's no need to get offensive," he said.

"Maybe it's just best if everyone calms down," I said. They both stopped arguing for a second and then the man carried on.

"It's ridiculous. If I hit you it'd be me that'd get blamed."

"That's because it would've been your fault," I said. "It's a long, clear, straight road."

"It's my insurance that'd go up."

"Yes, your insurance would go up and he'd be dead."

"It's not fair. The government are thinking of bringing in something that makes it always the driver's fault if a crash involves a bicycle. It was in this morning's Daily Mail."

"So you are a Daily Mail reader!" I said.

The man actually blushed and then smiled but at least he

stopped yelling. At last I'd met a Daily Mail reader with the decency to be ashamed of it.

We reached Holyhead and found a campsite. Elton had originally been planning to return home immediately but I tempted him to stay for a pint in the campsite's bar, a friendly, laid-back place. Elton had once had big dreams of an army career. He'd signed up at sixteen and had his career progression planned out but this was cut short when he was injured only four years later and had to leave. Craving the physical life he joined the local mountain rescue service, most of which was carried out on foot, but occasionally it involved helicopters supplied by the military and it was this that had enabled Elton to meet and work with Prince William on a few occasions.

"William's a nice guy," Elton said. "Very down to earth. Our station master gave William a wooden sword and asked to be knighted, and he did."

After a couple of pints Elton had to cycle the thirty miles back home. I'd only known him for about five hours but he already felt like a best mate.

I stayed on in the bar and got talking to an Australian called Greg. He'd just driven 5,000 miles around Britain.

"England's weird, mate," he said, "The first thing the English always tell me is how shitty the place is."

"Do you like England?"

"No, it's shit. But Wales and Scotland are nice."

The ferry arrived in Dublin on a grey, drizzly morning. I had an important appointment a hundred miles away at eleven the next day, which meant my exploration of Dublin was kept to a minimum. That was alright – I'd been here before – and the weather wouldn't have lent itself to a day of tourist bliss.

The city was packed. A big rugby game was on. The traffic

was at a standstill – the best sort of traffic for a cyclist – but this soon faded away as I was swallowed by Ireland's network of ancient country roads, narrow and winding and frequently very steep.

In Oldtown I stopped for something to eat at a small supermarket. A middle-aged woman, a real life Mrs Doyle, stood in the queue in front of me. She smiled. I smiled. She asked what I was doing there. I told her.

"Have you heard this, boys?" she said in her thick Irish accent to two bored-looking eighteen-year-olds playing with phones at a table at the end of the shop counter.

"He's cycling all the way to Scotland. It's twenty thousand miles." One of the lads grunted.

"Have you heard this, boys?" she repeated. They didn't look up. "Ah, c'mon." She rolled her eyes. "I bet you've a ton o' stories."

"Yes," I replied. She was expecting more but I was sick of talking about the ride. I'd been telling this tale three or four times a day for months.

"Have you heard this, boys?" They had and they didn't care.

We bought our stuff and left the shop. Her enthusiasm continued outside.

"I carn't believe this. Will we have a photo? I don't even know your name."

"Steven. And yours?" Go on, be as Irish as possible.

"Siobhan." Perfect.

She bungled her family out of her car – her nephew, his wife and child – and we assembled for a photo. Her nephew, only in his forties, walked with a stick.

"Aw, it was terrible," she said, speaking like a high speed train. "He caught swine flu in hospital three years ago. He was in there for four months, y'know. He had to learn to walk again. And, y'know, he had every organ wired up to some machine."

"That sounds bad." But she was off again.

"And, y'know, this is a very important historical place."

"Is it?"

"Just up the road there's a church that Cromwell used to go to."

"What's it called?"

"It's just around the corner there."

They got back in their car and drove off with the window down.

"And I bet you've friends all over Europe," she said as she drove away smiling and waving. "I carn't believe it!"

I'd wanted to set off as early as possible but the B&B in Dundalk wouldn't do breakfast earlier than half seven. I went downstairs at quarter past and sat in the dining room's lounge area just in case things kicked off a little earlier. Mrs B&B entered the room at twenty past, saw me there and glared.

"Stay there," she said, walking past. At exactly seven thirty I was given the green light.

I had to be in Clough, forty odd miles away, for eleven otherwise I'd miss out on completing a task I'd started in 1992. Mike, an Irish OU student, was going to walk me up Northern Ireland's highest peak. I'd already climbed Ben Nevis, Snowdon and Scafell Pike in a single weekend over twenty years earlier. Today I was hoping to add the 850 metre Slieve Donard.

I wolfed down my breakfast and left the B&B at exactly eight. It was a clear day with blue skies perfect for showing off Northern Ireland's rolling hills. Within ten minutes I was repairing a puncture – not today, please – and then ropey directions from a traffic warden in Newry added on a few unnecessary miles. Despite the hot sun and lumpy terrain, I gunned it and arrived just after eleven. The walk was on.

Mike and I got in his car and headed for the base of Slieve Donard. After parking up, we walked up the track through some woods at the bottom of the hill. Just as we'd broken cover and hit the shelterless moorland it started to rain but after a hot morning ride and a steep climb through the trees it was wonderfully refreshing.

Mike has had his share of problems. As a young student he'd been forced to drop out of a degree course because his gambling addiction had caused him to fail his exams. Since then he'd lost serious amounts of cash. His wife left him taking their daughter. His life had been in such tatters he'd twice tried to commit suicide.

But things were changing. He was making a determined effort to end his addiction. The internet connection in his house was disabled from midnight until half six in the morning, the period he used to creep downstairs for a sneaky game of poker. He'd been clean for four years. Seeing how serious he was, his wife had come back and sanity was returning. But once, while waiting for a car, he'd dropped a coin into the taxi office's fruit machine and felt the familiar urge. It'd scared him how close to the edge he'll always be.

He was now studying with the OU, an organisation that gives everyone a second chance. The courses were helping him with his addiction and providing structure to his life. He was studying maths. I just hoped he could skim-read the chapters on probability and not get too involved.

The rain stopped and the sun returned. Slieve Donard wasn't a difficult climb – it's more of a big lump than a mountain – but the views from the summit were worth it. As Mike cracked open a couple of celebratory beers he'd brought for us, I spied a young woman, arms outstretched, doing a tightrope act on the Mourne Wall that traverses the top. The crosswinds were making it an extra challenge. I took a snap of her. Later she came up to me and asked if I could send her a copy. She was a nineteen-year-old French student called Cleo, who was hitching and wild-camping her way around Ireland alone. She joined us as we walked down the hill.

"How do you find places to sleep?" I said.

"I just knock on people's doors and ask."

"And how many doors do you need to knock on before someone says yes?"

"Not many people say no. Only about one in ten refuses."

Maybe the Northern Irish people were universally kind, or maybe they saw this pretty, short-haired girl and didn't want to leave her at the mercy of others. I wondered what the hit rate would be for a dirty, smelly, hairy bloke. Speaking of smelly I asked her how she washed.

"I don't," she replied.

The next morning, after a truly humongous Irish breakfast with Mike and his family, I had a fairly uneventful ride towards Belfast. Halfway there a racing cyclist came alongside me.

"You look like that fella on telly this morning," he said.

"Who's that?"

"The one swimming from Land's End to John o' Groats."

Sean Conway, the round-the-world cyclist I'd met in Greece, had set himself a new challenge to swim the length of Britain. I'd been following his progress but I wasn't aware he was so close. The day I was on top of Slieve Donard he'd apparently come ashore in Newcastle, the town at the foot of the hill. My beard had been developing nicely but was surely no match for Sean's huge, ginger facial bush.

The weather was being very Irish. I cycled damply through Belfast, stopping to see the Europa Hotel, apparently the most bombed building in the world. Now there's an accolade to be proud of.

I'd made good progress. I could just about make it to the port town of Larne in time for the ferry to Scotland. The ragged loyalist villages on the outskirts of Larne had Union flags painted on the road with "God Save The Queen" in large letters. It was hard to understand how a woman randomly born into a life of truffle-flavoured toothpaste could inspire such devotion from people struggling to pay the lecky bill.

The ferry was just about to leave when I hit the port. I got on board, had a pint of Guinness and fell asleep, only waking as the boat rubbed up against the harbour in Troon.

Today I would reach my final capital, Edinburgh, but on the way I'd visit Blackburn, not my Blackburn but the much smaller, Scottish one and coincidentally the home of Susan Boyle. I didn't know what I was hoping to achieve by doing this but I figured this would become clear while I was there. I cycled through waiting for some revelation but within minutes I was out the other side and sure I'd achieved absolutely nothing.

I arrived in Edinburgh and quickly located the address on Clerk Street that I'd been given. I had a bed for the night, or rather a mattress on the floor, at the temporary home of Fenella, my co-rider on the cycle into London. In the two and a half years since we'd ridden together she'd left Radio 2 and had produced a show for the Edinburgh Fringe. She was also performing with a sketch troupe at the event. Unfortunately one of her team was down with tonsillitis and the sketch show was temporarily cancelled. The entire cast was living in this apartment for the month.

With the other housemates I completed my international menu of firsts that evening in a Malaysian restaurant. After laverbread in Wales, a fake plastic foam cone dodgily named a Creamy Pie in Ireland, soda bread in Northern Ireland, I had a plateful of hakka pork and black fungus in Scotland. Mmm, fungus.

After a handful of adequate shows I arrived around midnight at Fenella's cobbled together stand-up event – some of the acts had only been recruited that day – as part of the Free Fringe, the backlash against the corporate takeover of the original Fringe. Some of the acts didn't have much experience but it was a better laugh than most of the stuff I'd paid for. It's great to see people doing something for love rather than money.

The next morning I pointed the bike southwards. I crossed the gentle hills of the Scottish borders. In Carlisle, news stands told of another dead cyclist. Then I crossed the not so gentle hills of the Lake District to Kendal. Here I could've turned right and headed straight for Heysham and the ferry back to the Isle of Man to complete this massive ride. But I had one more place to visit, a little town called Blackburn.

Chapter 24: A place like home

Capitals visited: 52
Total distance: 21,943 miles

After 470 days of travel I only had two days' cycling left. One day from Kendal to Blackburn and then another back to Heysham. I could've saved myself 130 miles and headed straight for the ferry terminal but after what I'd experienced, after seeing all these amazing capitals, the finest places Europe had to offer, I wanted a city break in Blackburn. I would consider my home town with new eyes and an open mind. I wanted to give it a chance.

The previous evening I'd had a shorter than short live radio interview with Radio Lancashire from my tent. While I was waiting for my fifteen seconds of fame the station was broadcasting a weather report. Apparently today was destined to be awful. It looked like I wouldn't be seeing Blackburn in the same golden rays I'd encountered Rome and Istanbul.

I left Kendal and eschewed the more direct A6 for the scenic route of the A65, that took me past the pretty villages of Kirkby Lonsdale, Ingleton and Settle. This road was famously popular with motorcyclists. There was none out today. It was heaving it down, the green hills washed out by alternating drizzle and downpour.

I was getting close now. Just outside Clitheroe I passed a fishery that promised "The best view in the world...probably!" which is a spectacularly bold claim. I cycled through its gate to get a glimpse of this stunning vista. I was pretty sure over there in the foggy murk on the other side of their little lake was Pendle Hill but I'd have to wait for the weather to buck its ideas up before I could be sure. To dry off a bit I went into their café. While I ate a toasted currant teacake I looked at the caff's walls. They were plastered with photos of successful catches from the nearby water. I'm no fish expert but it looked to me like each and every photo showed a gurning angler with either the same fat carp, the same giant chub or the same massive pike. Perhaps the lake only contained three fish. The poor sods were getting plucked out on a thrice daily basis, photographed and chucked back in the water. Their lips had more holes than a Dan Brown plot.

I continued into Blackburn, through a leafier corner I'd rarely visited, through Langho and Wilpshire. As I approached the centre, things got ropier. Over the last few weeks, since diagnosing myself with Blackburn Syndrome, I'd been trying to recall my home town's redeeming features. One had been the old covered market, a large, dark and cavernous hangar. As little kids my brother and I had regularly gone to one of its cheese stalls where the owner would cut a tiny cube of whatever he was selling to our mum and give it to us as a taster. Then we'd go next door to the market's famous sarsaparilla stand for a glass of the black, fizzy pop. Aged four my brother was going through an odd phase of chomping down on whatever his drinks were served in. The stall holders looked horrified when they heard a crack and saw this little kid stood there with a mouthful of glass. I was looking forward to seeing the market again and maybe even having a glass of sarsaparilla. Then I cycled past a large space that I couldn't remember being there before. They'd only gone and demolished the bloody market.

I kept cycling. I saw the new market, all shiny and modern and characterless. The sarsaparilla stall had apparently refused to move. The old market was only open for three days each week. The new one was forcing longer hours on them as well as tying them to a three year contract. They'd sodded off to sell their drinks in another market elsewhere.

I continued under Darwen Street bridge and headed towards my auntie Rita's. Her place would be my base for this city break. On Livesey Branch Road some nutter started furiously beeping his horn. The car overtook me and slowed down beside me. Oh no, please don't shoot. But it was my mate Oz, a co-rider on many a cycling trip back in the 90s, with his family. He pulled over and we arranged to meet in a couple of days' time.

I arrived at my auntie's and we discussed Blackburn. It was fair to say neither Rita nor my uncle Alan, nor my cousin Danielle nor her husband Paul had anything nice to say about the place.

"Why don't you move?" I asked.

"Well, you know." I'm not sure what this meant. It could mean, "We would but we don't have the money" or "We can't really be arsed" or "Actually, it's not that bad but we do like moaning."

Greg, the Australian I'd met in the bar in Holyhead, had been perfectly correct when he'd said the English like to run down their own towns. The comedian Andy Parsons once said only in Britain could a publisher release a book called *Crap Towns* and receive so many letters from people complaining their home towns weren't included that they'd had to publish *Crap Towns 2*. The third book in the series was in the process of being written and the authors had shortlisted a new batch of victims. Blackburn was on it.

Jack Straw, Blackburn's MP, wasn't happy about this. He thought Blackburn didn't deserve such abuse. His comments might have been more convincing if he actually lived in his own constituency rather than in the Oxfordshire town of Witney, a convenient 200 miles away.

The Lancashire Telegraph, the local paper, also didn't like the fact Blackburn might be officially crap. They wrote an article listing *Six Reasons to Love Blackburn*. This was what I needed. Here were their reasons.

"We have The Mall." Blackburn, you won't be surprised to hear, has a shopping centre and, also unsurprisingly, it contains exactly the same shops as every shopping centre in the country. It used to be called, perhaps unofficially, 'the precinct' but was now The Mall. Someone on the council clearly thought Blackburn needed some Yankee spirit. But in reality it's the same old shopping centre, the same old precinct, that'd been there since I was a dot with a new bit tacked on. They'd cleaned it up a bit and given it some new lighting but I wasn't sure you could state a convincing reason to love Blackburn was because it had the same stuff as everyone else.

"There's the Cathedral." Yes, Blackburn has a cathedral, but it's a cathedral in name only. Until 1926 it was merely a church. It was extended in the fifties, sixties and seventies, with all the style those periods evoke.

"There's beautiful countryside around Blackburn." The quality of the surrounding countryside says nothing about the town itself. After all, Dachau's surrounded by pretty scenery.

"And there's Witton Park." Blackburn has a park. In fact it has a couple. I was warned not to walk through one of them because I'd get stabbed.

But my favourite reason to love Blackburn was this one:

"The town is forever immortalised in a Beatles song. We've been mentioned in a song by the greatest band EVER. 'Four thousand holes in Blackburn, Lancashire' the iconic John Lennon sang on the track 'A Day in the Life'."

Yes, folks, one of the top six reasons to love Blackburn is because the Beatles thought the town's roads were so Ukrainian they deserved to be ridiculed in song.

The local rag wasn't making such a strong case but there was one item on the list I'd never heard of – Blackburn Youth

Zone – where for 50p kids could go along and play football and video consoles on wide-screen tellies and probably, in the words of Blackburn council, 'hang out'. Absolutely everyone I talked to who had children thought Blackburn Youth Zone was pretty good. One out of six isn't bad.

Other sources of inspiration about Blackburn were equally poor. The last time I'd checked the website *hotelplanner.com*, it listed the second, third and fourth best attractions in Blackburn as a visit to Preston, a visit to Bolton and a visit to Wigan respectively.

I went for a ride around town, to the places I'd lived. There was little point visiting Harwood Street, my home until the age of six, as it was now an industrial estate. I cycled the seven or so miles to Great Harwood, where I'd lived from the age of fifteen, out of town really but still within the BB postcode. The house looked the same but the field opposite was overgrown with tall weeds.

Then I cycled to Knuzden, where I'd lived from six to fifteen. When I lived here it'd been a massive estate full of kids. It was surrounded by fields, flat ones for playing football and lumpy ones for playing army and being poked with sticks. There was also an old Second World War prisoner of war camp, full of smelly concrete shacks hiding puddles and piles of bricks. We'd play there until someone with a dog would walk past the edge of it and we'd all scream, "Tramp! Tramp!" and run home breathlessly. Today the camp is no more. The M65 destroyed it. The fields, both the flat ones and the lumpy ones, were empty, as were the streets. This was a pleasant weekday in the middle of the school summer holidays and I didn't see a single kid playing out in the whole time I was there.

As I cycled through Accrington I felt the familiar clicking sound coming from the chain, just as it'd done in Lithuania shortly before it fell apart but I couldn't stop to sort it out. I had people to meet.

Two of these were Penny and Ivor, old friends of my mum and dad's while Ray and Lona were the parents of a Blackburn friend who'd emigrated to Australia shortly after I'd moved to Austria. Ivor and Ray were cycle touring buddies. Despite being close to seventy Ivor was still cycling up mountains whereas Ray was feeling his age of late and taking it easier.

It was interesting to note the general demeanour of each person and then ask them what they thought of Blackburn. Both women seemed down about most things, Ray took the calmly considered middle ground while bubbly Ivor was upbeat on whatever topic you got him talking about, which, to be honest, didn't take much encouraging. These moods translated directly to their opinions of Blackburn, the women being the most negative about the place, Ivor the most positive and Ray in the middle.

Before popping to the pub to meet Oz later that evening I sat watching some telly with Rita and Alan. All the programmes seemed to be telling me how shit life was in the UK. There was Crimewatch and Fake Britain and the constant misery of Eastenders. If you sit around and watch this stuff for long enough surely it must seep into your psyche.

Even outside the house CCTV cameras warned you trouble was about, or perhaps you yourself were trouble. In one shop I went into, there were fake cardboard policemen stood at the ends of each aisle to keep an eye on me. Were they accusing or protecting? It was no wonder Crap Towns could produce sequel after sequel.

Oz has always been a happy chap. He's the same age as me and married with a couple of lads. I wanted to hear a dose of his optimism.

"Tell me something good about Blackburn," I said.

He thought about it for a minute and then pulled a face. I

read him the *Six Reasons To Love Blackburn*.

"No, the cathedral isn't anything special. It looks sixties. It's all concrete. But the Youth Zone is good. My kids go there."

"Can you think of anything else?"

"Ah yeah, the art teachers at Blackburn college are good." Oz is a keen artist. "And there are good sports facilities for the lads."

"What about the new market?"

"No, it's shit. It's too clean. It's just like Morrison's. I don't go there."

"So where do you shop?"

"Morrison's," he joked. Then he paused. "Y'know something? I don't think of Blackburn as a good or a bad place. This is where I work and where my family is. I can make the things happen here that I want to make happen. I have my art classes and my music. I'm happy. In fact, I'm happier than I've ever been. I'd say location is irrelevant but it isn't. I've been working in Bristol for three days every week for the last thirteen months. I wouldn't want to live in a city but I can live here and I can be happy."

Having spoken to Rita and Alan, to Danielle and Paul, to Ray and Lona, to Penny and Ivor, and to Oz, but also having seen the whole of Europe, I'd come to a conclusion. Blackburn wasn't hell. It didn't have the crumbling tower blocks of Romania. It didn't have the police corruption of Ukraine. It didn't have the judgemental off licence owners of Turkey. It didn't have the swarms of mosquitoes of Latvia. It didn't have the vast tracts of radioactive forest and dictatorial control of Belarus. It didn't have the eye-bleedingly expensive beer of Norway. Equally, it didn't have the spectacular mountains and crystal streams of Austria, the architecture of the Czech Republic, the silver coastline of Sicily or the liver-bleedingly cheap beer of Bulgaria. It was just a normal town, almost identical to anywhere else in Britain. It had little to commend it but nothing in particular to condemn it.

Blackburn could have been any British town, except perhaps London, and it still wouldn't have been big enough for me in my twenties. I wanted to escape to somewhere else and so I vilified Blackburn, turned the town into a bogeyman and blamed it for my inertia, for being stuck there. It was Blackburn Syndrome. I would've hated wherever I was.

There are people who live in Blackburn happily but these are already happy people, like Oz. He could live almost anywhere. As long as he had his family, his piano and his sketchpad he'd be happy. And there are people who live in Blackburn miserably – I'd been one of them – but there's nothing to say these people wouldn't be miserable wherever they went. It wasn't leaving Blackburn that'd made me happy. It was finding a fulfilling job, meeting people with different backgrounds from all over the world, immersing myself in a new and exciting culture, learning a new language, stretching myself. You can be happy anywhere and miserable anywhere.

I felt like I owed Blackburn something. I'd done it a disservice. I'd slagged it off unnecessarily. I'd done the opposite of look at it through rose-tinted spectacles. My spectacles had been brown-tinted. I wanted to give it a gift. Blackburn needed some love. I remembered back to the places I'd visited, places where love has been freely expressed. All it'd taken was some padlocks fastened to a bridge. I'd seen them in Paris, Prague, Graz and Ljubljana. Blackburn could use a love-lock bridge.

I went to Poundland – Blackburn wasn't short of them – and bought a collection of padlocks, some large, some small, and a jar of Tippex. I painted the locks with the initials of the couples around me, Rita and Alan, Danielle and Paul, Nina and me. Since religion had frequently found a way into this trip – the young Christian who'd insinuated I was homeless in Segovia, drinking holy water in the Vatican City, Ramazan in Turkey, Orthodox Easter and my attempted conversion in Ukraine – I even painted a love-lock for Jesus. It said "JHC 4 MM".

I took the padlocks to Blackburn's newish Wainwright Bridge. Given this was an act of low level vandalism I tried to play it coy. I cycled to the middle of the bridge and turned my bike upside down as though I was having technical difficulties and then, while sat on the floor, I attached the padlocks to the bridge's fence. Since the Lancashire Telegraph had been so impressed by that Beatles song, the last one I added was a larger padlock that read "All You Need Is Love".

Then I realised that perhaps I hadn't thought this through properly. Love-lock bridges usually straddle water. After clicking the padlock shut you're supposed to throw your key into the river below to seal the deal. Beneath the Wainwright Bridge is a railway line. I couldn't throw the keys down there. They might end up through the windscreen of the 1153 from Preston. I decided to visit another old haunt, a body of water where I'd fished as a lad. The keys ended up at the bottom of Rishton Reservoir.

It wasn't much but Blackburn had a new attraction. Or maybe the council were down there the next day with bolt-cutters. Still, I'd tried. Sorry, Blackburn. I mean it.

My city break was over. I wasn't sad to leave Blackburn but for the first time I wasn't escaping from it either. I set off at eight in the morning to give me plenty of time to cover the forty miles to reach the two o'clock ferry. Even if I had a puncture I could still pootle along without feeling the pressure of a deadline. I'd forgotten about the clicking chain but it didn't seem too bad. Surely it'd get me to the boat. Out of Blackburn and down the busy A59 I flew, across its roundabouts and out of the other side on my way to Preston.

And then something bad happened. There was a fizz and the back tyre was suddenly flat. No problem. I had a spare inner tube. But then I saw the state of the tyre. It had been shredded. I looked back on the tarmac for what might have caused it but could find nothing. The gash was six inches long.

I was still a good couple of miles from Preston. I pushed the bike. All was alright. I had plenty of time. All I needed to do was to find a bike shop and buy a new tyre. I passed some roadworkers and asked where the nearest bike shop was. They pointed me down a road about a mile away. I found the shop but it was shut. There was no sign on the door to say it was opening any time soon. Should I look for another or hope it was going to open in a minute?

A middle-aged woman turned up and waited outside with me along with her chubby, late teen son and his buckled back wheel. We asked a few passers-by. The consensus was it would open at ten, in half an hour. We waited. Ten came and the shop stayed shut. Fifteen minutes later we were just about to try elsewhere when the owner rolled up. He said he could swap the tyre and inflate it more quickly than I could and so I let him, but once my old tyre was off he was constantly interrupted by phone calls. It was another half an hour before I left.

Now I had a new deadline. I cycled like a pillock up the thankfully flat road to Lancaster with my chain clanking every few revolutions and made it to the ferry with only minutes to spare.

After a pleasant crossing on a calm, warm August afternoon I arrived in Douglas to be met by Dave and his son, Conor, both on bikes. We took the quieter, slightly hillier route back to Port St Mary, my start point. Although Conor was only fourteen he was the one struggling to get up the hills.

We had a job to complete, to discover the fate of the pretend meerkat I'd buried on Day One. We stopped at the Fairy Bridge and I located the spot but it wasn't there. Maybe one of those near death experiences – my passing out through low blood pressure in northern France, dopey Oleksandr and his car in Ukraine, my accident on Russia's broken roads, the truck on the way out of Oslo or the car in Cheltenham – would've spelled the end of me and the fairies had taken my gift and traded it for my one last chance at longevity. No, that was bollocks. I'd just been lucky.

A few miles later we weren't far from the village. With Conor wheezing up the hill behind, Dave suggested we finish with the prettier option, a track running along the seashore. Dave went ahead while I crunched with each turn of the pedals. It was getting worse. We twisted and turned for a minute then up ahead was the centre of Port St Mary and its little supermarket. There was a steep slope to reach the village road. I gave the pedals a burst of pressure to climb the track and, with less than a mile to go, my chain snapped.

The breakage had happened right beside the village off licence. I popped inside and bought two carrier bags full of celebration, one to dangle from each handlebar. I pushed the bike up the steep hill on the other side of Port St Mary, past the golf course, to the brow of the little hill before my mum and dad's house. It wasn't supposed to finish like this. I was meant to glide triumphantly into their driveway, not be sweatily pushing the bike and a load of booze, limping over the finish line. My little niece Shannon, a bundle of blonde hair and pink clothes, came running down towards me. My mum, dad, Dave and Conor were waiting outside for me. Everyone gave me a hug. Someone thrust a cold can into my hand.

It was over. I'd cycled 22,076 miles, or 35,528 kilometres if you prefer, and I'd climbed a total of 177,510 metres, over twenty Everests or 132 Ben Nevises. I'd visited 52 capitals in 53 countries in a trip that had lasted 472 days. Of the three degrees I'd started, one had been stolen from me, one was complete and the third wasn't far off. Since I'd first had the idea to do the ride, almost every thought had been experiencing it or, in the winter breaks, looking forward to the experience of the next leg. All my money – my savings and future pension – had been invested in it. And it was over.

What the hell was I going to do now?

Epilogue

While cycling around Europe, a lot of people told how they'd like to do something similar, not necessarily a bike ride, but a big trip, something life changing. Maybe you feel the same way. Perhaps it's not a trip at all. Maybe you want to start a business or write a book or whatever. It doesn't matter. I hope my story shows that by making that first step – whether that first step is the first revolution of a bike's wheels or a plane ticket away from a town you've perhaps unjustifiably come to loathe – what lies beyond is joyous. If my writing hasn't been sufficient to get this point across, I want to tell you something else.

Since I've been studying it, some people have told me that maths is useless. I want to show you it isn't and use it to tell you how unbelievably lucky we all are.

The chance of your winning the jackpot of the UK lottery is extremely low, 1 in 13,983,816 to be precise (or $49!/43!6!$ if you want the calculation). You'd consider yourself very fortunate indeed if you won but you've already defeated much longer odds than those. You won life.

For the sake of round numbers later down the line, let's assume the average woman is fertile from age nineteen to forty and has two and a half children that make it to sexual maturity. With one egg per month there's only a one in a hundred chance that, of those available to a mother, any particular egg will grow up and have children of its own. Let's also assume the average age to have a child, and therefore the average length of a human generation, is 33 years. It used to be a lot less than this, but 33 gives us a neat and tidy three generations per century.

We can now go back to any given year and work out the odds of your being here from that date. Let's choose the year

1600. Since that time you have had about twelve ancestors, each with a one in a hundred chance of being born, meaning that, given the situation in 1600, the likelihood of your existing was one in 100^{12} or, more simply, one in 10^{24}. And if that still doesn't mean much to you, it's quite a bit less likely than winning the lottery jackpot three times in a row.

If you want to calculate the odds of your being here from the year 300 AD – the year of Bruce Forsyth's birth – my scientific calculator gives up, but the odds are massive, something like one in 10,000,000,000,000,000,000,000, 000,000,000,000,000,000,000,000,000,000,000,000,000,00 0,000, 000,000,000,000,000,000,000,000. And that was only 1,700 years ago. Modern humans are believed to have been around for 200,000 years and so your chance of being here since then is one in 100^{6000}, which is one followed by 12,000 zeroes. Probability-wise that's roughly the same as winning the lottery jackpot every single Saturday from its launch in 1994 until the year 2027.

But this is only a tiny fraction of the real calculation. You also have to consider all the evolution, with its random mutations, that had to occur exactly as it did over billions of years for humankind to come about in the first place, all the tectonic plate movements that isolated some populations and enabled others to be wiped out by predators, the geological make-up of the Earth and its composition as a result of condensing gases from the remnants of the early Solar System, but also the cloud from which the Solar System emerged and the earlier stars that burned their hydrogen and helium to form the heavier elements within that cloud that were eventually necessary to make you exactly as you are. The chance of your being here is so infinitesimally small as to be zero, or no chance whatsoever.

You, me, any of us, shouldn't really be here at all. Make the most of it.

Printed in Great Britain
by Amazon